The Gates Foundation and the Future of U.S. "Public" Schools

Routledge Studies in Education and Neoliberalism

EDITED BY DAVE HILL, *University of Northampton, UK*

1. The Rich World and the Impoverishment of Education
Diminishing Democracy, Equity and Workers' Rights
Edited by Dave Hill

2. Contesting Neoliberal Education
Public Resistance and Collective Advance
Edited by Dave Hill

3. Global Neoliberalism and Education and its Consequences
Edited by Dave Hill and Ravi Kumar

4. The Developing World and State Education
Neoliberal Depredation and Egalitarian Alternatives
Edited by Dave Hill and Ellen Rosskam

5. The Gates Foundation and the Future of U.S. "Public" Schools
Edited by Philip E. Kovacs

The Gates Foundation and the Future of U.S. "Public" Schools

Edited by Philip E. Kovacs

Routledge
Taylor & Francis Group
New York London

First published 2011
by Routledge
711 Third Avenue, New York, NY 10017

Simultaneously published in the UK
by Routledge
2 Park Square, Milton Park, Abingdon, Oxon OX14 4RN

Routledge is an imprint of the Taylor & Francis Group, an informa business

First issued in paperback 2012

Typeset in Sabon by IBT Global.

Library of Congress Cataloging-in-Publication Data

The Gates Foundation and the future of US "public" schools / edited by Philip E. Kovacs.
p. cm. — (Routledge studies in education and neoliberalism ; 5)
Includes bibliographical references and index.
ISBN 978-0-415-87334-5 — ISBN 978-0-203-83494-7 (ebk)
1. Bill & Melinda Gates Foundation. 2. Educational change—United States. 3. Public schools—United States. 4. Endowments—United States. I. Kovacs, Philip E.
LC243.B55G38 2011
370.973—dc22
2010025198

ISBN13: 978-0-415-87334-5 (hbk)
ISBN13: 978-0-203-83494-7 (ebk)
ISBN13: 978-0-415-53663-9 (pbk)

Contents

Tables

Foreword

In an era when entire schools in Rhode Island and Georgia see their faculty members fired en masse, and in state after state thousands of teachers are being laid off because of the economic disaster caused by greed and risk on Wall Street, there seems to be a change occurring that is in keeping with what advocates of privatization have been arguing for since at least as far back as Milton Friedman, if not to Frederick Taylor or earlier. Specifically, business-minded leaders continue to act on economic assumptions regarding schooling: that schools exist to prepare people for jobs; that "efficiency" and "competition" are necessary elements of schooling; that global comparisons ranking countries based on their schools are logical and valid; and that "accountability" should be ubiquitous when talking about teachers and students.

These leaders, including Arne Duncan and Barack Obama, seem to understand schooling only or primarily in economic terms. Far from the "socialists" label Tea Party advocates hope to tar the current administration with, they are, in terms of schooling, among the staunchest capitalists in the world. And why shouldn't they be? They surround themselves with corporate leaders, eschew critical scholars, and play the political game of blaming schools that seems to be a standard and enduring part of political life. In order to understand the emptiness of Duncan's and Obama's rhetoric, we have to understand the reasons why the language they use is misguided at best and dangerous at worst. To put it simplistically, the language of business is suited for manufacturing, mining, franchising, technologizing, etc., and so on. The language of business is a language that myopically focuses on profit, often at the expense of human life (witness the Massey coal- mining explosion and the oil rig fire in the Gulf of Mexico). Applied to schooling, such a language minimizes human interaction among and between students and teachers. They become subsumed under the logic of profit (read: high test scores). According to this logic, "good" schools will stay in business and bad schools will fail. Again, the logic is flawed because businesses and schools are not of the same kind. Businesses exist to make money. Schools are places where learning, knowing, and growing are supposed to take place. Under the logic of business, however, learning, knowing, and growing—if they exist in any substantive way—are changed to meet the demands of economic expectations. Learning is not for the sake of understanding a wide and expanding body of information, unless it is tied to functionalist vocationalism. Knowing as an engaged and intricate epistemological inquiry is reduced to practice tests that are timed after students are fed red grapes and the thermostat is doubled-check to be sure it's at 72-degrees Fahrenheit. Growing as an active process becomes stunted under the language of business because growth is only understood in economistic terms (to develop skills, habits, and attitudes that will enable students to secure jobs in a technologically advanced global economy).

To combat the language of corporations and business means to look inwardly at ourselves and then to look around us at what constitutes our lives and our understanding of our lives. Contesting the logic of business means questioning many of the assumptions we take for granted. Is our capitalist society meritocratic? Can we succeed by boot-strap pulling? Are we a classless society, in the sense of permeability between and among the rich and poor? Philip Kovacs' book addresses questions like these and also does far, far more.

Themes within this work include, but are not limited to: venture philanthropy, teacher quality, and competitive privatization. Jim Horn, Ken Libby, Kenneth Saltman, and Michael Klonsky all provide important insight into the idea of philanthropy and how it is being exploited as (and thus morphed into) "venture philanthropy." As the authors note, venture philanthropy is not something that merely or already exists. It has been brought about strategically by wealthy capitalists: give money to schools in order to control schools. It is a simple strategy, actually, but one with enormous consequences. By allowing private interests to co-opt public schools, we risk losing the potential to achieve a well-functioning republic—and one that aspires to democratic ideals. Private interests, however, are not always understood as a threat to schools. Indeed, the contrary is too often true. Most people in the United States, I assert, see the wealthy people as "successes," if not capitalist American idols. As such, they are given leeway to make claims about schools that are rarely informed by educational research that is not tainted by think-tank sponsored research, paid for by foundations representing transpartisan corporate interests.

In practice, this means that citizens give over decision-making to those who already have power and influence of a particular (corporate) sort. It reifies as unquestionable whether competition, test scores, and international rankings are the primary aims of schooling. The result is acquiescence or, worse, hegemony: willingly and knowingly seeking private money to fund public schools. In an era of economic crisis, this dilemma only gets worse, of course. Facing massive budget shortfalls because capitalist greed (still promoted, though arguably a root cause of massive unemployment and economic strife), schools are all too willing to sell naming rights to their buildings, erect cell phone towers on school grounds, and plaster buses with advertisements enticing students to eat junk food. While the chapters in this book go into exceptional, grounded detail, I fear that readers will miss an important larger point: public schools may not actually (yet) be public. Instead, I fear that schools are already privatized spheres where venture philanthropists have infiltrated and, largely, won any battle (should it have even taken place at all) over what it means to be educated.

Said differently, too many U.S. citizens unthinkingly and uncritically accept a central tenet of venture philanthropy, namely, to code the discourse about schools with economic language. When Bill Gates and Eli Broad lament the state of public schools, they use a language of economics. Schools become factories, teachers become managers, and students become widgets. It is a simple shift, a sleight of hand, to get U.S. citizens to parrot back the assumptions and entailing consequences: schools should produce the same products, teachers should train those products, and students should learn what it means to be a commodity-statistic.

Teachers, as a second theme in this book, should become more critically engaged in the scholarship of teaching, but they rarely evidence critique. Perhaps they are now so demoralized (demonized?) by wealthy plutocrats that they see no recourse. The best teachers seem to know that there is a problem with the logic of business and the factory model of an advanced technological society that follows from it. But with whom are they supposed to confide? Since school leaders have already swallowed the Kool-Aid of business logic (CEO does not mean Chief Executive Officer, it means Chief Education Officer), they reinforce the problem far too often. Similarly demoralized are scholars in colleges of education. Part of the larger strategy of privatization, neoliberal politicians are increasingly making it easy for "educational leaders" to assume positions of power without certification or education in leadership programs. Teaching, too, has now been reduced to online distance courses that mirror correspondence courses far more than rigorous teaching and learning. Yet, we should not forget the ulterior motive: corporatists want to take power out of the hands of colleges and universities because corporatists are questioned in the academy. To get around critical engagement, we set up "alternative certification" routes that require less time, less engagement with important literature, less understanding of the dimensions and multiple constructions of good teaching.

Subsumed under a "what works" mentality, teachers, students, and their curricula are increasingly standardized and routinized—just like a factory assembly line. The myth here, of course, is that there is no single standard for teaching and learning. The recent push for a national curriculum seems odd in some cultural sense (we're all individuals), but it makes perfect sense in a commodities logic. National standards will mean, according to this logic, that there are no longer excuses to be given about not "preparing" students for their (economic) future. All schools will be held to the "same high standards" in order that they can be compared, ranked, and, if necessary, vaunted or closed. Schools as markets, then, are no different than

McDonald's franchises. The food is exactly the same, the delivery, interaction, dress, etc.and so on, are all coded and standardized. The success of "school-as-franchise" means that profits are compared and "customer satisfaction" scores are included in a profit-loss spreadsheet such that '"successes'" and "failures" result. Schools as spreadsheets. Students as products. Teachers as script readers ("Would you like fries with that?"). Why more people are not outraged by the corporate assault on students, teachers, and schools appears to be that they believe the language of business should be the language we used to talk about and evaluate schooling. This book contests such an assumption and calls on readers to look through a different lens, as it were, to see if there is a different narrative at play. Is it possible that the philanthropy identified in this book is not philanthropic after all? A critical analysis is needed and the collection of authors brought together in these pages are just the ones to raise legitimate, serious questions about the credit due to the Bill and Melinda Gates Foundation.

Even with the criticality brought to bear on the Gates Foundation, the state of schooling, and the problems facing democratically-oriented citizens, this book does far more than complain about the problems. There are myriad examples of ways to confront the reductionist logic of business. Craig and Aimee Howley, Jessica Schiller, Philip Kovacs and H.K. Christie, and David Gabbard, among others, each provide important analyses and details to substantiate the larger critique. They also offer challenges to action. Indeed, I think the reader should know from the beginning that the tone of this work is important. The scholars represented in this work are deeply troubled by what they see as an assault on democratic forms of living (*qua* schooling). They are fearful that schools are at risk of being changed into even more contrived spaces for corporate propaganda. Marion Brady laments the reasons why current education reform will not work, but the point is to combat the myths within school discourse. It is here, at least partly, where meliorism can be seen. While lamenting the corporate assault on schools by venture philanthropists, the scholars in this book also advocate and demonstrate agency. They offer different ways of viewing and understanding the "taken-for-granted" assumptions of a consumer culture. Nobody in this book is arguing that students should not be employed, *per se*, but that schooling is more than narrow utilitarianism and restrictive vocationalism.

Schools should not exist to provide Bill Gates with future workers at Microsoft nor future consumers of his product—at least not uncritical, unthinking, unconsequentialist ones. Schools should not be seen as preparatory places where the young are homogenized and assimilated into a narrow vision of "future worker" as this is limiting rather than broadening. In fact, a subtle irony may exist within the language of corporate culture that has been adopted by schools. When corporate leaders argue that schools are not producing graduates who can perform x, y, or z function, they also argue that they want workers who can think critically in order to solve complex problems. Firstly, while although I'm not sure that the degree of complexity that business leaders identify is all that complex, the larger point is the bifurcation they make between schools producing "skilled" workers who also can tackle complexity. Secondly, and more to my point, I seriously doubt that Bill Gates wants workers (for his company or otherwise) who would challenge the monopolist practice that netted Gates his billions in the first place.

Relating the Janus-faced nature of corporate criticism of schools to teaching, many good teachers find themselves trying serve multiple masters. They care deeply about their students while they are made to follow scripted curricula. They are energetic about their content, though they have to write out mundane lesson-plans that cohere with state mandates. They are often critical of the cycle of reform that sends them the same old stuff called something different that they then have to spend inordinate amounts of time pretending to be "trained" in during professional development sessions. Demoralized, many of the best teachers leave the classroom. How do venture philanthropists propose to deal with it? They argue that tenure should be abolished, merit pay should be instituted, and the "performance" for which they are to be rewarded are students' test scores.

The problem with such a list of expectations is the simplicity it presumes. Much like reducing schooling to a factory model (otherwise known as a competitive site for global entrepreneurship?), reducing teaching to a set of scripts, plans, and standards is also limiting. On the corporate view, it breeds completion. What it actually breeds is fear and a push to "cover" testable material rather than engaging in problem-posing for understanding. As though schooling, teaching, and learning are easily reduced to models, methods, strategies, and "best practices" means that the complexities of teaching and learning are disregarded and marginalized. This results in more and more teachers leaving the field of teaching, more students dropping out of school before graduating, and a corporate logic left to ask itself "Why are we requiring the very practices that have yet to work?" There is, after all, a long history of business meddling in school practice. From W.W. Charters, Franklin Bobbitt, and David Snedden all the way up to Arne Duncan, Bill Gates, and Eli Broad, the assumption that schooling is merely a puzzle to be figured out, once and for all, means that the complexities of learning, knowing, and understanding are not even on the table for consideration. They get subsumed under the overly simplistic logic of corporate expectations.

For those of us who study education and education policy, it is maddening to hear business leaders trumpet expectations for schools. They have no background, other than going to school themselves, to talk with any authority about schooling. This, perhaps, is the underlying point. Business leaders, no matter how ill-informed, should be included in conversation with others who actually know something about schooling. Instead of using huge sums of money to substantiate a skewed vision of schooling, which is precisely what the Bill and Melinda Gates Foundation does, they might consider anonymous donations to a variety of competing visions for schooling to see how well multiple means of approaching education might do for students and teachers. To donate anonymously, of course, defeats much of the self-aggrandizing purpose of the foundation itself, but the point here is to emphasize that schooling is not one thing. Teaching takes many forms. Learning, far from simple (or simplified), happens at various rates that need not be compared. Schooling for corporate aims limits the potential of students and, perhaps most ironically, entrepreneurialism itself.

Regardless, the chapters that follow are a unique collection of work from a variety of intellectuals and practitioners. Many of these chapters are consistent with academic scholarship insofar as they have multiple citations, support, and warrant for their arguments. Readers are encouraged to look carefully at the arguments and evidence that is brought to bear against the Bill and Melinda Gates Foundation. Those who automatically wish to defend the Gates Foundation, because they believe the work of the Foundation to be so genuine and good, should suspend such an optimistic outlook and consider the darker side to the work done by it, and other, moneyed organizations.

Deron Boyles, Atlanta, Georgia

Acknowledgments

I would like to thank the contributors of this book for their scholarship and their patience, but I would be remiss if I didn't single out a few people who helped along the way. Ken Saltman suggested I put this edition together, and Dave Hill quickly set me up with a contact at Routledge. Without them, this book would never have made it out of the theoretical stage. I would like to thank Deron Boyles for the patient guidance he's provided me over the past six years. Rahna Carusi deserves special thanks for helping with the indexing, as does Nick Wilbourn, who helped with early copy-editing. My colleagues at UAHuntsville are more than I deserve, and I realize how fortunate I am to be surrounded by critical, engaged, doers. Importantly, I need to acknowledge my partner and child. My child for providing me with breaks from what was occasionally dispiriting work, and my partner for providing me with breaks from our son who enjoys taking work and either (a) scattering it all over the floor and/or (b) eating it.

1 From Carnegie to Gates

The Bill and Melinda Gates Foundation and the Venture Philanthropy Agenda for Public Education

Kenneth J. Saltman

This chapter discusses the dramatic recent shifts in educational philanthropy of the last decade represented by the entry into educational policy and reform of the Bill and Melinda Gates Foundation and other 'venture philanthropists' in education. It explains the change in the underlying assumptions behind the recent shift as part of broader ideological and economic trends. Most significant, the discussion elaborates on venture philanthropy as an expression of neoliberal ideology applied to education and the shift in the logic of educational philanthropy accompanying the shift from an industrial economy to one that is service oriented. The chapter begins by discussing the rise of venture philanthropy (VP) typified by Gates and goes on to distinguish it from the prior philanthropy typified by Carnegie and dominant in education for the past century. What is at stake in this discussion are the ways that public governance over public schooling is shifted to private concerns through VP, the ways the public financially subsidizes privatization of public governance in education, and the broader political and civic purposes of public schooling in a democratic society.

VENTURE PHILANTHROPY

Venture philanthropy differs markedly from prior educational philanthropy dominant throughout the twentieth century, including large donors such as the Carnegie Corporation, the Rockefeller Foundation, and the Ford Foundation. These traditional philanthropic endeavors defined giving through a sense of public obligation. In the traditional view, the industrialist gave back some of the surplus wealth he had accumulated. Carnegie's *The Gospel of Wealth and Other Timely Essays* codifies this perspective that its advocates described as "scientific philanthropy."[1] As critics such as Robert Arnove, Joan Roelofs, and others have argued, the early educational philanthropy played a distinctly conservative cultural role of supporting public institutions in ways compatible with the ideological perspectives and material interests of the captains of industry rather than of the workers of coal, steel, oil, or automotive production.[2] This labor created the surplus wealth that was first extracted and then went into universities, museums, libraries, and trusts. As Slavoj Žižek emphasizes, to *give* the capitalist must first *take*.[3] Public subsidies through tax incentives not only encouraged but financed such public works to be developed and designed by fiscal and cultural elites rather than by the broader public.

Although educational philanthropy played a hegemonic role throughout the twentieth century, it was hardly unified in its approaches and offered funding for a wide variety of initiatives and projects that were not restricted to the conservative side of the political spectrum. There was a distance between the donors and the uses made of the money in education; once given, money was not closely controlled and directed in its uses. 'Scientific philanthropy,' though beholden to a logic of cultural imperialism,[4] was marked by a spirit of public obligation and deeply embedded in a liberal democratic ethos.

Venture philanthropy departs radically from the age of 'scientific' industrial philanthropy. Venture philanthropy is modeled on venture capital and the investments in the technology boom of the early 1990s. VP not only pushes privatization and deregulation, the most significant policy dictates of neoliberalism,[5] but it is also consistent with the steady expansion of neoliberal language and rationales in public education, including the increasing centrality of business terms to describe educational reforms and policies: choice, competition, efficiency, accountability, monopoly, turnaround, and failure. Likewise, venture philanthropy treats giving to public schooling as a 'social investment' that, like venture capital, must begin with a business plan, must involve quantitative measurement of efficacy, must be replicable to be 'brought to scale,' and ideally will 'leverage' public spending in ways compatible with the strategic donor. To name but some of the recasting of giving on investment, grants are referred to as 'investments'; donors are called 'investors'; impact is renamed 'social return'; evaluation becomes 'performance measurement'; grant reviewing turns into 'due diligence'; the grant list is renamed an 'investment portfolio'; charter networks are referred to as 'franchises.' Within the view of venture philanthropy, donors are framed as both entrepreneurs and consumers while recipients are represented as investments. One of the most significant aspects of this transformation in educational philanthropy involves the ways in which the public and civic purposes of public schooling are redescribed by venture philanthropy in distinctly private ways. Such a view carries significant implications for a society theoretically dedicated to public democratic ideals. This is no small matter in terms of how the public and civic roles of public schooling have become nearly overtaken by the economistic neoliberal perspective that principally views public schooling as a matter of producing workers and consumers for the economy and for global economic competition.

Although educational philanthropy accounts for just a fraction of educational spending in the United States, its institutions have recently acquired disproportionate influence and control over educational policy and practice.

The new philanthropy is at the forefront of a neoliberal movement that spans both political parties and aims to corporatize education at multiple levels. That is, venture philanthropy is contributing to both the privatization of public schooling as well as the transformation of public schooling on the model of corporate culture—from voucher schemes to charter schools to the remaking of teacher education, educational leadership, and classrooms. Educational philanthropy that appears almost exclusively in mass media and policy circles as selfless generosity poses significant threats to the democratic possibilities and realities of public education. Venture philanthropists are involved in all aspects of educational reform, policy, and practice from finance to administration, from pedagogy to curriculum.

Venture philanthropy has a strategic aim of 'leveraging' private money to influence public schooling in ways compatible with the longstanding privatization agendas of the political right, conservative think tanks such as the Heritage Foundation, the Hoover Institution, the Fordham Foundation; corporate foundations such as ExxonMobil; and corporate organizations such as the Business Roundtable and the Commercial Club of Chicago. The central agenda is to transform public education in the United States into a market through for-profit and nonprofit charter schools, vouchers, and 'scholarship' tax credits for private schooling or 'neovouchers.' Venture philanthropies such as New Schools Venture Fund and the Charter School Growth Fund are being financed by the large givers, especially the Gates, and aim to create national networks of charter schools, charter management organizations, and educational management organizations (EMOs). These organizations are explicit about their intent to transform radically public education in the United States through various strategies. Along these lines the venture philanthropists are also working in conjunction with large urban school districts and business groups to orchestrate such plans as New York's New Visions for Public Schools, Chicago's Renaissance 2010, and similar mixed income schools and housing projects in Portland, Oregon; Boston, Massachusetts; and elsewhere. These coordinate the privatizations of schooling and housing and gentrify coveted sections of cities. They are aggressively seeking to reimagine teacher education through online and onsite initiatives and educational leadership on the model of the MBA. The key players of venture philanthropy in education—including but not limited to such leaders as Gates, Walton, Fisher, and Broad—are able to exercise influence disproportionate to their size and spending power through strategic arrangements with charter and voucher promoting organizations, think tanks, universities, school districts, and schools. The seed money that underfunded schools desperately seek allows the venture philanthropists to 'leverage' influence over educational policy and planning, curriculum and instructional practices, and to influence the very idea of what it means to be an educated person. Though the implications for educational reform are vast, there has been scant scholarship on venture philanthropy in education.[6]

DECLARATIONS OF FAILURE TO JUSTIFY PRIVATIZATION: VENTURE PHILANTHROPY AND NEOLIBERALISM

In 2004, Bill Gates appeared before the National Governors Association and gave a speech, a version of which was reprinted in multiple newspaper op-ed columns. Gates stated, "Our high schools are obsolete. By obsolete, I don't just mean that they're broken, flawed or underfunded, although I could not argue with any of those descriptions. What I mean is that . . . even when they work exactly as designed, our high schools cannot teach our kids what they need to know . . . This is an economic disaster," he said, one that is ruining children's lives and "is offensive to our values."[7]

The other leading venture philanthropists have sounded the same alarm as Gates' declaration of the failure of public schooling and the threat that public education poses to the nation's economy. Even before Gates' speech, billionaire venture philanthropist Eli Broad announced that "public education is in many ways in a crisis that we can no longer ignore . . . We risk not only a lower standard of living and a weaker economy . . . We're in danger of becoming a second-class nation. I see the stakes as incredibly high. We're headed in the wrong direction."[8]

For Gates, Broad, and the Walton family (of the Wal-Mart fortune), who are the leading venture philanthropists in education, the 'right direction' is to treat public schooling like a market, to make public schooling into a market. They share a set of assumptions about public education that can be generally summarized as follows:

1. Public schools have 'failed' and the public sector cannot be relied upon for 'good' education.
2. Government is inefficient and markets are efficient.
3. Government involvement threatens rather than facilitates personal liberty.[9]

The declaration of the 'failure' of public schooling forms the backbone of the venture philanthropists' school agenda. In my prior work, I have elaborated on the destructive implications of describing public schools and public goods generally as private goods.[10] I have emphasized that terms such as 'failure,' 'choice,' and 'competition' (as well as 'consumers,' 'efficiency,' and 'monopoly') are part of a broader long-standing neoliberal agenda[11] that extends far beyond education: misrepresenting public goods as private consumables, replacing the collective purpose of general welfare with the misguided terminology of profit accumulation, and portraying citizenship as consumerism.

Venture philanthropy in education needs to be understood as centrally an expression of neoliberal economic doctrine and ideology. At its most basic, neoliberal economic doctrine calls for privatization of public goods and services and the deregulation of state controls over capital, as well as trade liberalization and the allowance of foreign direct investment. As an ideology, neoliberalism aims to eradicate the distinction between the public and private spheres, treating all public goods and services as private ones. It individualizes responsibility for the well-being of the individual and the society, treats persons as economic entities—consumers or entrepreneurs—and it has little place for the role of individuals as public citizens or the collective public responsibilities of democracy. Within the purview of neoliberal ideology, the state can only be bureaucratically encumbered and inefficient, and the market naturally tends toward efficiency and effectiveness. Despite the antipathy to the state, neoliberals aim to shift the use of the state from its caregiving roles to its repressive ones.[12]

In the last two decades, neoliberal ideology has taken hold with a vengeance in education. This has involved describing public schooling as a business: students as 'consumers'; schools ideally needing to 'compete' against one another, with this competition driving up 'efficient delivery'; administrators described as 'entrepreneurs' and schools needing to be 'allowed to fail' 'just like in business.' 'High-stakes' standardized testing and standardization of curriculum have been utterly central to the neoliberal education agenda, in part because of the ways it treats knowledge as a commodity to be produced by experts, delivered by teachers, and consumed by students. The critical and dialogic dimensions to learning and teaching are denied in this view that treats education as indoctrination of the 'right knowledge.' In the neoliberal perspective this anticritical view of knowledge and learning is labeled 'student achievement.' The metaphorizing of public education in the language of the market has confused the private enterprise of profit accumulation with the public and civic purposes of public education.

Within the neoliberal view of education, declarations of 'failure' have more than one function. As a rhetorical strategy, they make it seem as though the fault for low scores has to do with the low merits of students and the underperformance of teachers rather than excessive standardization, financial pressures on school systems, overstrained parents, economic disadvantages, or the overbureaucratization of knowledge. They thus redefine public schooling as private enterprise, and they naturalize private enterprise as the cure to public school 'failings.' As they conflate public and private sectors, they conceal how different levels of public investment result in different levels of educational quality and reflect historical inequalities in public investment.

The neoliberal declaration of a 'failed system,' which relies on the metaphor of business failure, is selectively deployed and both racially and class coded. It is not leveled explicitly against rich, predominantly White communities and public schools for whom high levels of historical investment and the benefits of cultural capital have resulted in high achievement, traditionally defined. Rather, the declaration of 'system failure' is leveled against working-class and poor, predominantly non-White communities and schools. As such, it misattributes educational inequalities and shortcomings to the public sector rather than to the private sector, which in the U.S. bears responsibility for them, as funding is linked to wealth through property taxes and local funding while the private sector has historically played a central role in engineering educational inequality.[13] For example, as Paul Vallas and then Arne Duncan in Chicago have pushed the neoliberal approach, the endlessly repeated suggestion has been that the public sector has 'failed' and now it is 'time to give the market a chance.' The market got a chance, however, when the business sector influenced and shaped school reform and policy in Chicago for over a hundred years prior to the business-designed and Duncan-implemented Renaissance 2010 plan. The neoliberal solutions of union busting, school privatization, the idealization of deregulation in the form of charter schools, the idealization of competition and choice, the business-led reform with events such as the Renaissance Schools Fund (the financial arm of Renaissance 2010) "Free to Choose, Free to Succeed: The New Market in Public Schooling," the implementation of 'turnarounds' as seemingly innovative solutions actively denies the ways the public system has a long history of business-led, engineered failure—not to mention a history of unequal resource distribution by being tied to property wealth.[14]

Peter Frumkin, a prolific author on venture philanthropy, highlights the link between the declaration of public school failure and blame for global economic competitiveness: "[O]ne of the most popular fields for venture philanthropy efforts has been K–12 education. Many business people see the failure of large parts of the public school system as a crisis that has the potential to erode America's long-term economic growth potential."[15]

So when Gates and the other venture philanthropists declare the 'failure' of public schooling as potentially causing a broader economic crisis for the United States in the world, they are calling for a turn to the private sector to redress the problems that too much private sector involvement in education created in the first place. Moreover, these business tycoons misrepresent their desire for an educated workforce wherein workers would compete in the global economy as a universally valuable vision rather than a class-specific one that benefits most those who own and control capital. Subjugating the public purposes of public schooling to primarily that of making competitive workers for the global economy presumes that the public interest is principally served by engaging in the global race to the bottom fostered by the neoliberal vision of trade deregulation and public sector privatization. Venture philanthropists openly talk about U.S. students ideally becoming workers who will compete for scarce jobs against workers from poorer nations. Values of worker discipline, docility, and submission to authority are injected into the corporate school vision as they represent the ideal of the disciplined, docile, and submissive workforce. This view of the national education system serving the interests of capital in a global economy is at odds with the public interest that would be better served by a critical pedagogy in which students develop the tools of social criticism and develop as critical intellectual citizens.

ECONOMIC AND POLITICAL MOTIVATIONS FOR EDUCATIONAL PHILANTHROPY

In his book *Against Schooling: For an Education that Matters,* Stanley Aronowitz bluntly writes a seldom-spoken truth about the motivation for Microsoft's giving and for the Bill and Melinda Gates Foundation. Namely, he says there are tremendous financial (especially tax) benefits for super-rich individuals such as Bill Gates to give away large portions of their fortunes to and through nonprofit organizations.[16] Of course, there are other significant self-interested motivations, including the public relations benefits of promoting oneself as 'socially responsible,' particularly as Microsoft sought to flout antitrust regulations and use its vast resources to pursue monopolistic consolidations in the software industry. (Attorney Joel Klein aggressively prosecuted Microsoft's monopolistic acts, went on to become head of New York City Public Schools, and received millions from the Gates Foundation.)

Philanthropy generally and educational philanthropy more specifically have long histories of functioning both as financial benefits for economic elites and ways of countering negative public perceptions and diffusing class antagonism. In an early public relations stunt to counter immense public antipathy, John D. Rockefeller was famously displayed in Depression-era newsreels handing out dimes to the indigent. Henry Ford built schools, worried not only about his public image but also about the dangerous thoughts his future workers might have on the assembly line. Left-wing critics of philanthropy, often coming from a Gramscian perspective,[17] have emphasized the crucial role played by philanthropy in cementing hegemony by producing consent for conservative economic arrangements and educating citizens to comprehend civil society in ways compatible with ruling-class interests. One such Gramscian, Joan Roelofs, points to Marx's recognition in volume three of *Capital* of how the ruling class is able to stabilize and extend its control by assimilating the intellectuals of other classes.[18]

Andrew Carnegie's exhortation in *The Gospel of Wealth* for the captains of industry to spend their surplus wealth for the benefit of the public appears less than thoroughly virtuous or generous from the critical tradition. The critical tradition recognizes that Carnegie first had to employ vast violence to amass surplus wealth through labor exploitation, wage suppression, attacking unions, and working workers to disablement and death while he used political clout to minimize public regulations that would impede wealth accumulation.[19] Carnegie's surplus wealth came first at the expense of the public and through the most aggressive means to exclude the public from participating in the processes of wealth creation.

Such exclusions required not only the state-supported economic monopoly over property but also a political monopoly to maintain the rules of the game. In sum, for the critics of scientific philanthropy, the cultural project involved assimilating the intellectuals of subordinated classes and groups into the dominant institutions, creating new dominant educational institutions (like schools, libraries, and museums), and instituting new mechanisms to produce knowledge in ways that reproduce social hierarchies. The 'gift' of philanthropy in the age of scientific philanthropy was predicated upon the state-coordinated capitalist plunder of the labor and lives of the working class.

In the early twentieth century, tax laws strongly promoted foundations. Such laws were the result of deliberate public policy decisions. The U.S. sustained and supported foundations by "permitting the creation of general-purpose perpetuities dedicated to serving an indefinite class of beneficiaries (through changes in state trust law) and by creating tax deductibility for donors (in both state and federal tax law)."[20] It is remarkable how little of the literature on either foundations generally or venture philanthropy in particular address this fundamental fact that foundations serve as mechanisms to minimize the taxation of wealth and as such largely serve as an entitlement for the richest citizens. Although roughly half of wealth given to foundations comes in the form of small donations, the real financial benefits principally go to the big givers at the top of the economy who are able to significantly reduce their tax burdens. For every ten dollars given by the Gates Foundation, four dollars is lost from the public wealth in taxes.[21] The philanthropist would otherwise give this money to the public in the form of taxes.

By giving to the foundation, particularly to the foundation the philanthropist controls, the philanthropist essentially evades the bulk of public control over the use of tax revenue. This means that first, venture philanthropy in education exists only through public financial subsidy; second, the forgone public tax revenue needs to be understood as being effectively, through the design of public policy, redistributed to the private controllers of the foundation; third, the foundation, which is almost always controlled or directed in its mission by economic elites, uses this public wealth for privately determined purposes; and fourth, these purposes tend to align with the material interests and ideological perspectives of private elite power.[22]

In the case of venture philanthropy in education, this public subsidy for private control of educational policy, practice, and administration can be seen operating in three domains: economic, cultural, and political. On the economic level, venture philanthropists in education pursue a multifaceted neoliberal agenda of school privatization and deregulation; these involve running schools for profit, lucrative real estate deals related to charter schools, and getting rid of unions that could threaten these plans. As for the impact on culture, venture philanthropists pursue a largely rightist form of educational policy and practice, emphasizing test-based accountability and expanded corporate school models such as teacher bonus pay for test scores,[23] school commercialism, corporate forms of school administration, and conservative anticritical curricula and school models. On the political front, venture philanthropists in education actively lobby legislatures and districts to establish a national network of charter franchises, expand charter schools locally, implement vouchers, and put in place education tax credits that function like vouchers, as well as to allow for remaking teacher education in ways that remove critical and intellectual content. The coordinated goal of all these efforts by venture philanthropists is to privatize the public school system by 'leveraging' the private foundation resources. In effect, then, the public pays to have its own educational system increasingly directed, controlled, dismantled, and owned by private interests.

For venture philanthropists such as Gates, Walton, Broad, Fisher, Dell, Milken, or others, the attraction is not only tax savings but the possibility of retaining control over the use of tax money that would otherwise go into the public wealth. It is not a coincidence that the central mission of preparing workers for their corporations is high on the venture philanthropists' agenda, nor is it a coincidence that educational visions organized by broad-based agenda of challenging social hierarchy would be largely excluded from the perspectives they support. As people who are extraordinarily successful in business, it is not surprising they would believe they know best what to do with money in a field such as medicine or education about which they may otherwise know little to nothing. However, such belief hinges upon the baseless assumption that all of these fields are like business or are indistinguishable from business. One of the primary casualties of such thinking is the inability to distinguish private goods from public ones. It is perhaps more accurate to say the venture philanthropists participate in redefining the public sphere as a private sphere. A prime liability of such redefinition is that society becomes increasingly understood as a collection of atomic individuals responsible only for themselves. Part of what public schooling represents is the care that each citizen has for the well-being of not just oneself and one's own children but for everyone else in the society as well as for the society as a whole. Although celebrated in libertarian literature (the books of Ayn Rand, for example) or popular film (via the action hero), the radically autonomous individual is an impossibility in that individuals are always situated in social contexts and cannot evade political, economic, and cultural relations and exchanges. The question becomes what kinds of such relations benefit both the individual and the society as a whole.

For venture philanthropists who understand the individual and the social through neoliberal ideology, every individual is to become an entrepreneur—that is, a business person in pursuit of private gain, always looking to start new enterprises and move on to the next hot opportunity. The teacher must hustle grants from foundations and test scores for bonus pay; the student must hustle grades to cash them in for further education and later cash; and everyone must hustle against each other. For the entrepreneurial educator and student, image becomes increasingly important. If one shifts the register from the market economy vision of the entrepreneur to the democratic political conception of the citizen, it becomes difficult to see how values of collaboration, deliberation, dialogue, and collective purpose have a role. Rick Cohen puts it well and succinctly:

> Privatizing public education transforms the educational environment from one that builds a sense of collective purpose and nurtures democratic ideals to one that emphasizes individual choice and makes education a commodity to be produced and consumed in the marketplace.[24]

The social costs of the venture philanthropy approach to schooling include a loss of the ability to grasp the limitations of applying the business metaphor to education but, more broadly, the limitations of an economy and ecology premised on unlimited economic growth.

FROM CARNEGIE TO GATES

A leading scholar on philanthropy, Stanley Katz specifies the particularly public understanding held by early twentieth-century leaders of 'scientific philanthropy':

> I want to use the term 'philanthropy' in the special sense originated by Carnegie and the senior Rockefeller: as the self-conscious donation of truly large sums of private wealth to do public good by addressing the causes (and also manifestations) of social problems of all kinds.[25]

It should be said from the outset that for critics on the Left, the causes of social problems are the social structures and systems that facilitate the vast amassing of wealth by few at the expense of many. The projects of Carnegie and Rockefeller were defined through the public interest and appear on one level to be concerned with redistributive efforts toward ameliorating inequalities in wealth and income as well intertwined cultural inequalities such as unequal access to education. However, as Katz among others points out, the scientific philanthropists were deeply conservative and understood their giving as having a practical use for themselves and others of their class:

> They believed that the private sector needed to step up to enhance the public welfare, both to relieve the political pressures of popular unrest and to reduce the chances that the state (especially the federal government) would rise to that task.[26]

Scientific philanthropists sought not simply to use private money for public gain but to serve ruling-class interests in a number of ways. These conservative intents include delegitimation of socialist politics and movements, establishment of institutions that directly served elites, assurance of social reform rather than radical structural change, and creation of social networks to secure the status of elites.[27] Additionally, foundations supported social programs such as social security to assuage Depression-era labor unrest, worked to support tax laws that prohibited giving to political parties, supported civil rights and minority education projects in part to diffuse minority interest in radical movements, and foundations supported 'democracy promotion' projects overseas that would promote liberal capitalism rather than socialism or communism.[28] Carnegie exhorted the super rich to found universities, and many did, such as Cornell, Stanford, Johns Hopkins, and Rockefeller's University of Chicago. Stanford and Chicago have been hotbeds of neoliberal thought. University of Chicago arguably was the birthplace of neoliberalism under Milton Friedman (some would claim London School of Economics and Hayek), and leaders of the push to privatize public schooling are associated with the Hoover Institution housed at Stanford. This is not to say there has been no progressive or radical political thought coming out of these universities but rather to highlight the centrality of foundations to the early formation of educational policies that have left a conservative legacy.

As Roelofs argues, nearly all public education reform of the twentieth century has its origins in philanthropy:

> Nearly all reforms in public (as well as private) education originated with foundations. The course credit system and centrally administered college entrance examinations came about as a requirement for the college teacher's pension program (now TIAA-CREF) started by the Carnegie Corporation for the Advancement of Teaching. These had a major effect on standardizing high school education throughout the United States, as college admission increasingly dictated curricula. Carnegie later initiated 'new math,' 'Sesame Street,' and 'service learning.' Ford, along with Carnegie, were the major promoters of educational television developers of the Corporation for Public Broadcasting, Headstart, Upward Bound, and alternative schools. In 1967, McGeorge Bundy, President of the Ford Foundation, was appointed by New York City's mayor as chair of a task force to plan for NYC school system decentralization.[29]

The scope of liberal and sometimes even progressive commitments to the public sector emerging from scientific philanthropy neither invalidates the conservative project of undermining radical movements for systemic change and genuine democracy, nor does this history invalidate the reality that the commitment to the public good did result in the strengthening of the deliberative aspects of the public sphere. Both aims can be found explicitly stated in Carnegie's *The Gospel of Wealth*. He writes that the best gift a philanthropy can give to a community is a free library, "provided the community will accept and maintain it as a public institution, as much a part of the city property as its public schools, and indeed, an adjunct to these." Carnegie emphasized the value to the public of the free access to knowledge and information, and he understood public knowledge institutions as ameliorative by allowing the poor opportunities for self-advancement.

Like the leading educationalist of his day, G. Stanley Hall (who is largely responsible for the late nineteenth century field of study of adolescence), Carnegie accepts the racially grounded doctrine of recapitulation theory. Recapitulation theory holds that the development of the human being repeats the development of the human race and that the successful development of the human race toward civilization depends upon youth being forced to undergo the trials of earlier stages of human development. These trials build character in middle-class White boys and prepare them to lead civilization forward.[30] Such movements as scouting and the YMCA typify such early twentieth-century thinking that viewed getting back to primitive nature as a necessary strengthening endeavor to prepare youth for stewardship of civilization. In the view of recapitulation theory, human development follows from primitive nature to animals to lower humans to higher humans. Within this schema, White European males are at the top of the upward chain of nature. However, White boys in particular need to go back down the chain to get toughened up for the stresses of governing advancing civilization. In the *Gospel of Wealth*, Carnegie celebrates his own impoverished childhood and the character he gained by working as a child laborer in the textile industry. He describes his adult visit to the home of a Sioux Indian chief and makes much of the fact that the lowliest Indian and the chief live in indistinguishable dwellings. For Carnegie, this illustrates the superiority of Euro-American civilization. The difference between the worker's cottage and the millionaire's mansion indicates for him an upward movement toward greater and greater civilization. He argues that capitalism raises everybody's quality of life and that the amenities of the worst-off in civilized society are superior to the living standards of kings in prior eras. However, competition and the refusal of aristocratic inheritance make possible the forward movement toward greater and greater innovation and civilization. Carnegie extols the virtues of poverty, the valuable lessons bestowed upon child laborers, and laments the misfortune of the children of the rich who do not benefit from the character-building blessing of destitution. Carnegie sees the Sioux as both stuck in the prior history of the human race and as communistic. Communism, Carnegie explains, is not progress but regress that brings humanity back to the life standards of 'primitives.' For Carnegie, capitalism produces both wealth and poverty. The dim and stultified aristocrats of old Europe have suffered from the mistake of inheritance. Carnegie exhorts his millionaire contemporaries to be ashamed to die with their wealth. Instead, they ought to give it to the public so those who can help themselves will do so. Those incapable of helping themselves should be left to the care of the state, he explains.

Central to Carnegie's view of philanthropy is the value of self-help but also the definition of human worth through economic productivity. Carnegie rails against the violence of frivolous giving of charity and suggests that the nickel given away on the street goes on to do compounded harm to the recipient whose productive energies will be drained by the possibility of unproductive acquisition. Scientific philanthropy for Carnegie must be highly rationalized based on its inspiration for fostering economic productivity. However, it also must contribute to the public good that cannot be strictly reduced to the economic. Indeed, Carnegie has harsh words for the wealthy person who flaunts wealth in conspicuous displays rather than by giving to the public. And Carnegie opposes the giving of vast private inheritances to children, seeing this as a diffusion of productive energies and a corrupting influence. Perhaps what is most significant in Carnegie's thought is the expansion of a perspective toward wealth found in Benjamin Franklin's autobiography. Franklin taught his readers to view money as having a life of its own and a reproductive capacity. The squandering of wealth was akin to killing productive offspring. Of course, both Franklin's and Carnegie's view of wealth as being strictly guided by rational utility typifies the increased rationalization of giving in accord with capitalism.[31] Carnegie's vision for philanthropy deeply displaced a value on dispensing wealth and marked a turn toward the shift from *charity* to *philanthropy*. Bill Gates and other venture philanthropists mark another significant shift in the Western understanding of giving.

Bill Gates read Carnegie in preparation for establishing his Bill and Melinda Gates Foundation. There are certain elements of Carnegie's thought that Gates continues, including the rationalization of philanthropy as necessarily fostering 'productive' individuals and greasing the inclusion of working people in the ideologies of a corporate-dominated economy that mostly undermines their own interests. However, there are numerous glaring differences between the social visions of Carnegie and Gates. Carnegie viewed public schools and public libraries as crucial for making knowledge and information freely available to individuals. While Carnegie idealized hard work, self-improvement, and self-reliance despite potentially punishing economic and material conditions, it was publicly and freely supported immaterial labor (self-education) that the individual could pursue for self-improvement and economic advancement. For Carnegie, while the public sector should certainly not redistribute access to public control over capital, the public sector should make freely available the means for individual access to information that would benefit the individual and contribute to the making of a more educated workforce and informed citizenry. On the contrary, Bill Gates earned his historically unmatched fortune specifically by using intellectual property laws to own, control, and license the products of immaterial labor, namely, software and digital information. That is,

Gates' wealth is principally the result not of the sharing and free exchange of knowledge in the public domain, celebrated by Carnegie as the route to freedom and a democratic public, but rather Gates' wealth is a product of the restriction and commodification of knowledge. In the 1970s, computer hobbyists freely shared their hardware and software innovations in a kind of hippy tech movement. Some of the software that would go on to result in spectacular profits for Microsoft, Apple, and other computer companies began as innovations freely shared by hobbyists. Bill Gates and Steve Jobs, among other early leaders of the nascent computer industry, were particularly adept at commercializing and monopolizing the innovations of others.[32] In fact, what would come to be called shareware or open source is closer to the spirit of the early software and computer innovators who were motivated less by the potential for profits than by intellectual curiosity, the technology itself, and the challenges of solving problems.

Whereas Carnegie eschewed conspicuous displays of wealth and excessive consumption, Gates champions a version of schooling that idealizes a corporate economy in which consumer spending on manufactured needs is at the core. So venture philanthropy intensifies the economic rationalization of giving by insisting that giving be more tightly controlled, especially in terms of its outcomes. Yet, it also departs from the ties that scientific philanthropy had to the ideals of a productive industrial economy. In a sense, the transformation of philanthropy reflects the transformation in the understanding of productivity and utility accompanying the shift in the U.S. from an industrial to a consumer- and service-based economy. To put it differently, as the core of the economy has become increasingly defined by the imperative for economic growth dependent on ever more frivolous consumer spending and the fabrication of ever new irrational consumer needs and desires, unplanned and unrationalized giving appears increasingly as a problem in need of eradication. One way to think about this is that as squandering and irrational expenditure of energy, wealth, and resources is increasingly central to economic growth in a consumer society, squandering and irrational expenditure, like the giving of charity, increasingly appear as a problem and must be rationalized and expressed through authorized, legitimate, planned, and orderly forms. Charity must appear as investment. The logic of this creeping rationalization in the irrational consumer economy is particularly evident in the aesthetic realm. A value on and celebration of utility, the display of usefulness can be seen, for example, in the long-standing popularity (from the early '90s to the present) of the SUV in which the individual sporting (display) of potential usefulness is both a kind of status and also carries with it a moralism about excessive expenditure: the luxury car is decadent, but it is acceptable when in the form of a useful truck. Of course, in reality what could be a more frivolous expenditure than using a large gas-guzzling truck to do errands around town. This became obvious only when the price of gas in the U.S. radically spiked to over four dollars per gallon in a short span of time in 2008.

The origins of the shift from scientific to venture philanthropy in education thoroughly coincides with the broader neoliberal shift in education that can be traced back at least to the landmark report of 1983, *A Nation at Risk: The Imperative for Educational Reform. A Nation at Risk* was significant for reframing the animating ideals of public education through national economic competition and declaring a "rising tide of mediocrity," prompting hundreds of task forces to reevaluate every aspect of public education in the terms of the role education could play for global economic competition and workforce preparation.[33] Richard Lee Colvin writes:

> Demographic, technological, and economic changes in the United States and worldwide had made education more valuable for individuals, and for the nation's economic well being, than ever before. It was that last development, brought into focus with stories of outsourcing jobs and the multiplying number of engineers and scientists emerging from universities across India and Asia, that motivated Gates and others to remain committed to addressing the problems of the public schools.[34]

Conservative writers such as Colvin, Hess, and others recognize the shift to a service economy behind the redefined purpose of public education for the economy. However, they affirm such an understanding of public education primarily in the service of a corporate dominated, service-based economy and accept the neoliberal assumptions that schooling should primarily serve an economic function. They do not consider how such an understanding redefines the public dimensions of public schooling in privatized ways.

CONCLUSION

Venture philanthropy is a bankrupt ideal in light of the collapse of neoliberal market fundamentalism with the economic crisis that began in 2008. The public bailouts of multiple private industries radically called into question the long-standing economic doctrine and its emphasis on markets as self-regulating and the neoliberal view of expanding the market model to all aspects of public life. The projects of applying business rationales to all aspects of public schooling ought to be recognized as a hangover from a speculative bubble economy, from neoliberal economic dictates and ideology. These business ideals and metaphors as applied to public schooling need to be not only dropped but replaced with a recovered public sensibility, a universal value for the public schooling as a crucial part of a democratic public.

I have suggested that the shift from 'scientific' to venture philanthropy ought to be understood not only as part of the expansion of neoliberal ideology into education, the importation of the venture capital model into different domains, and the diminishing sense of the public but also in terms of the transformations from a production-oriented industrial economy to a consumption-oriented service economy. As the U.S. economy has become increasingly 'frivolous'—that is, dependent upon the ever greater expansion of manufactured consumer desires rather than the use-value of commodities—'frivolous' giving in the form of charity without strings has appeared in need of eradication by venture philanthropy. Instead venture philanthropy seeks to rationalize all aspects of giving and to control the giving process. I call into question the economic rationale for public schooling based on the unlimited growth of a consumer economy.

Neoliberal educational reform promises the student the dreamworld of consumer luxury found in consumer society, a promise that dominates educational policy. Those reforms pushed by venture philanthropy—the call and implementation of high-stakes standardized testing, the standardization of curriculum, the vocationalization of schooling, hyper-rationalization of all aspects of schooling from teacher bonus pay and paying students for grades to the linkage of teacher and administrator preparation to student test scores, the calls to treat public schooling like a market—all of this is justified as leading to the promise of greater and greater consumption.

The promise is based on educational exchange. The individual who works hard to learn that which others have determined to be important is ultimately promised the exchange of grades for higher schooling and then the exchange of grades and graduation for work, the exchange of work for greater income, and ultimately the ability to maximize the self through the consumption of ever more goods and services. Within this view, knowledge is treated like cash to be earned and then exchanged for educational honors and eventually for economic rewards. In these examples, testing is used as if it is a neutral and objective 'market' that serves as the medium for the acquisition of, display, and exchange that rewards talent and work. Of course, not only are the politics of knowledge behind the framing, selection, and organization of knowledge denied in this view, but the broader public implications of learning and the public role of schools is evacuated in favor of a metaphor of markets and consumption.

This explicit equation of educational activity with the promise of greater and greater levels of consumption is made to the nation as well as to the individual. The nation's schoolchildren must work hard in schools to compete globally with other nations to maintain or increase our nation's consuming capacity. In this zero-sum game the losing, poorer nations end up with the role of doing the brutal labor necessary to produce the commodities in the retail stores of the richer nations. This educational promise has no way of dealing with the global race to the bottom for cheaper and cheaper labor and worsened labor conditions; nor does it deal with the structural push for cheaper and cheaper domestic labor. As some such as Stanley Aronowitz argue, expanded higher education enrollment becomes a way to disguise unemployment. As the U.S. economy has entered crisis, we find the largest venture philanthropies retooling their agenda to focus specifically on higher education preparation.

In both the case of the individual and the nation, the promise is driven by the idealized form of consumption, that is, luxury—luxury understood through greater and more glorious forms of commodity acquisition and consumer activity. The social costs of consumerism as the core educational promise includes not merely a crisis of meaning, the alienation of the individual from the self, from nature, and from others; but it also empties out the political and ethical possibilities of education as the only vision of social improvement becomes the individual promise of consumer commodity acquisition. The social costs are even greater in the sense that constantly increased economic growth as the guiding force of the economy guarantees ecological devastation and vast inequalities in standards of living. Unlimited economic growth as the economic and educational goal is an utterly unsustainable ideal that will only result in the current heading toward ecological collapse, natural disaster, and human catastrophe. In the neoliberal view there is no alternative to the present, and so the aim of education is to enforce the existing order—an order that is misrepresented as natural and inevitable rather than as being continuously enacted through policy. There is a kind of double violence involved in the neoliberal educational project promoted by Gates and the other venture philanthropists. On the one hand, it naturalizes the neoliberal economic uses of education and thereby naturalizes and misrepresents as inevitable what are in fact human policies and priorities for profit accumulation above all else. On the other hand, neoliberal educational reform undermines the development of critical forms of education that would serve as the conditions for a public with the intellectual tools and dispositions to collectively solve public problems and move the society on a different course than the dead-end guarantee of unlimited growth.

The anticritical and anti-intellectual forms of schooling that are being fostered by neoliberal educational reform deprive citizens of the capacities to imagine and enact alternatives for the future, in part because they fail to teach how to criticize and analyze the assumptions and ideologies undergirding claims to truth. The dispositions of curiosity, disciplined creativity, and investigation under attack by neoliberal educational reform are crucial for fostering in citizens the skills of interpretation and social intervention, for imagining and enacting alternatives to the present.

Educators and cultural workers as well as students, policy makers, union organizers, and those committed to education for social justice need to work for the following:

1. To end tax breaks for foundations and to erect a wall between giving and the use of money for education as part of a larger movement against business driven, antipublic educational reform. If money is given by private interests, then public control ought to be fully retained over the use of educational spending.

2. To stop the application of economism to educational reform. With the collapse of neoliberal assumptions we should stop applying business metaphors and logic to educational thinking derived from discredited market fundamentalism. Metaphors not only of deregulation and privatization but also market-based framings of 'competition and choice,' 'monopoly,' 'turnaround,' and 'efficiency' need to be dropped in favor of public language and assumptions including equality, the public interest, public pedagogy, and a renewed language of educational obligation grounded in public democratic values. The 'measure' of educational progress ought not to be test scores but rather social progress measured by the dismantling of oppressive institutions and practices and the making of institutions and practices that provide contexts for egalitarian social relations, democratic debate, and dialogue in strong public spheres.
3. We should nationalize foundation wealth and give it to public educational authorities. Consider the case of the Bill and Melinda Gates Foundation wealth. Microsoft's private wealth was the result first of billions of dollars of public subsidy for the development of the computer industries, the internet, and information technology. This has been a case of socialized funding and privatized profits. Once the public paid to develop the industries, the profit from the technologies was handed over to private companies. The public then subsidized super-rich individuals by giving tax breaks for foundations that essentially subsidized these private individuals to take control over educational policy steering. In essence, the public has paid to give control of public policy to elites who were already the beneficiaries of public funding for high-tech development, real estate riches, and retail fortunes. This circuit of privatization must be ended, and public control over public policy formation must be democratized.

NOTES

1. A. Carnegie, *The Gospel of Wealth and Other Timely Essays* (1886; repr., New York: The Century Company, 1901).
2. See R. Arnove, *Philanthropy and Cultural Imperialism: The Foundations at Home and Abroad* (Bloomington: Indiana University Press, 1982). See also J. Roelofs, "Foundations and Collaboration," *Critical Sociology* 33 (2007): 479–504.
3. S. Žižek, *Violence* (New York: Picador, 2008), 20–22.
4. See R. Arnove, *Philanthropy and Cultural Imperialism.*
5. Neoliberalism involves redistributing public goods to private controls while espousing market triumphalism. As David Harvey explains, it is a project of class warfare. See D. Harvey, *A Brief History of Neoliberalism* (Oxford: Oxford University Press, 2006).
6. Notable early exceptions to this include Frederick Hess's edited collection *With the Best of Intentions* from a neoliberal perspective and the liberal work of Janelle Scott such as "The Politics of Venture Philanthropy

in Charter School Policy and Advocacy," *Educational Policy* 23, no. 1: 106–36; and the work of Rick Cohen of the Center for Responsive Philanthropy. Mike and Susan Klonsky's book *Small Schools: Public School Reform Meets the Ownership Society* (New York: Routledge, 2008) and Philip Kovacs's scholarship on Gates stand out as some of the rare critical work on venture philanthropy. See for example, P. Kovacs, "Think Tanks, Foundations and Institutes," in *Knowledge and Power in the Global Economy: The Effects of School Reform in a Neoconservative/Neoliberal Age*, ed. D. Gabbard, 2nd ed. (Mahwah, NJ: Lawrence Erlbaum Associates, 2007); and P. Kovacs, "The Anti-School Movement," also in *Knowledge and Power.*

7. R. Colvin, "Chapter 1: A New Generation of Philanthropists and Their Great Ambitions," in *With the Best of Intentions*, ed. F. Hess (Cambridge, MA: Harvard Education Press, 2005), 21.
8. R. Colvin, *With the Best of Intentions*, 27.
9. These points are modified from those made by R. Cohen in "Strategic Grantmaking: Foundations and the School Privatization Movement," National Committee for Responsive Philanthropy, November 2007, http://www.ncrp.org/files/publications/ncrp2007-strategicgrantmaking-final-lowres.pdf (retreived August 20, 2010).
10. See, for example, K. Saltman, *Collateral Damage* (Lanham, MD: Rowman and Littlefield, 2000); *The Edison Schools* (New York: Routledge, 2005); *Capitalizing on Disaster* (Boulder: Paradigm Publishers, 2007).
11. As economic doctrine, neoliberalism calls for the privatization of public goods and services, the deregulation of markets, foreign direct investment, and monetarism. Neoliberalism represents an ideology of market fundamentalism in which the inevitably bureaucratically encumbered state can do no good and markets must be relied upon to do what the state has formerly done. Neoliberalism imagines the social world as privatized and suggests that economic rationality ought to be expanded to every last realm. In this view the public sector disappears, as the only legitimate collectivities can be markets, while the individual is principally defined as an economic actor, that, is a worker or consumer. The state in this view ought to use its power to facilitate markets. Democracy becomes an administrative matter best left to markets rather than to public deliberation.
12. P. Bourdieu, *Firing Back: Against the Tyranny of the Market* (New York: New Press, 2003).
13. See J. Spring, *Educating the Consumer-Citizen* (New York: Lawrence Earlbaum, 2003).
14. See D. Shipps, *School Reform Corporate Style: Chicago 1880–2000* (Lawrence: University Press of Kansas, 2006).
15. P. Frumkin, "Inside Venture Philanthropy," *Society*, May/June 2003: 4
16. S. Aronowitz, *Against Schooling for An Education That Matters* (Boulder, CO: Paradigm Publishers, 2008), 53.
17. See R. Arnove, *Philanthropy and Cultural Imperialism.*
18. See J. Roelofs, "Foundations and Collaboration."
19. See A. Carnegie, *The Gospel of Wealth.*
20. S. Katz, "Philanthropy's New Math," *Chronicle of Higher Education* 1F2, 2007, supp. 3.
21. S. Strauss, "The Robber Baron as Lord Bountiful: Bill Gates and the Capitalist Philanthropy Scam," *Freedom Socialist* 27, no. 4 (August–September 2006).
22. This point is made by multiple scholars of foundations, including Joan Roelofs and Robert Arnove.

23. Paying teachers bonuses linked to student test performance exacerbates the ways in which standardized testing contributes to the unequal distribution of cultural capital and the ways in which class and culturally specific knowledge is treated as universally valuable. In addition to fostering 'teaching to the test,' this undermines the possibility of critical forms of teaching and learning that connect claims to truth to questions of power and authority and broader structures of power.
24. R. Cohen, III, "Strategic Grantmaking: Foundations and the School Privatization Movement," National Committee for Responsive Philanthropy, November 2007, http://www.ncrp.org/files/publications/ncrp2007-strategicgrantmaking-final-lowres.pdf (retreived August 20, 2010).
25. S. Katz, "Philanthropy's New Math," 2.
26. Ibid., 7.
27. I. Silver, "Disentangling Class from Philanthropy: The Double-Edged Sword of Alternative Giving," *Critical Sociology* 33 (2007): 538.
28. These are discussed in J. Roelofs, "Foundations and Collaboration."
29. Ibid., 491.
30. This history is discussed in S. Gould, *Ontogeny and Phylogeny* (Cambridge, MA: Belknap Press of Harvard University Press, 1985); G. Bederman, *Manliness and Civilization: A Cultural History of Gender and Race in the United States, 1880–1917* (Chicago: University of Chicago Press, 1996); N. Lesko, *Act Your Age!* (New York: Routledge, 2001); and E. Brown and K. Saltman, *The Critical Middle School Reader* (New York: Routledge, 2005). The last contains an exemplary excerpt from G. Stanley Hall's book *Adolescence.*
31. G. Bataille, *The Accursed Share*, vol. 1 (New York: Zone Books, 1998), 126.
32. The PBS miniseries documentary *The Triumph of the Nerds: The Rise of Accidental Empires* (1996) provides a valuable history of the early commodification of the software and computer industry.
33. R. Colvin, *With the Best of Intentions*, 25. See A. Molnar, *Giving Kids the Business* (New York: Westview, 2001).
34. R. Colvin, *With the Best of Intentions*, 26.

2 Power Philanthropy
Taking the Public Out of Public Education

Michael Klonsky

I wish I wasn't [the world's richest man]. There is nothing good that comes out of that.

—Bill Gates
(2006 Interview with Danny Deutsch,
Times of London, 5/5/2006. Also Seattle Times 7/3/2007)

The world's largest private foundation, run by the world's richest man, Bill Gates, is part of a small group of omnipotent private foundations that currently play a disproportionate role in driving national public education policy. Virtually free from any government oversight and accountable to no one, the power philanthropists leverage multibillion-dollar reserve funds to drive a conservative agenda and threaten many areas of public life and public decision making.

Employing a top-down reform strategy, power philanthropy has taken upon itself the mantle of the world's social engineer and has particularly turned the arena of public education topsy-turvy. This new generation of billionaire private funders was spawned by the technology revolution of the 1980s. Armed with a few provocative ideas about schooling and social transformation, coupled with a penchant for the business model of market-based reforms, they have used their philanthropy to muscle their programs into school districts, schools, and indeed, into the federal government, calling into question the public nature and purpose of traditionally public institutions, and especially of public schools.

Giant foundations and corporate megafunds, such as the Bill and Melinda Gates Foundation and the Eli and Edith Broad Foundation, now underwrite much of what passes for educational reform. Their backing lends a measure of clout, political credibility, and favorable media attention to any program or strategy they anoint as a "model." As the largest foundations control ever larger concentrations of private wealth, their power over public institutions also grows larger. For example, the Broad Foundation now trains school superintendents and district CEOs in the *Broad model* of leadership and then uses its economic and political clout to have them placed at the top of dozens of major public school systems, both urban and suburban. Broad fellows currently hold leadership positions in districts such as Washington,

D.C., New Orleans, Philadelphia, Detroit, Green Bay, Boston, Durham, Prince George's County (Maryland), Providence, Houston, Chicago, Dallas, and Oakland, to name but a few.[1] The annual $2 million Broad Prize given to a chosen school district serves to sweeten the pot, which makes the selection of a Broad-connected CEO almost irresistible.

Another example: the Gates Foundation's growing influence in popular media in partnership with media giant Viacom, including collaboration on actual scripts and messaging. The Gates messaging experiment began on September 12, 2009, when BET, a division of Viacom, premiered an award-winning documentary called *Pressure Cooker* as part of the network's ongoing education initiative and Viacom's new Get Schooled platform. In one scene, an African-American teacher stands in front of a class full of inner-city students and delivers the foundation's message:[2]

> At a school where more than 40 percent of students don't even make it to their senior year, Ms. Stephenson's class stands in stark contrast, with 11 members of last year's class earning more than $750,000 in scholarships. She offers the kids her version of the American Dream: You choose a realistic goal. You work hard. You work the system. You get out of Northeast Philly.

Arango and Stelter go on to describe the Gates media intervention:

> The huge foundation, brimming with billions of dollars from Gates and Warren Buffett, is well known for its myriad projects around the world to promote health and education. It is less well known as a behind-the-scenes influencer of public attitudes toward these issues by helping to shape story lines and insert messages into popular entertainment like the TV shows *ER*, *Law & Order: SVU* and *Private Practice*. The foundation's messages on HIV prevention, surgical safety and the spread of infectious diseases have found their way into these shows . . . It could be called 'message placement': the social or philanthropic corollary to product placement deals in which marketers pay to feature products in shows and movies. Instead of selling Coca-Cola or GM cars, they promote education and healthy living.[3]

This disproportional power over public space and ideology is but a reflection of the rapidly widening gulf between the super rich and the rest of us. The family of Wal-Mart founder Sam Walton, for example, has a combined fortune of around $90 billion. Warren Buffett's and Bill Gates' personal fortunes are each estimated at around $46 billion to $60 billion. (Buffett gave half of his personal fortune to the Gates Foundation in the belief that Gates would be a wiser investor in public good than the government). Contrast this concentration of personal and family wealth with that of the bottom 40 percent of the entire U.S. population—about 120 million people—which is estimated to be $90 billion in the aggregate, and you begin to get the picture of the great social-political imbalance. But, one might well ask, isn't it a good thing that the nation's wealthiest few use their money to help the nation's poor? Isn't charitable giving a positive value, worthy of praise? Good question.

Since the start of the high-tech revolution, the nation's richest families have doubled their share of the nation's combined wealth. By the year 2000, they had accumulated a third of that total wealth. That's more than what is owned by 90 percent of the population. The most far-sighted of that top 1 percent obviously realized that without some sort of redistribution, this gaping Grand Canyon between them and the rest could be a formula for 'civil unrest.' Besides, they were going to have to give some of it up, either in taxes or in the relative shelter of charitable trusts, which enable them to use that otherwise taxable income to wield influence and shape public life while amassing public goodwill.

The Gates Foundation, which has become the vanguard force in this new era of top-down school reform, flexes its $66 billion muscles to influence global social and economic policies in areas ranging from health to public education. Their cadres fill key positions in both Republican and Democratic administrations, particularly within the Department of Education. For example, Secretary of Education Arne Duncan's Chief of Staff Margot Rogers served as the special assistant to the director of education at the Gates Foundation. In this position she managed and co-led the development of the foundation's five-year education strategy and staff realignment, and she served on the education division's investment committee and strategic leadership team. Assistant Deputy Secretary for Innovation and Improvement James Shelton previously served as a program director for the education division of the Gates Foundation and managed the foundation's national programs and work in the northeast region of the United States. Shelton has also been a partner and the East Coast lead for New Schools Venture Fund and cofounded LearnNow, a school management company that later was acquired by Edison Schools. This is not to imply that either Rogers or Shelton are moles of any sort, working in the direct service of the foundation. It simply illustrates the breadth of Gates' influence and the easy movement back and forth of top-level officials between government and power foundations.

Although the foundation, which is personally run by Bill Gates, has at times provided badly needed resources in areas where public funding can't or won't, that funding has often brought with it the disempowerment of local communities and an overreliance on the whims, predispositions, or simple misunderstandings of the world's richest man.

Nowhere has this antidemocratic wind of power philanthropy been blowing harder than over the stormy seas of U.S. public school reform, where power plays by the Gates, Broad, and Walton Foundations have often left piles of wreckage in their wake.

Today's power philanthropists are a far cry from predecessors like Andrew Carnegie—wealthy industrialists who basically believed that it was the moral duty and social responsibility of the super-rich to act like a charity and possibly help remake the poor while feeding them. As writer Bill Kauffman put it, "Carnegie's greatest legacy would owe more to old-fashioned charity than Social Darwinism. He gave away money to build small-town libraries and restore church organs."[4]

Others, like Rockefeller, donated millions in an attempt to clean up a tarnished public image as one of the most despised men in America. In other words, it made good political sense—not to mention being a giant tax shelter. Bill Gates, similarly, may have realized the need to run the world's biggest and most powerful foundation, following Microsoft's battering by international courts and regulators for the company's strong-arm and illegal practices within the high-tech industry.

In one interview, Gates admitted that billions of dollars in fines made him rethink his relationship with government.[5] At first Gates took pride in not having to deal with government. But he told the BBC that the long court battles made him see the need to exert greater influence over government and the public sector. It's worth noting here that the federal attorney who prosecuted and finally settled the Microsoft case in the U.S. was none other than Joel Klein, a Broad Fellow and now the chancellor of the nation's largest school district, New York City Public Schools, which currently receives more than $100 million in Gates and Broad funding.

One may well ask if there's any hope of restoring corporate legitimacy in the wake of the 2008 scandal-ridden near-collapse of global finance-capitalism and highly publicized fiascos like the Madoff scandal. Is power-philanthropy, or what some now call philanthro-capitalism, the driver of global social change in today's crisis-ridden world, as it claims to be?

In a speech that sent shock waves through corporate/philanthropic offices around the world, Bill Gates told the 2008 World Economic Forum in Davos, Switzerland, that "creative capitalism can and should help solve the world's problems of hunger, disease, and poor schools by building social capital into investments into profitable business enterprises." Gates tried to make the case that "businessmen and businesses are best placed to save the world."[6] Author Michael Kinsley, who was inspired by the Davos speech, describes creative capitalism this way: "It's using the idea of self-interest turning into the general interest—which Adam Smith wrote about—to address problems that have traditionally been addressed by philanthropy and government."[7]

The power foundations' destructive impact could be clearly seen in the promising community-based small-schools movement for high school reform in the 1990s. This movement initially received major foundation support that provided fuel and energy, and then, as suddenly as it had supported reform, the philanthropies abandoned it or imposed undemocratic control mechanisms, top-down mandates, arbitrary timetables, and inappropriate business models of replication and accountability. The small-schools movement became the centerpiece for a tug-of-war between public and ownership-society interests.[8]

During the eight years of the Bush administration, the vibrant, teacher-led small-schools movement that had arisen since the early 1990s was overtaken by chains of privately managed charter schools underwritten by the power philanthropists who used their influence to undermine competing public investment in the program.

In 2004, Bush's secretary of education Rod Paige moved to defund the federal Smaller Learning Communities (SLC) initiative in order to shift some $240 million away from public school restructuring and into support for private and parochial schools. The federal SLC grant had offered hope to teachers in many large, urban and suburban, violence-prone high schools. The grant program had originated in 2000, after the shootings at Columbine High School, with strong bipartisan support. After being placed on the Bush administration's chopping block, the program was saved only after intensive lobbying and congressional trade-offs in a highly contentious and polarized political climate. Several of the largest foundations, including Gates, began advising school districts and state departments of education to steer clear of SLCs and concentrate instead on closing low-performing schools and replacing them exclusively with new start-ups or charter schools. At the same time, Gates-funded "research" granting also began to shift away from high school reform. One report by Gates consultants made the claim that differences in school environments "had no clear impact on student learning" and warned that "SLCs can be very disruptive to the school."[9]

Gates' nearly $2 billion investment in the small-schools initiative was much more than a traditional foundation's attempt to push innovation into schools. In 1999, Gates had hired Tom VanderArk, the former school superintendent from Federal Way, Washington, to run the foundation's $6 billion education program. VanderArk, like Bill Gates, had been sold on the idea of small schools even though he had himself tried and failed to restructure Federal Way's large high school (1,600 students), unable to sell the idea to his teachers, their union, and conservative elements within the community.

VanderArk went about his new assignment with a vengeance, leveraging the foundation's money to create hundreds of new small schools and to restructure traditional, large urban high schools, first in the state of Washington and then across the nation. He went on a search for replicable models and found a few external and intermediary organizations and leaders whom he felt were capable of driving the process forward. They included the Bay Area Coalition of Equitable Schools (BayCES), headed by Steve Jubb, charter school guru Joe Nathan at the University of Minnesota's Center for School Change, and the Chicago-based Small Schools Workshop.

Pointing to "a growing body of research, including University of Washington education Dean Pat Wasley's study of Chicago's small schools movement, suggesting that students thrive in smaller academic settings,"[10] VanderArk at first used $350 million of the fund's money to push small schools into school districts, whether they wanted them or not. The grants, which marked the foundation's first gift to schools outside its home state, spanned the country from New York to Alaska. The biggest, $13.5 million, went to the Providence, Rhode Island, school district to devise ways to create smaller learning environments, as well as to improve teaching and strengthen community involvement. Nathan's group received $7.9 million to work with school districts in Cincinnati, St. Paul, and West Clermont (Ohio) to explore ways to reconfigure into smaller learning settings ten large high schools that served a total of 16,000 students. Other early Gates grant recipients included The Big Picture Co., headed by Dennis Littky and Elliot Washor, cofounders of Providence's ground-breaking progressive MET school (Gates pushed MET leaders to replicate the school in dozens of new districts); the Center for Collaborative Education in Boston, directed by Dan French, who would later become the driving force behind that city's innovative Pilot schools; and EdVisions, a progressive teachers' cooperative that ran the Minnesota New Country School in Henderson, Minnesota (to replicate that model at fifteen new schools).

In district after district, the foundation's arbitrary goals and timelines began to clash with those of local reformers and educators. Some district leaders had no real desire or capability to implement the Gates model, especially if they had to keep to the foundation's timeline. Strict implementation could mean facing a revolt by teachers and principals. In some districts, such as Cleveland and San Francisco, the threat of a Gates invasion led to the departure of veteran superintendents.

Gates funding was so large and so widespread, it seemed for a time as if every initiative in the small-schools and charter world was being underwritten by the foundation. If you wanted to start a school, hold a meeting, organize a conference, or write an article in an education journal, you first had to consider Gates. So it's understandable that small-schoolers were shaken when they first began to hear of fickle shifts in Gates' funding strategy and when stories began to appear in the education journals that indicated the foundation's interest in high school restructuring was fading and funding might move in another direction—possibly toward another magic bullet, such as teacher training or early college. The foundation that had recently seemed to hold out the greatest hope of help and support for major school-change efforts now appeared to favor closing hundreds of urban high schools and turning them over to private management companies.

The first public clue was a 2004 article in which VanderArk was extensively interviewed:

> As a strategy for reforming secondary education in America, small schools have gotten big. Prodded by an outpouring of philanthropic and federal largesse, school districts and even some states are downsizing public high schools to combat high dropout rates and low levels of student achievement, especially in big- city school systems. For longtime proponents of small schools, the groundswell of support for their ideas was making for heady times.[11]

Then the other shoe dropped:

> Despite the concept's unprecedented popularity, however, evidence is mounting that "scaling up" scaled-down schooling is extraordinarily complex. A sometimes confusing array of approaches is unfolding under the banner of small high schools, contributing to concerns that much of the flurry of activity may be destined for disappointing results. "It's very, very difficult to do this well," said Tom Vander Ark, who heads the Bill and Melinda Gates Foundation's mammoth initiative to create small high schools. "Small is not a panacea. It's a platform that helps you do the things you need to do to help kids succeed." Vander Ark surmised that Gates' reform would have to shift gears. Rather than converting large high schools into smaller learning communities or small schools, said the Gates leader, "we need to close a thousand schools."[12]

Most small-schools activists, teachers, and researchers had long appreciated the fact that small schools weren't a "panacea" and that high school restructuring was arduous, demanding work. After all, they had been doing the work for about a decade in most cities. Many suspected that VanderArk's gloomy assessment of the prospects for high school reform, particularly for the conversion of large high schools, was a reaction to the failed Gates-funded small-schools project at Denver's Manual High School.

The Manual Project was a top-down attempt at high school restructuring. In a bygone era, Manual had been the flagship high school of Denver's black community. In recent years, the impoverishment of the surrounding community and of Manual's student body, accompanied by a middle-class exodus, had helped turn Manual into a poverty-stricken school with a population that was 86 percent low-income students of color including a growing percentage of Spanish-speaking immigrant students.

The school fell into decline and disrepair. Its problems were those common to low-income schools: a revolving-door series of principals, a shrinking school population, and a shortage of highly qualified teachers. The school was ill-equipped to provide needed services to its new English Language Learners. A *Denver Post* story described the plight of one of the long line of Manual principals, Nancy Sutton:

> Sutton tried almost everything to improve Manual: small learning communities, off-campus internships, and group learning. High school reform was still relatively new. "[We were] ahead of the national knowledge base, ahead of what people knew what to do," Sutton said. "I was doing everything, we all were, that I thought was research based." But teachers felt pulled in different directions . . . Manual was at the very bottom of all Colorado high schools on the 2000 Colorado Student Assessment Program tests. Sutton and some of her school leaders in 2001 decided to take a stab at one more school reform, applying for a Gates Foundation grant to break up Manual into three small schools. At the time, Gates was investing hundreds of millions of dollars across the country, mostly in urban areas, in small-school reform. These schools were believed to save at-risk students by giving them personal relationships and high expectations. The school board approved Manual's 'breakup' in the spring of 2001. Most teachers found out about the plan in April from a note in their mailboxes. They had until August, when school started, to figure it out. "We resented it," said Mario Giardiello, who taught at Manual from 1999 to 2003. "Everything felt like it was being done to us . . . All of this was done without the students' or teachers' input."[13]

With little knowledge or understanding of the unique needs, history, and conditions within the rapidly changing Manual community, the Gates Foundation jumped into the fray armed with a boiler-plate restructuring plan to turn Manual into three completely autonomous schools: The Millennium Quest Science Academy, The Arts and Cultural Studies Academy, and the Leadership Academy (http://www.elpueblointegral.org/The_Manual_Story.pdf). Through its intermediary, the Colorado Children's Campaign (CCC), the Gates Foundation pushed its own completely arbitrary timeline for change, propelled in part by its need to quickly identify a national, replicable model for the foundation's new high school initiative.

But in Denver, a resistant district leadership pushed back, unwilling to cede power to outsiders. Teachers, who felt left out of the decision-making process, also resisted. Most important, students, parents, and community groups expressed anger—not so much at the small-schools plan but at the top-down way in which it was imposed upon them. The Gates Foundation's 'model' was never really implemented. Its vision of pure, autonomous small schools soon turned into three amorphous programs, with kids and teachers trying to make up for shortages by crossing over from school to school for needed classes and programs. Finally, Gates and the district gave up. The funding was pulled. The district announced that Manual would be shut down, its kids shipped to schools throughout the city. Teachers lost their jobs. The community lost a precious resource.

The shock waves from the Manual debacle reverberated throughout the small-schools movement, leaving some national and local advocates in despair: How could something so promising and so well funded turn so sour? VanderArk concluded that the problem wasn't with the Gates Foundation's model of change, but rather something inherent in high schools like Manual. VanderArk summed up the Manual experience in a *Business Week* article, estimating that up to 1,000 of the nation's 20,000 neighborhood high schools would have to be closed down, a disaster for some communities, potentially on a par with Hurricane Katrina.[14] Restructuring high schools, creating smaller learning communities, working for school change with existing faculties and students, and engaging communities in the process, were knocked off the top of the Gates Foundation's funding agenda.

Although the Gates Foundation never did a critical self-assessment of the debacle at Manual, a group of University of Colorado researchers did. Three years after the closing of Manual, the researchers found that 558 students had been forced to relocate to new schools, which destabilized their lives as well as the Manual school community. Relationships that had been years in the making, between students and adult educators and among the students themselves, were torn apart. Nearly a third of those students are now classified by the district as withdrawn. They are either dropouts, have moved to a different state, or their whereabouts are unknown. One student has died, and 94 transferred out of Denver Public Schools. Their progress is no longer tracked.[15] The study also found that:

- Only 52 percent of the students who were juniors when Manual closed went on to graduate. Manual had previously graduated 68 percent of its seniors.
- Historically, Manual students had a 6 percent chance of dropping out of school. After closure, the chance that a displaced Manual student would drop out soared to 17 percent.
- Colorado Student Assessment Program test scores among displaced Manual students dropped between 3 and 38 points in reading, writing, and math. Historically, Manual students typically gained between 8 and 19 points each year in those subjects.[16]

Fast forward to today: Education Secretary Arne Duncan is calling for the closing of at least 5,000 more high schools. The legacy of the Gates Foundation's reform strategy lives on.

When a relatively small activist group of neoconservative ideologues took hold of the U.S. Department of Education in 2001, they sought to consolidate their *ownership society* agenda by exercising control over the $60 billion K–12 federal education budget to drive state and local spending priorities; they also sought to recruit a growing and increasingly active sector of private educational philanthropists. Frederick Hess of the American Enterprise Institute aptly dubbed this activist tendency "muscular philanthropy," which he considered a compliment. The group includes a broad spectrum of private funders both large and small that ranges from

Walton and the Milwaukee-based Lynde and Harry Bradley Foundation on the political right to the liberal/centrist Ford, Carnegie, Broad, and Gates Foundations; the latter is so big that they consider themselves above traditional Left/Right political alignments.

During the past decade, power philanthropy has attached itself to that ownership society line of the Bush administration's No Child Left Behind policies. It has become, in effect, the sugar daddy for a new class of politically aligned corporatists and educational entrepreneurs. Its influence to a large degree carried over to the new Obama administration through its Department of Education and appointed Secretary of Education, Arne Duncan. This carry-over was confirmed by Vander Ark, who in a blog post described the current administration's Race-to-the-Top (RTTT) initiative and its "coherent education agenda" as a "mostly unified eight-year policy push by the new money foundations."[17]

While education director at the Gates Foundation, Vander Ark helped shape many of these policies; yet today, he echoes the assessment made by many of the Obama/Duncan critics on the Left, who find it difficult to distinguish between the current education program and that of the previous administration. Vander Ark points out:

> The "new" education agenda didn't get written last month: it's been a decade in the making . . . Since 2001, the charter school movement has become a powerful force backed by funding from Gates, Broad, Walton, Fisher, and Robertson foundations. Active charter advocates include The National Alliance of Public Charter Schools, Center for Education Reform, and funding coalitions including New Schools and Charter School Growth Fund.[18]

VanderArk goes on to describe the foundations' "human capital" agenda, which he says, "has also matured in the last eight years with the scaled success of foundation favorites Teach for America, New Leaders, and New Teacher Project. Accelerated progress on national college ready standards began with a 2004 Gates Foundation orchestrated National High School Summit, a shotgun marriage of Achieve and NGA."[19]

The power philanthropists continue to view government, schools, and all public space primarily as inefficient bureaucracy-bound inferiors as compared with the corporate and technocratic visionaries in a world run by "the smartest guys in the room."[20] The reference here, of course, is to privatization pioneer Enron, which, before its scandalous collapse, had helped drive the great public-to-private shifts in the economies of Britain under Thatcher and the U.S. under Reagan.[21] As Enron V.P Rebecca Mark told Harvard researchers, "We are bringing a market mentality and spreading the privatization gospel in countries that desperately need this kind of thinking."[22]

Emergent power philanthropists display the same Enron zeal for influence over public education. The Walton Family Foundation, for example, dwarfs all other funders in the school privatization movement, having provided more than $25 million each year for five consecutive years. Other major supporters of so-called 'school choice' are the Lynde and Harry Bradley Foundation, which gave over $6 million in 2005 to the organizations studied; and the Sarah Scaife Foundation, which gave nearly $4 million in 2005. Both these foundations are widely known to promote conservative causes, says Aaron Dorfman,[23] executive director of the National Committee for Responsive Philanthropy (NCRP), a watchdog organization.

Surprisingly, the Gates Foundation was the fourth-largest donor to organizations promoting vouchers in 2005, granting $2.6 million to organizations studied in the report. An NCRP study found that each of the foundations had its own reasons for supporting privatization, which makes it difficult to classify them as one group. But most had expressed frustration with what they believe to be the "failure of public schools" and pushed the concept of free-market competition as a way to leverage better outcomes.[24]

Says Dorfman, "Some of the more zealous conservative funders in the report are strongly anti-government and/or anti-union and see this issue as an opportunity to reduce the size of government and weaken teachers unions."[25]

Because the power philanthropists enjoy lucrative tax benefits, with the tab being picked up by the tax-paying citizenry, Dorfman concludes that it's right to consider these massive accumulations of funds to be at least "partially-public."[26] He insists that there could and should be more public oversight and democratic accountability over how foundation dollars are spent. Predictably, Gates, Broad, and Walton have all pushed back on this notion and in fact reversed it, forcing public entities like school districts instead to be accountable to them, the private funders. Their critique of public institutions is deep, thorough, and self-interested.

In his 2008 *Testimony before the Committee on Science and Technology, U.S. House of Representatives*, power philanthropist Bill Gates made clear his wishes for a fluid supply of foreign technical labor to be brought into the U.S. to work for companies like Microsoft. He also faulted U.S. public schools for not turning out enough competent engineers and scientists and called for even greater emphasis on standardized testing, or what Gates refers to as "metrics."[27]

In his self-assigned role as world changer and power wielder, however, Gates has remained fairly neutral and above the fray so far as partisan politics are concerned. He gives mightily to both parties and finds a sympathetic ear within each. Case in point: the Wall Street Journal reported that employees at Microsoft and the Gates Foundation bundled large contributions to the Obama inaugural celebration.[28] For an event where Wall Street employees were actually banned from giving, Gates made sure his people were among the largest group of bundlers.

Many progressive educators and school reformers find it difficult to make a critical assessment of these new power philanthropists. For one thing, the more liberal wing of corporate philanthropy is already under attack from free-market ultraconservatives who argue that the role of business is strictly profit making and that caring for the sick or feeding the hungry in the Third World is not good business.[29]

For another, if it weren't for the likes of Gates, Broad, and the Walton family, many of these would-be critics would lack valuable resources for their own badly-needed reform efforts, charter schools, and university-based research projects. Numerous school districts around the country would become operationally dysfunctional in this period of giant budget cuts, were it not for concentrated and targeted, multimillion-dollar gifts from those previously mentioned.

But particularly in times like these, marked by a global financial meltdown, it's easy for some to see philanthro-capitalism as a necessary if problematic force to be reckoned with as we watch underfunded public institutions, school systems, being forced to accept a Faustian deal—to surrender public ownership and decision-making in exchange for their very survival. Many school communities and supportive educational reform organizations have already succumbed. Others are bravely resisting.

Even where direct self-interest isn't involved, some reform activists can be heard defending or apologizing for the power philanthropists. As one of my colleagues put it, if it weren't for Gates, half of the countries in Africa wouldn't have a medical system, and AIDS and malaria would be twice as devastating as they already are.

It's hard to disagree with that line of thinking without seeming like an uncaring sophist or ideologically driven academic. Being neither of those, I would argue that those facing epidemics in Africa as well as those suffering from poor educational resources here in our local communities, can ill afford dependency upon the benevolence of the world's five or six richest men for their health care, public schools, or other basic needs. In a democratic society, health care and education should be part of the public domain, part of public space, and run with a high level of public decision-making and public accountability.

In some respects, the expression of concentrated financial power determining public need differs little from that being exercised by governmental elites. In a certain sense, the behavior of power philanthropists is no different from the way government grants or foreign assistance programs function, often driving a narrow partisan or ideological agenda attached to badly needed health, birth control, or education programs. A great recent example was the implementation of the so-called Mexico City Gag Rule, by which the Bush administration barred the use of funds for those nongovernmental organizations (NGOs) who dared perform or even mention abortion services as a method of family planning. The policy became a political wedge issue in the abortion debate, as Republicans adopted it and Democrats rejected it. President Obama rescinded it as one of his first acts in office.

Obviously, even within the public domain, the struggle to maintain a public voice continues. But it could be argued that having so much power over the lives of millions of people is an even more egregious violation of democratic ideals when that power is held singly by one man or a few corporate foundations.

None other than Bill Clinton's labor secretary, Robert Reich, who once preached that "social responsibility and profits converge over the long term," now believes that the giant corporations "cannot be socially responsible, at least not to any significant extent." (Reich, R. (2007) Supercapitalism: The Transformation of Business, Democracy, and Everyday Life, p. 172. New York, Vintage).

In his book *Supercapitalism*, Reich makes the case that the current appeal to corporate social responsibility is directly related to decreasing confidence in our democracy's responsiveness to the common good.[30] Although Reich says little about the role of power philanthropy, he goes so far as to call the whole idea of *corporate social responsibility* a dangerous diversion that is undermining democracy. One reason, says Reich, is the effectiveness of corporate lobbyists who prevent the government from forcefully responding to societal or scientific problems, such as climate change, and who use corporate power as leverage against aid programs unrelated to America's corporate interests.[31] Asks Reich: "So why would the same corporations that block effective action on the environment voluntarily embark on their own efforts to improve the environment?"[32]

But at Davos, the new class of corporate and Wall Street billionaires answer Reich this way: If, as Milton Friedman argued, the "social responsibility of business is to increase its profits,"[33] then the establishment of giant and well-endowed philanthropies can incentivize the world-changing agendas of their socially conscious leaders. Not only that, they argue, philanthro-capitalism can do it more effectively and efficiently than can big bureaucratic government agencies or small, local NGOs, since the philanthropies are not hampered by requirements for democratic decision making or oversight.

Philanthropy may well have a pivotal role to play in today's civil society. But hopefully, the role will not be that of sole or even primary source of funding for society's basic needs. Especially in these times of deep economic crisis, shrinking tax bases, and tightening budgets in the public sector, schools and communities are increasingly reliant on big philanthropy, not just for innovative pilot projects or supplemental program development, but for the essentials. Along with this dependency has come a shrinking public sector, as public space is sold off or contracted out and with it, a steady erosion of public voice and input into the most important decisions that affect the lives of our communities.

The purpose of this examination is not to attack the philanthropists for being philanthropists or even to doubt their motivation for giving away billions of dollars from their personal or corporate vaults. But that motivation plays a role in society and is worth close scrutiny. For if the public space and public control over democratic institutions diminishes in proportion to the growth of influence of power philanthropy, then we need to examine critically the current system of public and private resource distribution with a view toward systemic change if our democracy is to survive these difficult times.

Over at Microsoft, the Gates people would say that mega-giving is good for their corporate image. Others might make the case either biblically, medically, or psychologically that it's better to give than to receive; it's good for one's soul, health, or brain. Matthew Bishop claims that giving motivates the brain's mesolimbic pathway and generates the feel-good neurotransmitter dopamine.

Bishop is an award-winning journalist and the coauthor with Michael Green of *Philanthrocapitalism: How the Rich Can Save the World*. After reading about Warren Buffett's $30 billion contribution to the Gates Foundation, thereby doubling its assets and making it by far the world's largest philanthropy, a star-struck Bishop interviewed billionaires like Gates, George Soros, and other so-called "influentials" including Bill Clinton, Angelina Jolie, and Bono to find out their motivation.[34]

Several of the dot-com billionaires spoke about philanthropy as a solution to what some psychologists call "sudden wealth syndrome."[35] Bishop and Green point out that never before in history has there been such a rapid and massive transfer of wealth into the hands of such a small number of individuals. Although their book is selling like hot cakes, which reveals the nation's widespread interest in philanthropy as a potential crisis buffer, Bishop and Green may have picked an inopportune time to gush over a seemingly never-ending stock market bubble. They go so far as to claim that the wealthy are simply "more generous" by nature than poor people, and even calculate the structure of a billionaire's life as divided into two great periods: their "wealth-creating" and "wealth-disbursement years."[36]

The largest power foundations, including Gates, invest most if not nearly all of their assets in for-profit ventures rather than in public giving. After Bill Gates decided to come over from Microsoft to run the foundation directly, a *Los Angeles Times* article revealed that nearly 95 percent of the Foundation's tax-free funds were being spent on profitable private investments that did great harm to the environment in countries around the globe.[37]

While the foundation was pouring $218 million into worldwide polio and measles immunization and research, including in the Niger Delta—while funding inoculations to protect health—its stock portfolio included investments of $423 million in Enid, Royal Dutch Shell, Exxon Mobil, Chevron, and Total of France—the same companies responsible for most of the flares blanketing the delta with pollution beyond anything permitted in the United States or Europe.

The foundation was far from alone in its destructive investment practices. However, many large foundations engage in far more socially conscious and ethically consistent investment practices. Several major foundations that make social justice, corporate governance, and environmental stewardship key considerations in their investment strategies include the Ford Foundation,[38] which has a clearly defined "social justice" funding strategy[39] and, with $11.6 billion, is the nation's second-largest private philanthropy. Others include the John D. and Catherine T. MacArthur Foundation, the Rockefeller Foundation, and the Charles Stewart Mott Foundation.

The global financial crisis is bound to have an effect on philanthrocapitalism. The most influential donors have lost an estimated 15 to 20 percent of their assets in recent months. Although the current crisis is expected to constrict foundation support for education and school reform initiatives, it could indirectly increase the leverage these giant foundations have in influencing education policy from the top down. The sharp decline in housing prices, for example, has reduced the assets held by education foundations and threatens the very existence of many school-based reform initiatives.

Then there's the question of power-foundation strategies and models for change, which often flow from the corporate mindset and the style of work of one man or a small group of 'expert' consultants. Bill Gates, for example, has created his own bureaucracy with a staff of 700 to run the $60 billion dollar foundation. He reserves all the big management decisions for himself and a small team of close advisors, including his wife, Melinda. All his management team members come from the corporate world. None are educators. Patty Stonesifer, the foundation's former senior Microsoft executive, recently stepped down only to be replaced by Jeff Raikes, another top Microsoft executive.

Ford Foundation director Michael Edwards is a critic of power philanthropy. Edwards estimates that a handful of super foundations will spend an estimated $55 trillion over the next forty years. In his book *Just Another Emperor?* he notes that in the foundation world, "a meager 5.4 percent of philanthropic resources in the United States are spent on activities defined as 'public and societal benefit,' as opposed to religion, opera and the like, a figure that rises to 7 percent for money that is channeled to 'communities of color' and 11 percent for 'social justice grant making' by U.S. foundations."[40]

Financial Times writer Andrew Jack recalls how Bill Gates bristled at critics' suggestions that the foundation should broaden the number and diversity of those who set strategy. " 'Corporations have a CEO. We have a CEO. Corporations have a board. We have a board,' he says. 'It's not a gigantic board . . . It doesn't avoid mistakes, but I think we've really made our best effort on those things.' "[41]

Gates seems surprised at suggestions the foundation could do more to improve transparency, pointing out that it is posting ever more information on its website, from details of grants provided (required by law, of course) to the (still limited details of) lessons learned from those that failed and succeeded alike.

Gates also focuses on "technical changes," says Jack.[42] Since he's not an educator or health professional and knows little about teaching or the lives of the students and families impacted by the change strategies he leverages, he will fall back on what he knows best and that which fits within his comfort range. To say that the worldview of power philanthropists like Gates naturally shapes their approach to school or health care reform and their molding of public policy would be an understatement. In global health care, for example, many health professionals have repeatedly claimed that Gates' interest in technological solutions focuses on particular diseases rather than building up the health systems of developing countries.[43] More important, their monopolization of public space pushes out the smaller players and eliminates competition, including competing approaches to problem solving, thereby stifling innovation. The making of major grants to just one group in approaching a scientific problem can distort the entire scientific process, overlooking other possible avenues of thought and action, and reshaping the research agenda of a nation or of a scientific community.

Is it possible to reform the distribution and accumulation policies of the power philanthropists and, in particular, the Gates Foundation? Probably not, in the short term. Their sheer size and embedded power within the current political system should keep them immune from external pressures for some time to come. Neither does there seem to be the political will within either political party to impose even the mildest constraints on the foundation as they once tried to do on parent company Microsoft.

The best we can hope for is that at some point, resistance will build to philanthropic paternalism at the community level and that public pressure will force some sort of reassessment from within the philanthropic community itself.

NOTES

1. Broad Superintendents Academy, "Map of Fellows," http://www.broadacademy.org/fellows/map.html (accessed August 12, 2009).
2. T. Arango and B. Stelter, "Messages With a Mission, Embedded in TV Shows" New York Times, April 1, 2009, http://www.nytimes.com/2009/04/02/arts/television/02gates.html
3. Ibid.
4. B. Kauffman, "Darwin in the New World," Wall Street Journal, January 9, 2009.
5. BBC, "Bill Gates Part 5 Interview with BBC," YouTube video, http://www.youtube.com/watch?v=5OLgcdgOmsk (accessed July 5, 2009).

6. R. Colvile, "Creative Capitalism by Michael Kinsley—Review," Daily Telegraph, January 13, 2009, http://www.telegraph.co.uk/culture/books/bookreviews/4223668/Creative-Capitalism-by-Michael-Kinsley-review.html
7. H. Benson, "Kinley's Mantra: Capitalism for Common Good," San Francisco Chronicle, December 18, 2008, E-1, http://www.sfgate.com/cgi-bin/article.cgi?f=/c/a/2008/12/18/DD0Q14LRS5.DTL&type=books#ixzz0UakD4PWy.
8. M. Klonsky and S. Klonsky, Small Schools: Public Reform Meets the Ownership Society (New York: Routledge, 2008).
9. J. Fouts et al., Leading the Conversion Process: Lessons Learned and Recommendations for Converting to Small Learning Communities (Bill and Melinda Gates Foundation, 2006), 1, http://www.spu.edu/orgs/research/Leading%20the%20Conversion%20Process%2010-6-06.pdf.
10. See M. Klonsky and S. Klonsky, Small Schools, 131.
11. C. Hendrie, "High Schools Nationwide, Paring Down," Education Week, June 16, 2004, http://www.edweek.org/ew/articles/2004/06/16/40small.h23.html.
12. Ibid.
13. A. Sherry, "Manual's Slow Death," Denver Post, May 7, 2006.
14. J. Greene and W. Symonds, "Bill Gates Gets Schooled," Businessweek, June 26, 2006, http://www.businessweek.com/magazine/content/06_26/b3990001.htm.
15. J. Meyer, "High School Interrupted for Manual Students," Denver Post, May 24, 2009, http://www.denverpost.com/firstinthepost/ci_12438681 (accessed August 12, 2009).
16. Ibid.
17. T. Vander Ark, "A Long Trek before a Race to the Top," Huffington Post, August 9, 2009, http://www.huffingtonpost.com/tom-vander-ark/a-long-trek-before-a-race_b_254979.html (accessed August 10, 2009).
18. Ibid.
19. Ibid.
20. P. Elkind and B. McLean, The Smartest Guys in the Room: The Amazing Rise and Scandalous Fall of Enron (New York: Portfolio Trade, 2004).
21. Ibid, 48.
22. Ibid., 72.
23. A. Dorfman, "How Public Is Private Philanthropy: Separating Myth from Reality" (press release, National Committee for Responsive Philanthropy), http://www.ncrp.org/news-room/press-releases/558-ncrp-statement-on-how-public-is-private-philanthropy (accessed June 30, 2009).
24. Ibid.
25. Ibid.
26. Ibid.
27. B. Gates, Testimony before the Committee on Science and Technology, U.S. House of Representatives, March 12, 2008, http://www.microsoft.com/Presspass/exec/billg/speeches/2008/congress.mspx (accessed January 14, 2009).
28. C. Cooper and B. Mullins, "Wall Street Is Big Donor to Inauguration," Wall Street Journal, January 9, 2009, http://online.wsj.com/article/SB123146096981566339.html?mod=googlenews_wsj (accessed January 9, 2009).
29. M. Maiello, "Should Business Save the World?," Forbes, January 12, 2009, http://www.forbes.com/2009/01/12/gates-creative-capitalism-oped-cx_mm_0112maiello.html

30. R. Reich, Supercapitalism (New York: Alfred A. Knopf, 2007).
31. Ibid.
32. H. Davies, "A New Take on Giving," The Guardian, January 10, 2009.
33. M. Friedman, "The Social Responsibility of Business Is to Increase Its Profits," New York Times Magazine, September 13, 1970.
34. M. Bishop and M. Green, Philanthrocapitalism (New York: Bloomsbury Press, 2008).
35. S. Kitchens, "How to Be a Good Billionaire," Forbes, December 25, 2008, http://www.forbes.com/home/2008/12/24/intelligent-investing-philanthropy-jolie-bonoDec25.html (accessed December 25, 2008).
36. M. Bishop and M. Green, Philanthrocapitalism, 28.
37. C. Piller, E. Sanders, and R. Dixon. "Dark Cloud over Good Works of Gates Foundation," Los Angeles Times, January 7, 2007, http://articles.latimes.com/2007/jan/07/nation/na-gatesx07
38. Ibid.
39. S. Berresford, "Social Justice Philanthropy and U.S. Political Traditions" (Ford Foundation, 2003), http://www.fordfound.org/newsroom/speeches/131 (accessed August 11, 2009).
40. M. Edwards, Just Another Emperor? (New York: Demos, 2008).
41. A. Jack, "Profitable Philanthropy," Financial Times, January 12, 2009, http://www.ft.com/cms/s/0/a767d91a-e0c9-11dd-b0e8-000077b07658.html?nclick_check=1 (accessed January 12, 2009). In Gates Keepers blog, http://gateskeepers.civiblog.org/blog/_archives/2009/1/12/4054864.html
42. Ibid.
43. M. Bishop and M. Green, "What They Are Saying . . . Billanthropy: Good or Bad?" USAID FrontLines, 2009, http://www.usaid.gov/press/frontlines/fl_jul09/p2_billanthropy070904.html (accessed July 31, 2009).

3 The Gates Foundation's Interventions into Education, Health, and Food Policies

Technology, Power, and the Privatization of Political Problems

David Hursh

The Bill and Melinda Gates Foundation is reshaping the way in which society provides for education, health care, and food. Founded in 1994 as the William H. Gates Foundation, their initial philanthropic initiatives focused on "global health and community needs in the Pacific northwest."[1] Initial education programs supported increasing public library users' access to the internet and college scholarship funding. During the last election, the Gates Foundation teamed with the Eli Broad Foundation and the Rockefeller Foundation to fund Strong American Schools, a "nonpartisan campaign aimed at elevating American education to the top of the presidential campaign agenda between now and November 2008."[2] In recent speeches Bill Gates has trumpeted Knowledge Is Power Program (KIPP) charter schools as the model for education reform. In 1998, the Gates Foundation entered the health arena by funding programs to develop childhood vaccines; and in 1999, the foundation funded programs to develop an AIDS vaccine. In January 2003, the Gates Foundation launched the Grand Challenges in Global Health initiative to stimulate researchers to "develop solutions to critical scientific and technological advances against diseases of the developing world."[3] Reasoning that improved health also required improved nutrition, the Gates Foundation began funding research on and distribution of genetically engineered crops and the commercialization of agriculture through the use of modern varieties of fertilizer and pesticides. In 2006, the Rockefeller and Gates Foundations jointly formed Alliance for a Green Revolution in Africa (AGRA).[4]

INTRODUCTION

Because the Gates Foundation is the largest philanthropic organization in the world with an endowment that exceeds the gross domestic product of many countries, few academics are willing to criticize it for fear they will reduce their chances of receiving funding.[5] However, we need to ask whether the initiatives are likely to result in their stated goals or whether the initiatives undermine more promising programs and efforts. Although

Bill and Melinda Gates would argue that their efforts are well intentioned, I suggest that the Gates Foundation's philanthropic efforts have several negative consequences:

1. The initiatives ignore that to improve education and health, and reduce hunger, we need to decrease economic inequality and change social structures. For example, hunger is not caused by lack of food but because the poor cannot afford food. India now produces more food per capita than before, but because of the focus on exports rather than local consumption, and the corporate monopoly over bioengineered seeds rather than those saved by farmers, more people are going hungry than before.[6] Similarly, hunger in Africa has increased because the World Bank's and International Monetary Fund's economic policies undermined local farmers' ability to grow food for local consumption. During the 1960s, "Africa," writes Bello, "was not just self-sufficient in food but was actually a net food exporter, averaging 1.3 million tons in food exports a year between 1966 and 1970. Today, the continent imports 25 percent of its food, with almost every country being a net importer." [7]
2. The reliance on markets and technology substantially oversimplifies the problems and subverts our ability to situate our health, food, and education systems within the political, social, and economic issues that must be addressed if we are to improve them.
3. Philanthropy is a private solution to pubic problems. Because of its size, the Gates Foundation's funding undermines if not preempts discussion and activities in response to the issues of hunger, health, and education.
4. The approaches endorse market-based and individual solutions to the problems and therefore weaken efforts to find structural solutions, such as developing affordable health care systems; or as Patel, Holt-Gimenez, and Shattuck write, the Gates Foundation's approach "ignores the structural and political causes of Africa's hunger." [8]

Therefore, I will begin with a brief overview of the Bill and Melinda Gates Foundation and then analyze the key features of their efforts in health, agriculture, and education. I will conclude by showing how their approach incorporates a neoliberal rationale that particularly favors private enterprise over governmental responsibility and technological solutions over changes in the economic and political system.

GLOBAL HEALTH AND AGRICULTURE

As described above, the Gates Foundation's first forays into health began with research on vaccines.[9] In 2003, "the Foundation launched a 'Grand Challenges in Global Health' initiative to stimulate scientific research into developing solutions to critical scientific and technological problems that, if solved, could lead to important advances against diseases of the developing world."[10] The foundation poses fourteen 'Grand Challenges' to global health: six focus on improving vaccine delivery and creating new vaccines, two focus on controlling insects that transmit agents of disease, one focuses on improving nutrition, three address drug resistance and the developing cures for latent and chronic infections, and two call for more accurate and economical measurement of disease and health status.

In the Gates Foundation's recent annual letter, Bill Gates conveys that the Global Health Program accounts for about 50 percent of their funding and focuses on twenty diseases. "The top five are: diarrheal diseases (including rotavirus), pneumonia, and malaria—which mostly kills kids—and AIDS and TB, which mostly kills adults."[11] The emphasis on vaccines and other technologies as the solution to disease is also evident. In the same letter, Gates writes:

> there are opportunities for big breakthroughs—from discovering new vaccines that can save millions of lives, to developing new seeds that will let a farming family have better productivity, improve their children's nutrition, and sell some of the extra output.[12]

Gates later reiterates his faith in technology:

> I have been talking a lot in this letter about technological solutions like new seeds and vaccines. Our optimism about technology is a fundamental part of the foundation's approach. Advances in science have played a huge role in improving the living conditions in the rich world over the last century.[13]

However, a recent report in the *British Medical Journal* (*BMJ*) raises questions about the Gates Foundation's involvement in global health. Brown states, "critics suggest that its [the Gates Foundation's] reluctance to embrace research, demonstration, and capacity building in health delivery systems is worsening the gap between what technology can do and what is actually happening to health in poor communities."[14] The author cites David Sanders, director of the School of Public Health at the University of the Western Cape, South Africa, as stating that the foundation's "vertical, disease specific funding strategies . . . damage health systems in developing countries."[15]

Other critics include Anne-Emanuelle Birn, professor of International Development Studies and Canadian chair of International Health at the University of Toronto, who faults the Grand Initiatives for their heavy reliance on technology and for ignoring the more complicated but necessary political and economic issues. Birn states that the foundation's Grand Challenges in health

> share an assumption that scientific and technical aspects of health improvement can be separated from political, social, and economic aspects. Indeed, the Grand Challenges initiative has made this division explicit by excluding the problems of poverty, access to health interventions, and delivery systems. [16]

Birn argues that without examining social, political, and economic inequalities, efforts to improve global health are likely to fail. She states that "redistribution measures . . . play a key role in the successful implementation of medical, public health, educational, and household measures."[17] Without decreasing poverty, Birn adds, global health is unlikely to improve. "Relative poverty—as reflective of hierarchies of access to material, social, and political power—demonstrates a clear gradient effect, whereby each step down the ladder is associated with worse health."[18]

Recognizing that vaccines have their use but should not be overemphasized, Birn suggests, "global health might be better served through political support for universal, accessible, and comprehensive public-health systems (to ensure vaccine coverage, among many activities) in the context of overall improvement in living and working conditions."[19] She writes, "the world leading authorities on global health hold that two-thirds of child deaths and four-fifths of all deaths in developing countries are preventable through existing measures."[20]

Some of those existing measures include providing clean water and sanitation. In *Stunted Lives, Stagnant Economies*, Eileen Stillwaggon writes, "Every day around the world illnesses related to water supply, waste disposal, and garbage kill 30,000 people and constitute 75 percent of the illnesses that afflict humanity."[21] But, writes Birn, the Gates Foundation's focus "on effective vaccines against diarrheal diseases would probably mean that the problem of extending clean water and sanitation to half of the world's population without access would seem far less pressing."[22] Such a diversion ignores the major role of improving the world's infrastructure and that lack of clean water and sanitation play a major role in causing disease.

In contrast to focusing on vaccines, Birn would concentrate on improving the environment in which people live. For example, she notes that tuberculosis prevention can be achieved through "the simplicity, dignity and cost effectiveness of a 'healthy housing' approach."[23]

In the same way that vaccines are an effort to provide a scientific solution to a political and economic problem, the Gates Foundation's approach to solving one of the Grand Challenges of reducing hunger and improving nutrition rests on a scientific solution. The foundation aims to improve nutrition through the development of a "single plant species" that would provide all the required nutrients. Birn again asks whether the Gates Foundation is ignoring more central issues. She writes:

> This approach also overlooks key distributional questions. Many of the regions with the worst malnutrition problems—such as Central America, the Andes, East Africa, and India—have extremely fertile growing conditions and produce some of the world's most nutritious fruits and crops. As Nobel-winning economist Amartya Sen had demonstrated, malnutrition and famine are not caused by technical roadblocks but rather by political and economic ones: local populations are priced out of their food entitlement due to poor income distribution and market shifts, such as production for export, that have little to do with food supply or nutritional content.[24]

The Gates Foundation's efforts to reduce hunger extend beyond the Grand Challenges in Global Health initiative. In October 2006 they announced a "joint $150 million Alliance for a Green Revolution in Africa (AGRA)" that focuses on improving agricultural output. In the recent annual report, Bill Gates writes:

> New seeds and other inputs like fertilizer allow a farmer to increase her farm's output significantly, instead of just growing enough food to subsist. This innovation is just as important as developing and delivering vaccinations. The additional output means her children get better nutrition, which improves their health and ability to learn.[25]

In a Food First Policy Brief for the Institute for Food and Development Policy Holt-Gimenez, Altieri, and Rosset present ten reasons why AGRA will not solve the problems of poverty and hunger in sub-Saharan Africa.[26] Likewise, Vandana Shiva criticizes similar efforts in India for exacerbating the problem of poverty and hunger. In both sub-Saharan Africa and India, the critics point out, AGRA has benefited corporate farms to the detriment of small farmers.[27]

Shiva states that AGRA pushed "farmers into debt. It left the land desertified. It destroyed variety. Punjab used to grow 250 crop varieties. Today it grows monocultures of wheat and rice during two separate seasons and a monoculture of genetically engineered cotton."[28] As Holt-Gimenez et al. point out, because the genetically engineered seeds have degraded the soil and required heavy irrigation and heavy use of pesticides, the result has been depleted natural fertility, an "increase in pest damage, drying up of aquifers and reduction of agrobiodiversity. In doing so, the Green Revolution increases environmental risk and exacerbates the economic vulnerability of poor farmers."[29]

Shiva explains how AGRA has undermined traditional farmers in India and resulted in thousands of farmers committing suicide, including 16,000 farmers in 2004.[30] The rise in suicides results from the corporatization of agriculture that began in the late 1990s when the World Bank's structural adjustment policies forced India to open up its seed sector to global corporations, including Cargill and Monsanto. Shiva writes:

> The global corporations changed the . . . economy overnight. Farm-saved seeds were replaced by corporate seeds, which need fertilizers and pesticides and cannot be saved. Corporations prevent seed savings through patents and by engineering seeds with nonrenewable traits. As a result, poor peasants have to buy new seeds for every planting season and what was traditionally a free resource, available by putting aside a small portion of the crop, becomes a commodity. This new expense increases poverty and leads to indebtedness.[31]

Shiva fears that AGRA that has been so harmful to Indian agriculture is now precisely the same program that Gates wants to bring to Africa. She states: "Gates, the Rockefellers and their corporate affiliates would like to bulldoze over Africa a green revolution like they bulldozed on India in 1965."[32] Shiva describes the Gates Foundation's use of the agricultural crisis in Africa as a means "to sell more chemical fertilizers to Africa, and then commercialize the food supply for Africa."[33] The crisis has also been used to benefit the genetic engineering lobby.

Like Birn, Holt-Gimenez et al. argue that "hunger is not primarily due to lack of food, but rather because the hungry are too poor to buy the food that is available."[34] They add that "without addressing structural inequalities in the market and political system, approaches relying on high input technologies,"[35] such as AGRA, fail. The growing hunger in Africa is largely due to the increased impoverishment of the same rural people who once grew food but have now left farming. Today's African farmers could easily produce far more food than they do, but they don't because they cannot get credit to cover production costs, nor can they find buyers nor obtain fair prices to give them a minimal profit margin. Under such circumstances, what difference will a new "technology package" make? Without addressing the causes of why African farmers leave farming—or why they underproduce—AGRA will have little impact on this trend. Amaytra Sen adds that famine is fundamentally a problem of democracy, poverty, and food distribution and recently "lamented that hunger was not enough of a political priority here. India's public expenditure on health remains low, and in some places financing for child nutrition programs remains unspent."[36]

Moreover, the Gates Foundation's support of AGRA and health care may not be as altruistic as it seems. For example, the Gates Foundation recently pledged $25 million to the World Cocoa Foundation, a foundation funded by the world's largest chocolate companies known for using "cocoa harvested by child and trafficked labor."[37]

Similarly, Piller, Sanders, and Dixon reveal that the Gates Foundation invests in drugs and companies that contravene its good works. They describe, for example, that while providing vaccines to a Nigerian child against polio and measles, the same child faces increased chances of respiratory problems from the toxins produced by a nearby oil plant owned by the Italia oil giant Eni, of which the Bill and Melinda Gates Foundation is a major investor. Indeed, local leaders blame oil development for fostering many of the very afflictions that the foundation combats.[38]

If the Gates Foundation sincerely desires to improve global health, Birn suggests that the "Gates Foundation take up a larger challenge: to integrate social and medical/technical means of improving global health" that would include examining:

> housing stock, sanitation coverage, schooling, social security, income distribution, neighborhood characteristics, imports, exports, and production, workplace and environmental protection, public revenues and spending, debt and banking patterns, migration flows, medical services coverage, and employment patterns.[39]

This would require that the Gates Foundation, which has amassed its wealth through the current economic system, to take on the existing local and global power structures. "At its most ambitious level," writes Birn, "the Gates Foundation could take on its concern for poor health as an impediment to international development by addressing 'inherently global health issues' relating to international trade, finance, and economic exploitation."[40]

EDUCATION

In education, we can see many of the same themes that are evident regarding health and agriculture: an oversimplification of the problem that ignores the larger social, economic, and political context; a reliance on technological remedies, including standardized tests; and concentration of decision-making power in either the corporate or institutional leaders while marginalizing teachers, parents, students, and other community members.

In this section, I begin by describing Gates' initial involvement in funding small learning communities and then in developing small schools; I show how these efforts often failed to improve student achievement, in part because they were top-down efforts that excluded teachers, parents, and students, and in some cases were abandoned. Consequently, Bill Gates has shifted his strategy from reforming schools to creating new ones with decision-making power concentrated in the hands of administrators. In his January 2009 Annual Report and February 2009 talk at the annual Technology, Entertainment, Design Conference (TED), Bill Gates extolled the virtues of the Knowledge Is Power Program (KIPP) charter schools and suggested them as the solution to increasing educational achievement.

Although the Gates Foundation's model asserts that teachers should have little input on educational goals or school organization, teachers are almost entirely responsible for student achievement. Differences in student achievement, he claims, result not from differences in resources provided to schools or social and economic inequalities such as lack of health care or adequate housing, but because of differences in teacher quality. Students who do well do so, he argues, because they have better teachers.

Furthermore, he asserts that superior teachers are created not through teacher education programs or professional development, but because they use students' test scores for the feedback necessary to improve. He states that testing is the only objective measurement of our students and that test scores inform teachers how to improve.[41]

The Gates Foundation entered into school reform efforts in 2001, when Congress appropriated $48 million for creating smaller learning communities (SLCs) in larger high schools in response to the student shootings in Columbine, Colorado. The advantage of SLCs, Congress argued, were that they would allow teachers to better know students and that schools would therefore be safer. Congress allotted $125 million for this initiative, to which the Gates Foundation added $1.5 billion.

In Chicago, the funding enabled groups of teachers, led by William Ayers, to develop the Small Schools Workshop in which teachers, administrators, and parents developed small schools. The principles that guided their work were taken from successful small schools, such as Deborah Meier's Central Park East in New York City, that included having teachers work together to design schools in which teachers would team teach, develop curricula that builds on students' interests, and collaboratively assess students' learning.

However, the Gates Foundation's approach to developing SLCs undermined their strengths. In their book *Small Schools: Public School Reform Meets the Ownership Society*, Michael and Susan Klonsky detail how the Gates Foundation's efforts at creating small schools contradicted the principles developed by practitioners such as Deborah Meier and Chicago's Small Schools Workshop. The Gates Foundation views teachers as a group to be controlled rather than consulted. In Chicago, in response to a question of whether teachers would be part of a Gates-funded board that now governed the public schools, a Gates Foundation representative declared that teachers could not be part of the board because that would be a conflict of interest, "like having the workers running the factory."[42]

Eventually, as the Klonskys describe, the Gates Foundation's top-down approach to school reform met with disaster. The Gates Foundation attempted to develop three SLCs within Denver's Manual High School through a process that reflected "little knowledge or understanding of the unique needs, history, and conditions"[43] within the community. Teachers, parents, and students were left out of the process, and they consequently resisted the reform efforts; the Gates Foundation and the district ultimately gave up, the school closed, and the funding ended.

The debacle in Denver led the Gates Foundation to decide it would no longer support the conversion of large high schools into small learning communities. Instead, the director of the foundation's school reform projects argued for closing "a thousand schools,"[44] and they turned their attention to starting new schools from scratch as either charter schools or corporate-run schools. For example, in Chicago, the Gates Foundation became a principal supporter of Renaissance 2010, which included closing 100 schools and reopening two-thirds of them as either charter schools or schools run by outside agencies. The foundation contributed $100 million to the Chicago reform effort.

In his recent annual report, Bill Gates reflected on the changes in their reform approach:

> Nine years ago, the foundation decided to invest in helping to create better high schools, and we have made over $2 billion in grants. The goal was to give schools extra money for a period of time to make changes in the way they were organized (including reducing their size), in how the teachers worked, and in the curriculum. The hope was that after a few years they would operate at the same cost per students as before, but they would have become more effective. Many of the small schools that we invested in did not improve students' achievement in any significant way . . . We had less success trying to change an existing school than helping to create a new school.[45]

Subsequently, the Gates Foundation advocates establishing charter schools characterized by top-down administration and standardized curricula and tests. In both the annual report and the TED lecture, Gates argued that the difference between students succeeding or failing is in the quality of their teachers. Although there is some truth in the claim that teacher quality makes a difference, Gates concludes that the differences in student success from school to school has to do almost entirely with the quality of teachers, therefore ignoring differences in resources provided either in the school or at home such as educational resources, local government's commitment to enriching educational programs outside of school, a time and place to study, and access to free or affordable medical care.

In his talk at TED, Gates concludes:

> the more we looked at it, the more we realized that having great teachers was the very key thing. And we hooked up with some people studying how much variation is there between teachers, between, say, the top quartile—the very best—and the bottom quartile. How much variation is there within a school or between schools? And the answer is that these variations are absolutely unbelievable. A top quartile teacher will increase the performance of their class—based on test scores—by over 10 percent in a single year.[46]

Gates' thinking is more than a little circular. He assumes that high tests scores prove that the teacher is of high quality, a characteristic that remains undefined, and then claims that if we only had high-quality teachers, students' tests scores would increase, so that "if the entire U.S., for two years, had top quartile teachers, the entire difference between us and Asia would go away."[47]

Furthermore, in response to the question of how to create high-quality teachers, he argues that neither advanced degrees, such as a master's degree in education, nor years of teaching make any difference. Rather, he says the best predictor of whether a teacher will be a good teacher is their previous performance. Such thinking leaves unanswered how a teacher becomes good in the first place.

However, later in his TED address he suggests we use the model of KIPP schools to understand how to create good teachers. KIPP schools, of which there are currently sixty-six in nineteen states (plus the District of Columbia) and which serve some 16,000 students, are characterized by a longer school day that includes school on some Saturdays, a standardized curriculum that emphasizes behavioral modification techniques and repetition, and teachers who are on call at all times. Parents are required to sign a contract to pledge that their child will comply with requirements and disciplinary measures. As we note below, what data we have about the schools indicates a high attrition rate for both students and teachers.

Gates argues that teachers in KIPP schools improve because they look at the data and conclude that their teaching is the cause of increased learning. However, as we know from statewide standardized tests, tests often inflate student achievement and are not a reliable indicator of student achievement from one year to the next.[48] Further, higher test scores do not by themselves tell teachers exactly what about their teaching is leading to the increased learning.

Moreover, although students who graduate from KIPP schools may have higher test scores on average than other students in the district in which the school is located, the schools are characterized by a high attrition rate. In a study undertaken at four San Francisco area KIPP schools, 60 percent of the entering fifth graders had left by the end of the eighth grade.[49] If, on average, those students who are either pushed out or drop out of KIPP schools are the lower achieving students, as they are likely to be, then the remaining students are likely to be more capable and to perform better on tests.

Not only do KIPP schools seem to push out students at a high rate, the same is true for teachers. The San Francisco study (and there are few such studies because KIPP schools do not routinely make their test results available to outside researchers), the "annual turnover rate for faculty ranged from 18 percent to 49 percent from 2003–04 to 2007–08."[50]

As such, KIPP schools resist accountability and marginalize parents, students, and teachers. Parents and students are forced to sign a contract that states what they will do in order to stay in the school. Teachers who, as stated earlier, are perceived as workers who should have no say in shaping curriculum and pedagogy are disempowered. In New York, where charter schools over a minimum size are required by law to allow teaches to unionize, KIPP schools are resisting the teachers' unionization efforts.[51]

CONCLUSION

The Gates Foundation's efforts in education parallel their efforts in health and agriculture. They ignore the larger economic and social context that affect whether people have access to or can afford health care or food. Instead, the Gates Foundation funds development of new seeds or vaccines rather than builds on the existent infrastructure. In the education sphere, they assume students will learn and the achievement gap will close if we just privatize education through charter schools, place all the responsibility for student achievement on teachers who merely exist to carry out administrators' directives, and ignore the economic and social inequalities that contribute to unequal achievement.

Their technological and top-down solutions—whether reflected in their efforts to develop vaccines or their assumption that test scores provide all we need to improve education—marginalizes farmers and medical and educational professionals, as well as the wider community. Instead, it is a view that the philanthropist, along with corporate officers who run multinational agricultural corporations and private schools, know best.

The Gates Foundation undertakes a neoliberal approach to social problems. They believe the social problems can be solved without governmental intervention, that private initiatives and markets provide solutions. Moreover, not only are teachers, farmers, and medical professionals perceived as irrelevant and eliminated from the process, but so is the public as a whole.

Furthermore, the Gates Foundation's sheer size stifles public discussion. As relates to health care, the foundation has a larger budget than the World Health Organization. In agriculture, more sustainable approaches such as those proposed by Vandana Shiva[52] or Food First[53] are marginalized as the foundation and its corporate allies (Monsanto, Cargill, etc.) introduce new grains and technologies to farming. In education, what we have learned about developing successful schools, whether the small schools described by Meier[54] and the Klonskys[55] or teaching and assessment as described by Darling-Hammond[56] are ignored. Moreover, the foundation's giving limits discussion as school districts clamor for its funding.

Rather than building on what we have learned about successful small schools, sustainable community agriculture, or the necessity of clean water and air for healthy communities, the Gates Foundation imposes its own top-down agenda on communities and schools.

In response, we need to critique the Gates Foundation's efforts to show how they undermine serious democratic examinations of the problems we face in health care, agriculture, and education. In all three cases, the Gates Foundation ignores the underlying structural issues that contribute to people not being able to afford life's basics such as health care and food. Instead, the Gates Foundation imposes more costly remedies that leave communities dependent on technological fixes and the largess of wealthy philanthropists.

Regarding education, we need to understand that improving our schools is necessary but not sufficient. Schools by themselves cannot significantly reduce societal inequality, and teachers cannot inspire every student in their classrooms to learn. We need to develop a society in which students know that doing well in school leads to well-paying, meaningful work. Many students, particularly those of color, know all too well that school success too often leads to little more than a minimum wage job. Even college graduates struggle to find positions that provide a livable income and health care.

Furthermore, students may graduate from KIPP knowing how to provide the teacher with the answer that he or she is looking for. But learning requires an ability to ask questions, weigh evidence, and provide solutions. We need to create schools modeled after successful small schools in Chicago and New York wherein students are encouraged to think critically, engage in questioning, and write and speak with clarity and grace.

We need to demand an end to top-down decision making by the wealthy and develop public participatory methods of governance that include and build on the expertise of the affected population: students and teachers, health care workers, community activists, farmers and families. Improving education, health care, and access to food will require a wide variety of solutions that are tailored to the local situation but aim to transform our agricultural, educational, and health care systems.

Last, as implied above, all of these problems are interconnected and their cause resides in the current inequalities in power and resources and the ways in which those are reproduced through social structures. We need to work together to critique and reform our political and economic systems that perpetuate political and economic inequality and create new models of governance, democracy, and economics. Given the great wealth of the Gates Foundation, these shifts in power will not be easy. But they are necessary.

I would like to thank Professors Camille Martina and Ted Brown, both from the University of Rochester, for their assistance on this chapter.

NOTES

1. Foundation Timeline and History—Bill and Melinda Gates Foundations. At http://www.gatesfoundation.org/about/Pages/foundation-timeline.aspx. Accessed August 10, 2010.
2. *Strong American Schools Campaign Launches to Promote Education Reform in 2008 Presidential Election.* At http://www.gatesfoundation.

org/press-releases/Pages/2008-presidential-campaign-education-070425-2.aspx. Accessed August 10, 2010.

3. See Grand Challenges in Global Health website, http://www.grandchallenges.org.
4. Foundation Timeline and History—Bill and Melinda Gates Foundations. At http://www.gatesfoundation.org/about/Pages/foundation-timeline.aspx. Accessed August 10, 2010.
5. S. Doughton, "Not Many Speak Their Mind to Gates Foundation," *Seattle Times*, August 3, 2008.
6. V. Shiva, *Earth Democracy: Justice, Sustainability, and Peace* (Cambridge, MA: South End Press, 2005).
7. W. Bello, *Food Wars* (New York: Verso, 2009), 68.
8. R. Patel, E. Holt-Gimenez, and A. Shattuck, "Ending Africa's Hunger," *The Nation*, September 21, 2009, 17–18, 20–22.
9. *Foundation Timeline and History—Bill and Melinda Gates Foundations.* At http://www.gatesfoundation.org/about/Pages/foundation-timeline.aspx. Accessed August 10, 2010. 10. A-E Birn, "Gate's Grandest Challenge: Transcending Technology as Public Health Ideology," *The Lancet* 366 (2005): 514–19.
11. B. Gates, "2009 Annual letter from Bill Gates" (2009), 6. At http://www.gatesfoundation.org/annual-letter/Pages/2009-united-states-education.aspx. Accessed August 10, 2010.
12. Ibid., 2.
13. Ibid., 9.
14. H. Brown, "Great Expectations," *BMJ* 334 (April 28, 2007): 874–76.
15. Ibid., p. 874.
16. A-E Birn, "Gate's Grandest Challenge," 516.
17. Ibid., 514.
18. Ibid., 515.
19. Ibid., 516.
20. Ibid., 517.
21. E. Stillwaggon, *Stunted Lives, Stagnant Economies: Poverty, Disease, and Underdevelopment* (Piscataway, NJ: Rutgers University Press, 1998); M. Davis, *Planet of Slums* (New York: Verso, 2006), p. 95.
22. A-E Birn, "Gate's Grandest Challenge," 516.
23. Ibid.
24. Ibid.
25. B. Gates, "2009 Annual Letter."
26. E. Holt-Gimenez, M. Altieri, and P. Rosset, "Ten Reasons Why the Rockefeller and the Bill and Melinda Gates Foundations' Alliance for Another Green Revolution Will Not Solve the Problems of Poverty and Hunger in Sub-Saharan Africa," *Food First Policy Brief No. 12* (Oakland, CA: Institute for Food and Development Policy, 2006), http://www.foodfirst.org/en/node/1527 (accessed May 20, 2010).
27. G. Null, "Globalization and Poverty: An Interview with Dr. Vandana Shiva," *Share the World's Resources: Sustainable Economics to End World Poverty*, 2009. At: http://www.stwr.org/food-security-agriculture/globalization-and-poverty-an-interview-with-dr-vandana-shiva.html. Accessed August 10, 2010.
28. Ibid., 6.
29. E. Holt-Gimenez, M. Altieri, and P. Rosset, "Ten Reasons Why."
30. V. Shiva, *Earth Democracy*.
31. Ibid., 121.
32. G. Null, "Globalization and Poverty."

33. Ibid., 5.
34. E. Holt-Gimenez, M. Altieri, and P. Rosset, "Ten Reasons Why," 3.
35. Ibid., 4.
36. S. Sangupta, "As India Growth Soars, Child Hunger Persists," *New York Times* (2009), A-1.n, March 3, 2009.
37. T. Newman, "Will Gates Foundation Help Cocoa Farmers?" *Voices from Africa*, 2007. At http://www.oaklandinstitute.org/voicesfromafrica/node/7. Accessed August 10, 2010.
38. C. Piller, S. Sanders, and R. Dixon, "Dark Cloud over Good Works of Gates Foundation," *Los Angeles Times*, January 7, 2007.
39. A-E Birn, "Gate's Grandest Challenge," 517.
40. Ibid., 518.
41. Winik, L.W. (September 11, 2007). Can Bill Gates fix our failing schools? *Parade Magazine*. At http://www.parade.com/articles/editions/2007/edition_09-23-2007/Intelligence_Report. Accessed August 10, 2010.
42. M. Klonsky and S. Klonsky, *Small Schools: Public School Reform Meets the Ownership Society* (New York: Routledge, 2008), 13.
43. Ibid., 135.
44. Ibid., 134.
45. B. Gates, "2009 Annual Letter," 11.
46. B. Gates, "How I'm Trying to Change the World," *Technology, Entertainment, Design*, 2009.
47. Gates, B. "Bill Gates speaks at the 2009 TED conference in Long Beach, CA. (February 4, 2009). http://www.gatesfoundation.org/videos/Pager/default.aspx-video=speeches-commentary/Pages/bill-gates-ted-talk-2009.aspx&pager=0&filter=&autostart=true. Accessed August 10, 2010.
48. D. Hursh, *High-Stakes Testing and the Decline of Teaching and Learning: The Real Crisis in Education* (Lanham: Rowman and Littlefield, 2008).
49. E. W. Robelen, "KIPP Study Finds High Student Attrition amid Big Learning Gain," *Education Week* 18, no. 5 (September 28, 2008): 10.
50. Ibid.
51. J. Medina, "Teachers Say Union Faces Resistance from Brooklyn Charter School," *New York Times*, February 7, 2009, http://www.nytimes.com/2009/02/07/education/07kipp.html (accessed May 20, 2010).
52. V. Shiva, *Earth Democracy*; V. Shiva and G. Bedi, *Sustainable Agriculture and Food Security: The Impact of Globalization* (New York: Sage, 2002).
53. E. Holt-Gimenez, M. Altieri, and P. Rosset, "Ten Reasons Why."
54. D. Meier, *The Power of Their Ideas: Lessons for America from a Small Urban School* (Boston: Beacon, 1995).
55. M. Klonsky and A. Klonsky, *Small Schools*.
56. L. Darling-Hammond, "Securing the Right to Learn: Policy and Practices for Powerful Teaching and Learning," *Educational Researcher* 35, no. 7 (October 2006): 13–24.

4 Marketing New Schools for a New Century

An Examination of Neoliberal School Reform in New York City

Jessica Shiller

Increased choice increases competition, which drives up the quality of all schools.

—E. Einhorn and M. Kolodner[1]

INTRODUCTION

After the recent presidential election, expectations have been high for some kind of sea change in the United States. Hopes for the end of the war in Iraq, a resuscitation of the middle class, and stemming the problems caused by climate change have all been discussed on the blogosphere. But as pundits ponder and debate whether we are in a new era, some critics see a continuation of past ideologies. Most telling, the recent collapse of the stock market has not brought criticism from the new administration regarding the centrality of the market in our lives, rather only a desire to reform its ways. As one observer noted, "Obama's ideology reflects the developing synthesis, one that attends to both the power of market forces and the need for government action to ameliorate the dislocation that those forces create."[2]

The new president retains strong faith in the market as the engine for our society,[3] carrying on a neoliberal ideology that gained ground when Keyensian economics fell out of favor and faith in an unfettered market moved toward the center of public life. For the past three decades, market-based strategies have not only guided our economic policy but have also driven our entire domestic agenda, including education. Market-driven policies and practices in education are easy to see: the proliferation of private education ventures like vouchers and charter schools nationwide, hiring of business leaders (CEOs) to run large urban school systems, instituting merit pay systems for teachers, and the growth of a multimillion dollar testing industry.[4]

In spite of scant data to support the argument that these market-based strategies work,[5] there is little desire to shift course. The new administration has thrown its weight behind them. For instance, the Race to the Top Fund, made available to states through the federal government, provides funding to states only if they implement market-driven strategies, like removing the cap on charter schools.[6]

Without evidence that these strategies work, we need to examine the problems inherent in market-driven education policies. To that end, this chapter looks closely at a neoliberal school-reform project that has taken hold in New York City over the past seven years, the New Century Schools Initiative (NCSI). A largely privately funded venture, since 2002 NCSI has opened 239 new small high schools in poor urban communities in New York City.[7] Funded by the Bill and Melinda Gates Foundation, along with the Carnegie and Soros Foundations, NCSI has been a central feature of New York City's Department of Education reform effort aimed at phasing out all of the city's large comprehensive high schools and replacing them with new small high schools.

Like other neoliberal, or market-driven, school-reform projects, NCSI is led by a group of business and political elites able to pour millions of dollars into an initiative without consulting the communities being served, paying close attention to the history of similar reforms, or carefully considering the complexity of the work of creating schools. Rather, NCSI founders have a simple theory of change steeped in neoliberal thinking. To solve an intractable problem like failing high schools, they generate funding, which attracts talented people new to the school system and untainted by its bureaucracy, who in turn create successful schools competing against others doing the same. Under this theory, competition ultimately improves the quality of schooling.

To start, they opened as many schools as possible so as to have the greatest impact on the system. Unlike some of the previous initiatives for small schools, which were smaller and operated as alternatives to the regular public schools,[8] NCSI schools have opened, as one observer compared, at "the pace of Starbucks franchises"[9] in order to remake the school system. Using the market as a model, NCSI's founders have tried to change the landscape of the school system by creating a wide range of school choices for families. As a Gates Foundation report stated, "Moving to a system of small schools would create greater choice for students and their families. Since high schools would be small, there would have to be significantly more schools than there are today. This change would foster competition and promise quality schools."[10]

Like all neoliberal reformers, NCSI founders have linked school choice with democracy and claim choice empowers all families to choose to which school they send their children.[11] However, this chapter argues that by leaving school improvement up to the market, NCSI has actually limited democracy by making schools accountable to funders rather than families and by putting decision making in the hands of school reformers rather than sharing it with parents and community members. Additionally, with an interest in short-term outcome gain, such as improved test scores, NCSI schools have not even met their own goal of improved educational equity but have significantly narrowed the focus of schools to practices that will maximize their short-term gain of improved outcome data, which limits the quality of education they provide.

By bringing critique of neoliberal theory to bear on the emergence of the initiative, examining evaluations conducted of NCSI schools, and evaluating my own qualitative study of three Bronx-based NCSI schools, I contend that NCSI has had deleterious effects on poor communities in spite of its enthusiastic support from politicians and business leaders. This chapter concludes with an alternative vision for more democratic schools that offers scholars, policy makers, and concerned citizens ways to challenge and terminate the neoliberal policies that have dominated education policy for decades.

THE EMERGENCE OF NEOLIBERAL SCHOOL REFORM

Larry Cuban has observed that business leaders have been involved in school reform practically since the inception of public schools. As far back as the 1880s, he noted, business leaders actively participated in school reform and sought a solution to what they perceived as a waning American competitiveness.[12] By the turn of the century, the ability of business to influence public schooling was in full swing. Frederick Winslow Taylor's notion of scientific management,[13] perhaps one of the most far-reaching business-inspired plans for public schools, suggested that schools should be made more efficient to produce students who are best prepared for a growing industrial economy.[14] Taylor's model influenced organizational structures that are now commonplace in many public schools today. At the time, educators like John Dewey fiercely argued against Taylor's model and contended that schools should be places that cultivate democracy and intellectual and moral development, not simply places that give students skills for work.[15] Yet the notion that the purpose of public schooling is to prepare young people for their future roles in the workforce has remained strong, in part because it appeals to an American desire for education to have an immediate and practical application rather than an intellectual one. The argument becomes even more persuasive at times when we perceive weakening of our global economic competitiveness.[16]

We currently are in one of those moments. The current context of rapid changes brought on by globalization has caused Americans to worry about their economic security, which fuels economic arguments for improving education. As Blackmore states:

> Education has, in most instances, been reshaped to become the arm of national economic policy, defined by both as the problem (in failing to provide a multi-skilled flexible workforce) and the solution (by upgrading skills and creating a source of national export earnings.[17]

By framing education as an economic problem in need of an economic solution in a time of economic insecurity, current neoliberal school reformers have been able to take an economic argument for school improvement to a new level, suggesting we not only improve students' skills for the workforce but also that we model school systems on the market itself. Under this construct, parents and students as consumers seek out the best services available, and schools compete for clients. To expedite this decision making, neoliberals propose limited intervention by government bureaucracies or regulation. For them, government has created cumbersome red tape and has protected the interests of groups resistant to change (i.e., teachers unions). As Pauline Lipman has stated:

> Neoliberalism asserts that societies function best when individuals make decisions in competitive markets rather than having governmental organizations make decisions for them . . . Furthermore, policy should promote economic growth by eliminating restrictions on corporate investment . . . social institutions, such as schools, also exist to promote economic growth. As a result economic conditions will improve for all, and there will be more equality for everyone.[18]

Under this model, neoliberal educational policies aim to give families choice in the school market without any government intervention. Neoliberal reforms, which position families as customers, are already in place across the country through vouchers programs[19] and charter schools. Neoliberal ideology has infiltrated schools by opening their doors to corporate sponsorship of activities and resources in public schools,[20] as well as placing highly paid CEOs at the helm of urban school systems.[21] All of these efforts turn schools into commodities and parents and students into 'consumers' whose educational opportunities can be improved by eliminating 'inefficient bureaucracies' and broadening their range of choices in the school 'market.'

Given the recent failure of the market, it is essential to question the wisdom of education policies that argue for neoliberal reforms. Critiques have pointed to the problems with neoliberal influence on schooling, claiming that it waters down the education that students receive,[22] turns teachers into technicians,[23] props up a commercial testing industry plagued by unreliable measurement,[24] and eliminates public accountability from school policy making.[25]

NCSI AND THE NEOLIBERAL MODEL

NCSI is a perfect case study for this examination since it has explicitly followed the neoliberal model (a summary is provided in table 4.1). First, NCSI has created a large market of schools from which to choose. The creation of hundreds of schools would produce competition, celebrated by neoliberal reformers as the best method to create quality schools. In a recent report funded by the Gates Foundation, the process of the NCSI is described as working with New York City's Department of Education:

> In developing and supporting small schools, the district aspires to improve public education for all New York City children by: increasing the supply of schools that provide outstanding educational opportunities for all of their students; fueling innovation within and attracting new resources (individual, community, and financial) to the public school system; creating a diverse portfolio of "existence proofs" (i.e., new schools that succeed where others have not) that will spur healthy competition across the district; and, identifying and supporting the district wide transfer of best practices from the new schools, including those related to instruction, accountability for student success, and decision-making autonomy.[26]

Gates and other NCSI founders contended that their strategy of introducing competition to the school system would improve achievement, producing more high school graduates that are prepared for a competitive workforce.[27]

Second, NCSI treats parents as consumers who need a basis on which to compare like products, schools in this case. Through the use of test score data and other quantifiable indicators, there is a constant flow of data coming in. The city's Department of Education (DoE) serves as auditor. They collect test scores as well as other data in order to issue report cards that grade schools on an A through F scale. These grades are made public for everyone to view on the DoE website,[28] which allows parents to decide which school is best for their child by using a similar set of indicators to provide a basis for comparison.[29]

The third way we see a neoliberal model in action through NCSI is perhaps the most important since the other two may not be possible without it: the collaboration of political and business elites to push forward their reform agenda. Similar to how Pauline Lipman[30] has described the school reforms under Chicago Renaissance 2010, NCSI is the result of an intertwined effort between business and political elites, both of whom shared an enthusiasm for market-driven reform and a mistrust of the public. The best example of this is evidenced in the makeup of the board of New Visions for Public Schools, an educational management organization (EMO)[31] that has been one of the largest conduits for NCSI funding and supervises 86 of its schools. Represented on its board are JP Morgan Chase; Black Rock, a global investment firm specializing in hedge funds; Evercore Partners, a firm that advises multinationals on corporate strategy; the head of the New York City teachers union; a former city council member; and Caroline Kennedy, who has privately fundraised for the schools but who has also been considered for public office.[32] There are no parents or community advocates on this board, which eliminates local decision making and community participation in the creation and monitoring of NCSI.

New York City does have a policy board and local community education councils, but the former has been staffed with supporters of the mayor[33] and the latter has very little decision-making power.[34] The elimination of public participation in the schools was easy after the state gave the mayor control of the school system in 2002. Shortly after, the mayor, a former CEO put in charge of the school system by the state government, did away with local school districts. An immediate consequence of this decision was the elimination of district superintendents and support staff, as well as school boards, previously one of the only outlets for public participation in the schools. Once the schools were under his control, Mayor Bloomberg and his chancellor of schools, Joel Klein, were then free to pursue their agenda, and implementation of NCSI was at the top of the list.[35]

A CRITIQUE OF THE NEOLIBERAL MODEL

Under a neoliberal model, advocates contend that people will have more choice, and therefore quality of service will increase. Some go as far as to say that individuals will be able to exercise their freedom under a neoliberal system, which they are prevented from doing under any other system.[36] However, in practice we do not all have the same freedom of choice, and therefore we do not enjoy the same access to quality services.

The idea of choice needs to be examined first. In reality, there is no free and equal market of schools from which to choose, even when there are many more choices. Because of the pressure on schools to show improvement in their data, schools narrow the types of students they serve, which prevents broad access to students who might pull down school data, such as special-education students, English Language Learners, or even students who have low grades or poor attendance as eighth graders. As Sharon Gewirtz's study of London schools found, increased competition among schools forced schools to shift priorities from educating all of their students to recruiting students who they think will be successful at the schools.[37] Clear evidence for this has been found in New York City by the group Parents for an Inclusive Education, a city-based nonprofit who published a report in which they found special-education students are not being served by the NCSI small schools in proportion to their citywide numbers.[38] Ironically, the wide range of choices combined with the public reporting of data has limited rather than expanded the school choices for families.

Neither has competition improved the quality of service that NCSI schools provide. With demands on the schools to keep improving test scores, competition has pushed schools to limit the kind of instruction they provide to students. Under restrictions to improve test scores, Linda McNeil and Angela Valenzuela found that teaching in Texas schools became synonymous with test prep, especially among schools that served poor students and students of color.[39] Data has shown the same to be true in New York City. Policy Studies Associates (PSA), a research firm contracted to study of twenty-six New York NCSI schools, reported that most NCSI schools "had accepted if not fully embraced the Regents exams[40] as a way of focusing their curriculum. In most NCSI schools, teaching to the Regents was viewed as teaching to standards, not teaching to the tests."[41] This emphasis on outcome data was seen as "academically focused"[42] but has had the unintended effect of limiting the kinds of things that schools did with students. In their classroom observations, PSA researchers documented NCSI teachers asking factual or procedural questions 51 percent of the time, whereas only 30 percent of the time was spent on inferential or more analytical questions.[43] Moreover, although PSA researchers reported that several schools were engaging students, there was a notable absence in the study of any teacher developing students' critical thinking skills at NCSI schools.[44] Therefore, although a school may have very strong test-score data, an A on their city's report card, that score does not mean the students are engaged or developing the strong critical thinking skills claimed by reformers such as Bill Gates to be vital to success in college or the workplace.

By leaving the success or failure of the schools to the market, some schools will fail, which has already happened in New York.[45] By not drawing on past successes effectively, failure may be inevitable. To begin with, in creating its initiative for small schools NCSI founders did not build on the long history that New York City has had by not including mentoring, training, or support from those experienced with small schools. NCSI leaders may have wanted to leave education to the 'experts,' but the problem is that the majority of teachers[46] and principals[47] in NCSI schools are new to their jobs and are not experts. Compounding this, the new small schools are situated in poor neighborhoods, and the teachers generally are not familiar with the students whom they serve; they need support to teach skills essential for the success for poor students and students of color.[48] There is very little guidance and support to do this very complicated work, yet there are serious consequences for not making improvements in their students' academic outcomes. Consequently, some schools succeed, some flounder, some fail; but unless we ensure that all schools succeed, we are not ensuring equity, which neoliberalism promises will happen (at least in theory).

NCSI has received some criticism[49] but still has had wide support across the political spectrum. In 2007, New York City's Department of Education received the prestigious Broad Foundation Award[50] based on its small school reform effort and is being studied as a model by other cities and even other countries.[51] In spite of the fact that there are serious flaws in the outcome data,[52] there is continued enthusiasm for opening more small high schools throughout New York City. Support for neoliberal school reform initiatives in general is broad even though there have been negative results.[53] For example, evidence from performance data from charter schools has shown that school reform initiatives are not improving student achievement.[54] Moreover, reports of charter initiatives in Cleveland; Washington, D.C.; and New Orleans describe how they have cleaned out the public coffers, provided shoddy schools, and excluded public accountability.[55]

Why do neoliberal reforms have so much support? Scholars have offered several explanations. Ken Saltman has argued that through the "shock doctrine of disaster capitalism," neoliberal policies are able to pass because they take advantage of the disorientation and overwhelm the public feels, especially with regard to urban education, and impose clear plans that offer a sense of order, efficiency, and simplicity.[56] Michael Klonsky has argued that neoliberal policies have been passed by co-optation. Using the language of social justice and invoking the civil rights movement, proponents of neoliberalism have managed to railroad their policies through, as has been evidenced by the Bush administration's policy making.[57]

Michael Apple and Tom Pedroni have a different take and suggest that recipients of neoliberal policies have not been duped by neoliberal elites, but instead have been proponents of market-based school policies themselves because of a perception of the possibility that they might have better school options and may even be able to have control over them. Pedroni found this to be the case among African Americans in Milwaukee who support vouchers.[58] The same was true initially about NCSI. As one parent exclaimed about her child's new school:

> I feel so good because the school knows me by name; they know my child. You just get the feeling everybody cares. It got me involved. At my son's old school, I didn't even bother. You couldn't even get through to the school; the phone just rang.[59]

This parent's experience lends some evidence to Pedroni's theory that constituents cooperate and support policies that are sometimes not in their best long-term interests. In this case, the need for better schools coincided neatly with political and business elites' agenda for large-scale school reform in New York City.

In addition to these theories, the broad base of support from liberals and conservatives for neoliberal strategies are responsible for their ubiquity. For instance, although they were unlikely partners, progressive educators were initially excited about the initiative. Many of them who had opened small schools under earlier initiatives saw the potential to expand a model they viewed as having the capability for schools to get to know students and families, to strengthen teaching and learning for students in poor communities, and to respond to the needs and concerns of the communities they served. Their goals were not market oriented but were social justice oriented.[60] With their early support,[61] neoliberal reformers had a broad coalition of support to push through their market strategies.

Moreover, as a country, our faith in the market has equaled if not surpassed our faith in democracy and equality. The market may be the only place where people feel as though they have agency, since they feel so powerless to turn against it. Consequently, it is imperative to replace democratic structures that provide the same agency people feel in the market. In a public system with public accountability, everyone is invested in seeing the system itself succeed. Without that investment, only the savvy consumers will succeed, which virtually guarantees a failing group.

THE NEW CENTURY SCHOOLS INITIATIVE'S NEOLIBERAL SCHOOL REFORM: A REPORT FROM THE GROUND

I conducted my own qualitative study of three Bronx-based NCSI schools to confirm the suspicions raised by the reports of the schools and NCSI's weak theory of change. The data collected describes the experience of people working in and attending schools founded under a neoliberal model (see table 4.1).

The schools, which I have called Team Academy, City Prep, and Vision High School,[62] are located in the South Bronx. They were selected because they were successful by neoliberal standards: they were improving outcomes on which they were being measured, including test scores and attendance rates, with poor students and students of color (see tables 4.3 through 4.5). To balance this picture, my aim was to capture the students' and teachers' voices, typically silenced in the current political discourse around school reform. Their experience brought an important counternarrative to the positive spin being placed on NCSI schools by the New York City Department of Education and a reality check to the rosy picture painted by the mainstream media.[63] As a result, the bulk of the data for this study came from interviews, classroom observations, observations of professional development and staff meetings at the three schools, and focus group interviews with students from each school to understand their experience with instruction throughout the 2005–2006 school year (for a detailed description of the data collection, see table 4.2).

When analyzing the data, I looked for evidence for where the problems with the neoliberal model were exposed. In particular, I looked at the quality of education offered by the schools, including curriculum and instruction and support for teachers, as well as who was served by the schools, all of which emerged from the critiques of neoliberal school reform, in order to see what the data revealed about these typologies.[64] I also evaluated the schools on their own measures; I looked at the degree to which they improved outcome data to see whether the market model would have any influence on how well the schools performed.

A Choice for Higher Quality: NCSI Schools' Classrooms

Under a neoliberal model, consumers are responsible for making their own choices about schools. Thus, hard data is required to compare and rank schools. The New York City Department of Education (DoE) has provided this service to NCSI schools by monitoring, collecting, and publishing data on a series of indicators, including test scores, attendance, and graduation rates. Schools were under pressure to show progress and improvement in their data at the end of every school year. Understandably, the schools in the study did whatever they could to improve their test scores, the main criteria upon which improvement was measured.

The main way this impacted the schools was that it made teaching essentially test preparation. High school students in New York City are required to pass five standardized exams in their major subjects—math, history, English, science, and foreign language—in order to graduate. To prepare for these tests, teachers did anything they could to get the students ready for testing. For instance, a ninth-grade science class at Team Academy provided evidence of how the Regents exam displaced any attempt to get students thinking about anything beyond the exam content. In this class, students were rarely engaged in any discussion, and their questions were quickly answered so the teacher could resume the lesson. For example, in one class the students were learning about taxonomy. The teacher was so intent on delivering the content that she silenced students. She shouted several times during class, "Stop talking while I teach." She insisted that she needed to get through the lesson and threatened students who disrupted with detention. During her lecture, she declared, "You don't have to understand what taxonomy is. You just have to understand how to do the Regents question."

Teachers felt a great deal of pressure to get students to pass the battery of standardized tests required to graduate, and they did not stray from the content of the tests in their teaching. However, even they acknowledged that their students were not learning much. As one interviewed teacher said:

> Teachers feel a great deal of pressure. Certain goals are set for the schools: 80 percent pass rate for courses, going up to 90 percent soon; teachers are concerned about these rates. So there is a hesitancy to get excited. We just have to pass more students, but that doesn't mean they'll be learning more.[65]

This was clearly seen in classrooms where there was a race to cover content, as one social studies class revealed:

> *Teacher:* What is white man's burden?
> *[Students do not respond.]*
> *Teacher:* What were the British trying to export around the world?
> *Student:* Teaching people to be civilized.
> *Teacher:* Why would a British poet write this in 1898? What famous war was going on in America?
> *Student:* Spanish-American War.
> *Teacher:* This was the beginning of what?
> *Student:* Colonies.
> *Teacher:* Which group had Sun Yat Sen? Who was he?
> *Student:* He wanted equality, democracy.
> *Teacher:* Right. What does it mean when we talk about Westernize? Sun Yat Sen wanted to Westernize China.
> *Student:* Modernize, make it like the West.
> *Teacher:* More like colonizing an old civilization, making trade agreements.
> *Student:* Like trying to profit off of them?
> *Teacher:* Who can share information on the Suez Canal? Why would the French put up millions for a canal?
> *Student:* Trade.
> *Teacher:* It was a shortcut for trading. Egyptians did the work. Turn to the "Rise of Modern Japan." Let's read aloud.[66]

In this classroom excerpt, the class covered a lot of disparate content, but that content did not get discussed. In other words, most of the teacher's questions had one-word or one-phrase answers. The students were not asked to think about why something happened or to make connections between events.

My observations confirmed data collected by Policy Studies Associates, which documented the amount of time teachers spent on different kinds of questioning techniques.[67] The bulk of time was spent asking students to recall rather than to analyze. With the emphasis on tests put on schools by the city's Department of Education and NCSI founders to document their progress, there was little incentive for teachers to do anything other than drill students on their content knowledge. Characteristic of a neoliberal model, test-driven instruction limits the ability of any teacher to engage students on a more sophisticated level, which severely limits the quality of the education that students received. Under a more democratic school model (see table 4.1), the curriculum and instruction would reflect the needs and interests of the students and would peak their interest and engage them in the content of the class. Sleepy heads on desks in classroom after classroom showed that the opposite was happening in the schools I observed.

Limiting Who is Served: Does Everyone Get a Choice?

The need to document continually improved test scores and graduation and attendance data had another consequence. Schools adopted many informal practices to limit the population of students they served so as to show progress on data indicators. One of the informal practices schools engaged in to narrow the student populations they served was a process of 'counseling out.' This process involved identifying students who were achieving at low academic levels or had attendance problems and moving them out of the schools by the end of ninth or tenth grade. That way, schools would not have a low-performing group to drag down their performance data. Since the teachers did not have the skills to deal with the academic needs of these students, this practice made sense to them, and it was widely supported at the three schools.

After a few interventions—meeting with the student's parent, offering academic support, or both—the schools took steps to find 'alternative placements' that would meet 'student needs better.' What this amounted to, however, was an effort to push out students who would drag down outcome expectations for the school. Guidance counselors, assistant principals, and social workers talked about this informal practice with students who appeared to be unable to complete the requirements to move from grade to grade, claiming it was in the students' best interests. As the numbers of students in the ninth grades swelled, counselors would start the process in the spring semester so the fall rosters would come down. In most cases, the students being 'counseled' were special-education students and English Language Learners (ELLs). This phenomenon has also been found by Elaine Garan, who documented the pushing out of over 160,000 students in New York City schools due to the pressure schools feel under high-stakes testing policies.[68] The constant need for improved data by neoliberal reformers puts schools in a precarious position, and so it is not a surprise that schools do what they can to show improvement in their performance data. In so doing, injustices and inequities are perpetuated, not resolved, as is shown with the practice of 'counseling out.' Yet neoliberal reformers would have us believe that equality is gained by holding schools accountable for their performance data.

Leaving Them up to the Market: Lack of Support for NCSI Schools

Under a neoliberal model, supplying schools with teachers has little to do with building a professional community, longevity in the profession, or hiring staff that are able to respond to community needs. To meet the great demand for new teachers, programs like Teach for America or the New York City Teaching Fellows[69] were enlisted to fill the vacancies produced by the hundreds of new schools created under an initiative like NCSI. By definition, these teachers are not asked to commit to teaching for longer than two years, are from outside the communities they serve, and are not provided with much support beyond their required courses.[70]

This resulted in schools being staffed by brand new principals and teaching staffs that were also largely new to teaching (see table 4.6). There was no place to get advice on how to improve instruction, how to work with struggling students, or how to design effective curricula. Since the schools served many students who were in need of additional support, this posed particular problems for improving their achievement.

The expectations teachers had for students was one obvious area that needed improvement. In many classrooms I visited and meetings I attended, teachers expressed low expectations of their students and had little desire to connect with their students. In a Vision High School English class, a tenth-grade teacher dismissed the need to connect the curriculum to students at all, saying that "People want her to teach 'ghetto literature' when she should be teaching 'real literature' like Steinbeck or Shakespeare." She did not think that connecting the content to students' lived experience was worthwhile and saw her curriculum as a binary of either focused on literature that her students could relate to or with literature that was completely removed from them, not both.

Many teachers, young and new to the communities that they were teaching in (see table 4.6), held a deficit view[71] of students. One teacher said that the only way to improve student achievement was to spend twenty-four hours a day with the students. He said, "That's the only way they will learn." He suggested going to their homes, telling them when and where to study. "They need a life coach," he added. Another teacher said, "We still have not brought the parents in, and we're still not connected and connecting the home to school. We're still not truly engaging the students. You know, it's hard because academics are not supported outside of the school."[72] Other teachers even expressed a paternalistic view of students. As one Team Academy teacher succinctly said, "I really believe that we have to be as teachers, you know, like physicians. You have to try to help your patient get well." In another case a teacher was frustrated and did not understand why students traveled with their families during the school year. As she expressed in a meeting of her colleagues:

> During a planning meeting, a group of teachers joked around about students who did nothing in each others' classes, and the art teacher said sarcastically that each student had his own learning style. The group then moved onto the projects they were working on in class. One teacher said that her students had to hand in papers early if they were going away before the Christmas break. She went on to say that some students have already left to go to Puerto Rico or the Dominican Republic. The science teacher continues, "Or Africa or wherever they're from." Another White teacher says that she was never allowed to miss school.[73]

This teacher's attitude toward her students was condescending and expressed a disinterest in understanding an important aspect of her students' lives—close family members outside of the United States—that clearly would prevent her from getting to know her students deeply and developing a caring relationship with them. Her comments suggested a rejection of students' cultural norms and values.

Staffing the new small schools with young and inexperienced teachers was not uncommon.[74] It was consistent with a neoliberal strategy since it allowed schools to maximize their resources to hire more staff while keeping costs down. However, with little experience to manage challenging classrooms, new teachers were not able to handle all of the responsibilities put on them. Having to help create a school, learn to teach, and work in unfamiliar communities was extraordinarily difficult. Consequently, at the end of each year several teachers left the schools, close to a third of the staff at Team Academy and Vision High School. Many that remained did not know how to navigate and undervalued the students, perhaps because they felt they were being undervalued by the NCSI schools.

Ironically, time was set aside for professional support. Called professional development, this allotted time was an opportunity to support the new teaching staffs and to address their attitudes and expectations. Generally, teachers across the schools expressed dissatisfaction with professional development. At Vision High School, for example, one teacher explained that when the school first opened, the staff had time to strategize together around problems they faced, but after the first year the principal replaced that with professional development (PD) meetings:

> The staff meetings were contentious. As we started to challenge the principal, they were replaced by PD. PD was decided by the principal for the staff. There was no room for conversation of any kind. This is the safest kind of staff meeting. A PD committee was formed of newer staff and staff who supported the agenda of the principal, which was not bad in theory, but ideas are never explored, challenged, or discussed among the staff anymore.[75]

The principal, herself inexperienced, erred on the side of controlling the time and the situation rather than rolling up her sleeves with the staff to solve problems. She had only been a teacher for four years prior to becoming a principal, and she did not have much knowledge or experience to lead the group.

At Team Academy, professional development time was dominated by a discussion of how to improve discipline policies and was the subject of a month's worth of staff meetings. For the administration and much of the teaching staff, punishments were seen as a solution to what they perceived as behavioral problems, but these could have been academic or other sorts of problems. For example, at Team Academy, students received detention when they did not do homework, which could have been incomplete for a variety of reasons, including after school work or family commitments or lack of understanding. In spite of the whole new set of administrative tasks created by the detention systems, teachers did not feel better about the professional support at the school. As one teacher said, "I can't believe we are not talking about the graduating seniors. They are not ready for college!" She was upset that the focus of teacher conversation was not on academic achievement of students. Her concerns were overshadowed by those articulated by another staff member who said, "It is not a perfect solution, but it's the only one we have."

In terms of helping students with their academic progress, professional development in all of the schools rarely addressed students' academic achievement. As one teacher put it, "The students who don't have the skills, I don't feel like I have much support with them." Very little was provided. As another teacher said in frustration, "No one has ever stepped in and said, 'Look I'm going to show you how to improve a curriculum.' I think people are looking for miracles." Without professional development that helps inexperienced teachers improve their practice, it is very hard to expect teachers to improve.

As a neoliberal reform, NCSI left professional support to the individual schools despite their clear need for guidance. Neoliberal school reformers often underestimate the complexity of teaching and think that competition by itself will motivate schools to improve, but the evidence from individual schools revealed that this was not even close to being enough. Under a democratic school model, veteran and new teachers would work together to develop their practice and would draw from community resources to improve their work. The staffs at the NCSI schools worked alone for the most part and did not even consult school staff in the same building.

The Failure of Competition to Improve Schools

Taking a look at the New York City Department of Education's website, one sees nothing but praise for the new small schools. City education officials have claimed that they have raised graduation rates, attendance rates, and test scores.[76] However, the improved numbers are not as dazzling as city officials would have readers believe.[77] The three schools examined in the study offered an important example of what is going on at the NCSI schools. They were typical of the small schools in that they served mainly poor students and students of color and have made remarkable gains with them. Graduation rates, for instance, have far surpassed those from the late 1990s, prior to NCSI.[78]

Despite the strong showing on some outcome data, students were not performing well in their classes. Looking beyond the graduation and attendance data, we see a much bleaker picture of student outcomes at the three schools. Students struggled to pass their courses and their exams. An examination of student transcripts showed that most students were receiving course grades of 65 and 70.[79] On their standardized Regents exams, students were able to pass with grades of 55, which the large majority did. With these low passing grades,[80] students could still earn local high school diplomas: only 25 percent at City Prep and Vision High schools and slightly higher at Team Academy earned Regents diplomas.[81] A report by Policy Studies Associates confirmed this finding and concluded that among the class of 2006, only 46 percent of students across twenty-six NCSI schools received Regents diplomas, as compared with 61 percent of citywide graduates who received them.[82] If one takes this standardized test seriously as a measure, at least as a minimum standard, the data suggests weak academic preparation among students attending NCSI schools.

As a study conducted by one of the City Prep teachers revealed, students from the 2006 graduating class were not staying in college in spite of relatively high acceptance

and enrollment rates. Approximately 70 percent had enrolled, but 30 percent of those had not actually started college in September or had dropped out after their first semester.[83] He concluded that the school needed to provide students more support during the processes of admissions, enrollment, and attending college. Students also complained that they were unprepared. In focus groups, students reported that their classes were too easy. Among seniors at the schools, this was a particular concern. Seniors only had to take two classes, English and social studies, because the state requires four years of study in those subjects but not in math or science. They worried that the limited course schedule was not what "kids going to other schools was doing."

Under a more democratic model, schools would be held accountable to the families they serve and would use multiple measures to show how they are doing. Since NCSI schools see themselves as accountable to the DoE for reporting improvements in outcome data, they only have an interest in meeting the minimum standards of those demands. If schools reported to families, they might be held to a higher standard than a minimum passing score. If dissatisfied, families could also directly communicate with the school about their expectations and standards. Additionally, parents could advocate for the use of multiple measures of assessment so that their child's evaluation and progress does not hinge on a single test score.

Summary

The evidence from the three NCSI schools indicates that contrary to the data publicized by the NYC DoE, the schools are not turning out better students. The students are learning mainly through test prep, and there is little evidence that they are mastering the content they are being taught since they are only meeting minimum standards. Students who are not meeting minimum performance standards are counseled out of attending the schools. Moreover, teachers get little support to provide high-quality instruction to their students.

Although my data was collected from only three NCSI schools, larger studies confirm my findings in a broader range of NCSI schools.[84] Policy Studies Associates found that across twenty-six schools, NCSI schools were neither teaching students critical thinking nor skills they might need for college.

Some critics might say that despite its shortcomings, NCSI has raised graduation rates in poor communities, which have been low for decades; but as educators well know, improved numbers does not translate into more learning and more content and skill mastery among students. Maybe more to the point, when closely examined, the data does not support that conclusion. Jennings and Dorn's 2007 findings show that test score improvements have not made the gains the DoE has claimed, and graduation rates are also much weaker than the DoE claims, especially among Black and Latino students.[85]

The wild praise NCSI has received is misleading because it masks problems and leads to uncritical support of small schools. In reality, NCSI does not guarantee high-quality schools to the very families that it promised it would. There may be a group of high-quality small schools available, but in a neoliberal system only the most savvy consumers are able to access these schools. For most, educational equity is still a pipe dream.

CONCLUSION: WHAT CAN BE DONE?

In a 2009 speech, Bill Gates admitted that developing the small schools has not been a success. He conceded that his foundation underestimated the constellation of factors that can influence the quality of a school.[86] NCSI's single-minded approach focused on the creation of a product and measurement of its quality without the necessary supports or sensitivity to context required to creating schools. Realizing its mistakes, the Gates Foundation has announced that it will refocus its efforts on teacher quality.[87]

Given this epiphany, there is an opportunity to make changes that would improve teacher quality across the nation. First, we need to end the punitive culture that censures schools for not meeting standardized testing targets. That will require an end to or serious revision of No Child Left Behind legislation to allow the use of multiple assessments to measure student progress so that teachers are not simply prepping students for tests. Moreover, we need an increase in funding and resources allocated to meaningful teacher training.[88] This strategy needs to be coupled with a decrease in crash courses in teaching, like Teach for America, which does little to prepare its "corps members" to have success and longevity in teaching.

Beyond the mandate for better teachers, a moratorium needs to be called on opening any new small schools until a full evaluation of the current schools can take place. Opening more and more unsuccessful schools will not help anyone. Yet this is exactly what the DoE is doing by dangling a gazillion-dollar carrot in front of local school districts.

Finally, and most important, we need local campaigns to combat the exclusion of public participation and accountability that market-based initiatives create and to promote democratic schools. Parents and community voices must be included in decision making regarding schools. In New York City, there is at present no mechanism for this. At the very basic level, we need a community-led decision-making body to put checks and balances on the mayor and his appointed staff. Going beyond this, we need to eliminate mayoral control of the school system. I am not suggesting that we return to a mythological good old days of community school boards, as they were rife with problems,[89] but I am suggesting that we need to have more democracy in our schools (see table 4.1) and in our society. Only by creating public spaces for multiple voices in decision making can we push democracy forward. That means genuine agency for community members and parents so that they do not need to seek it in the market.

We must begin with a healthy skepticism of market initiatives and a look at who truly benefits from them. The failure of the market has brought long overdue but growing criticism of the market's power to deliver social equality. We need to turn that skepticism and critique into action that will reinvigorate democracy and resist the encroachment of the market on our public institutions.

Table 4.1 Contrasting a Neoliberal School System with a Democratic One

	Neoliberal school system	Democratic school system
Parents	• Seen as consumers exercising their choice and comparison shopping for best product	• Responsible for holding schools accountable for educating their children • Involved in decision making at individual schools
Students	• Regarded as consumers who can move schools if they are unhappy with services provided • Measurable achievement documented by increased test scores	• Central to the culture and operation of a school • Teachers' instruction relies on knowledge of them personally and culturally and integrates that knowledge into curricula • Involved in decision-making processes
Teachers	• Responsible for improving student achievement as measured by test scores and sometimes paid more for the degree to which they make improvements • Need to find support to improve their level of instruction	• Professionals who collaborate with each other as well as with parents and students to drive what they do • Receive support to develop skills they lack
Curriculum	• Seen as the domain of experts from which schools may purchase packages that are appropriate for the context of the school • Ideally increases students' test scores	• Reflects the community interests, desires, and goals • Created by teachers in a collaborative fashion • Students' engagement a central component
Assessment	• Regularly collected data made public for parents to compare schools • Tied to assessments used and classroom practice, producing uniformity across classrooms and schools • Schools held accountable for improving outcome data or closed	• Multiple assessments used to track student learning • Individualized to school, class, and student

Table 4.2 Data Collection

Participants	Data collection method	Description of participants	Number in group
Teacher leaders	Semi-structured interviews with each teacher, informal conversations, andobservations of staff meetings and other professional meetings	Teachers who were the union chapter leaders at the three schools in the study	3
Teachers	A cycle of professional development meetings	All teachers at each of the three schools	66
Teachers	Three classroom observations with NCSI teachers in varying subject areas and grade levels using a rubric to evaluate the quality of teaching in the classrooms	A range of teachers from each school representing a mix of subject areas, grade levels, and experience	15 total, 5 from each school
Students	One focus-group interview with each group of students at three NCSI high schools	A random sample of students, ranging in grade level, from each of the three schools	45 total, 15 from each school
Archival/ quantitative data	Student transcripts; school-level data, including attendance rates, standardized test scores, suspension rates, course pass rates, graduation rates, college acceptance rates; and demographic information, including poverty rates measured by the percentage of students receiving free lunch		

Table 4.3 Demographic Data from Three NCSI High Schools

School	Race and ethnicity of students[a]	Free lunch eligibility of students	Total number of students
Team Academy	African American 33%	89.4%	303
	Latino 66%		
Vision High School	African American 35%	93%	332
	Latino 64%		
City Prep	African American 40%	71.8%	328
	Latino 60%		

Source: Data collected from Columbia University's Teachers College National Center for Teaching Excellence.

[a]Data excluded White and Asian-Pacific Islander categories because the numbers are so negligible. At City Prep, there are no students who are White or Asian-Pacific Islanders; and at Team Academy and Vision High School, the numbers fall below 1 percent.

Table 4.4 Attendence Data at the Three Schools

School	Attendence Rate for the 2005–2006 School Year
Team Academy	87.10%
Vision High School	82.70%
City Prep	85.30%

Source: Data collected from reports given to the New York City Department of Education by the schools.

Table 4.5 Comparison of Regents Pass Rates across Schools for 2005–2006 School Year

Regents exams	Team → Vision → City
ELA	90% → 81% →→ 77%
Math	90% → 65% →→ 69%
Global	91% → 72% →→ 73%
U.S. History	81% → 72% →→ 63%
Biology	86% → 68% →→ 73%

Source: Data taken from NYC Department of Education Annual School Report Cards.

[a]Data from Bronx High School taken from the 2000–2001 school year right before the school closed.

Table 4.6 Teacher Experience across Schools in Years

School	Teacher experience in years
Team Academy	53.3% of teachers $\leq$ 5 years
Vision High School	50% of teachers $\leq$ 3 years
City Prep	50% of teachers $\leq$ 4 years

Source: Data collected by Columbia University's Teachers College National Center for Excellence in Teaching.

Table 4.7 Race and Ethnicity of Teachers across Schools

School	Race/ethnicity of teachers[a]
Team Academy	African American 20%
	Latino 26.7%
	White 46.7%
Vision High School	African American 26.3%
	Latino 5.3%
	White 47.4%
City Prep	African American 22.2%
	Latino 38.9%
	White 16.7%

Source: Data collected by Columbia University's Teachers College National Center for Excellence in Teaching.
[a]Data excludes Asian and Pacific Islanders because that category included such a small percentage of the staffs.

NOTES

1. E. Einhorn and M. Kolodner, "42 New Public Schools to Open in Fall, Mayor Bloomberg Says," *New York Daily News,* March 1, 2009, http://www.nydailynews.com/ny_localeducation2009/03/01/2009-03-01_42_new_public_schools_to_open_in_fall_ma.htm (accessed March 2, 2009).
2. D. Leonhardt, "Obamanomics" August 20, 2008, http://www.nytimes.com/2008/08/24/magazine/24obamanomics-t.html (accessed April 23, 2009).
3. D. Leonhardt, "Obamanomics," *New York Times*, August 24, 2008, sec. MM30.
4. See D. Hursh, *High-Stakes Testing and the Decline of Teaching and Learning: The Real Crisis in Education* (Lanham, MD: Rowman and Littlefield,

2008); M. Klonsky and S. Klonsky, *Small Schools: Public School Reform Meets the Ownership Society* (New York: Routledge, 2008); P. Lipman, *High Stakes Education: Inequality, Globalization and the Urban School Reform* (New York: Routledge, 2004).

5. See M. Apple, *Ideology and Curriculum, 3rd ed.* (New York: Routledge, 2004); D. Hursh, *High Stakes Testing*; A. Molnar, "The Commercial Transformation of Public Education," *Journal of Education Policy* 21, no. 5 (2006): 621–40; K. Saltman, "Schooling in Disaster Capitalism: How the Political Right Is Using Disaster to Privatize Public School," *Teacher Education Quarterly* 32, no. 2 (2007): 131–56.
6. A. Klein, "To Duncan, Incentives a Priority," *Education Week*, February 4, 2009, 1. See also US Department of Education, http://www.ed.gov/programs/racetothetop/faq.pdf, which provides criteria for Race to the Top grants.
7. J. Shiller, "No Easy Answers: The Creation of Small Schools in the South Bronx" (PhD diss., New York University, 2007), 56.
8. This will be described more in a later part of the chapter, but as Michael Klonsky has explained in a recent book (Klonsky and Klonsky, 2008), earlier initiatives for small high schools came from a desire for democratic schools that are closely connected with the communities they serve.
9. S. Freedman, "From Distinguished to Extinguished, *New York Times*, May 25, 2005, sec. B8.
10. Gates Foundation, "High Schools for the New Millennium," 2004, 10, http://www.neincc.com/Documents/GatesFdnWhitePaper.pdf (accessed June 3, 2004).
11. A. S. Wells, J. Slatyton, and J. Scott, "Defining Democracy in the Neoliberal Age: Charter Schools Reform and Educational Consumption," *American Educational Research Journal* 39, no. 2 (2002): 337–61.
12. L. Cuban, *The Blackboard and the Bottom Line: Why Schools Can't Be Businesses* (Cambridge, MA: Harvard University Press, 2004), chap. 2.
13. This came to be known as Taylorism. Scholars have argued that Taylorism has led to the reproduction of inequality since it presumes one's future social class position is based on current class status and prepares students to assume the very same positions they already occupy. See S. Bowles and H. Gintis, *Schooling in Capitalist America: Educational Reform and The Contradictions of Economic Life* (New York: Basic Books, 1976); H. Giroux, *Theory and Resistance in Education: Towards a Pedagogy for the Opposition* (Westport, CT: Bergin and Garvey, 2001); M. Carnoy, Schooling in a Corporate Society: The Political Economy of Education in America (New York: McCoy, 1975).
14. F. Taylor, *Principles of Scientific Management* (New York: Norton, 1911), 12.
15. J. Dewey, "Untitled," *The New Republic* 3, no. 42 (1915): 3.
16. The most poignant example of this was the period after Sputnik launched in 1957 during which American schools focused on science education to make sure young people were prepared to compete with our Soviet counterparts.
17. J. Blackmore, "Globalization: A Useful Concept for Feminists Rethinking Theory and Strategies in Education," in *Globalization and Education: Critical Perspectives*, ed. N. Burbules and C. Torres (New York: Routledge, 2000), 137.
18. P. Lipman, "Renaissance 2010: The Reassertion of Ruling-Class Power Through Neoliberal Policies in Chicago," in D. Hursh, *High-Stakes Testing*.
19. Originally proposed by Milton Friedman in his seminal book *Capitalism and Freedom* (Chicago: University of Chicago Press, 1982).

20. See A. Molnar, "Commercial Transformation," 622; D. Garcia and A. Molnar, "The Expanding Role of Privatization in Education: Implications for Teacher Education and Development," *Teacher Education Quarterly* 34, no. 2 (2007): 13.
21. See Klonsky and Klonsky (2008); P. Lipman, *High-Stakes Education*; K. Saltman, "Schooling in Disaster Capitalism."
22. A. Molnar, "Commercial Transformation," 638.
23. M. Apple, *Ideology and Curriculum*, 62.
24. S. Ohanian, "Capitalism, Calculus and Conscience," *Phi Delta Kappan* 84, no. 10 (2003): 737.
25. P. Lipman, *High-Stakes Education*, 103–4; M. Klonsky and S. Klonsky, *Small Schools*.
26. T. Huebner, *Rethinking High School: An Introduction to New York City's Experience* (San Francisco: West Ed, 2005), 3.
27. Bill and Melinda Gates Foundation, "High Schools for the New Millennium, Imagine the Possibilities" 2004.
28. For more information, see schools.nyc.gov.
29. While this role for a government agency may be counterintuitive to some advocates of neoliberalism, a strong and centralized state power ensures independent participation in the market by maintaining order so that markets can operate freely and without interruption, implementing a uniform accountability system, which creates efficiency and easy comparisons of like products, also central to smooth market operation. As theorist David Harvey has explained, market processes "entail a deepening of the state's grasp over certain facets of the social process." D. Harvey, *Spaces of Hope* (Berkeley CA: University of California Press, 2000), 180.
30. P. Lipman, *High-Stakes Education*, 23–41.
31. Educational management organizations (EMOs) are private organizations now responsible for supervising and managing NCSI schools, a job that was once done by superintendents in local school districts, which no longer exist.
32. This information can be found at New Visions for Public School's website, http://www.newvisions.org/about-us/board-of-directors (accessed July 31, 2010).
33. J. Hernandez, "School Panel Is No Threat to Mayor's Grip," *New York Times*, April 22, 2009, sec. A1.
34. J. Baum, "Setbacks and Successes for Education Councils," *Gotham Gazette*, July 21, 2005, http://www.gothamgazette.com/article/education/20050721/6/1487 (accessed December 6, 2008).
35. Mayoral control was renewed in June of 2009. It was hotly contested as parents and community advocates wanted to eliminate or at least add more room for public participation in the school system, while the mayor and chancellor along with a host of business leaders, charter school advocates, and others supported the continuation of mayoral control (J. Medina, "Klein Defends Mayoral Control of Public Schools," *New York Times*, February 6, 2009, sec. A18).
36. This definition of freedom has been articulated best in M. Friedman's *Capitalism and Freedom*, in which he articulates freedom as freedom from constraint to pursue our self-interest (see note 19).
37. S. Gewirtz, *The Managerial School: Post-Welfarism and the Social Justice in Education* (London: Routledge, 2002), 66–71.
38. S. Garland, "Study: New Small High Schools Are Failing on Special Education," *New York Sun*, October 13, 2006, http://www.nysun.com/new-york/study-new-small-high-schools-are-failing/41544 (accessed December 3, 2008).

39. See L. McNeil, *Contradictions of School Reform: Educational Costs of Standardized Testing* (New York, Routledge, 2000); A. Valenzuela, *Leaving Children Behind: How "Texas-style" Accountability Fails Latino Youth* (Albany: State University of New York Press, 2005).
40. A set of five Regents exams are required for students to graduate from high school with a local diploma. Eight such exams are required for a Regents diploma, a more prestigious diploma for which college-bound students aim.
41. Policy Studies Associates, *Evaluation of New Century High Schools Initiative: Report on the Third Year*, June 2006, http://www.policystudies.com/studies/school/NCHS%20Evaluation%Report.pdf (accessed September 12, 2006), 51.
42. Ibid., 63.
43. Ibid., 51.
44. This includes goals for cultivating critical thinking and a sense of agency among students as well as culturally relevant pedagogy. Pauline Lipman discusses the implications of eliminating these from school curricula in *High-Stakes Education*.
45. J. Hernandez, "To Close a School: A Decision Rooted in Data but Colored by Nuance," *New York Times*, February 2, 2009, sec. A15.
46. M. Weinstein and others, *Stability in Student and Teacher Characteristics in the First Ten Years: A Study of Small High Schools in New York City* (New York: New York University Institute for Education and Social Policy, 2007).
47. E. Gootman, "Principal Ranks Undergo Heavy Turnover," *New York Times*, May 22, 2006, sec. A1.
48. G. Ladson-Billings, *The Dreamkeepers: Successful Teachers of African-American Children*, 1st ed. (San Francisco: Jossey-Bass,1994); J. Jordon-Irvine, *Educating Teachers for Diversity: Seeing with a Cultural Eye* (New York: Teachers College Press, 2003).
49. M. Fine, "Not in Our Name: Reclaiming the Democratic Vision of Small School Reform," *Rethinking Schools* 19, no. 4 (2005); J. Kozol, "Segregated Schools: Shame of the City," *Gotham Gazette*, January 16, 2006, http://www.gothamgazette.com/article/2006011/202/1718 (accessed January 18, 2006).
50. J. Medina, "Klein Defends Mayoral Control," sec. A18.
51. S. Chan, "For Bloomberg, in Los Angeles to Discuss Education, Admiration and Talk of the Presidency," *New York Times*, September 21, 2006, http://www.nytimes.com/2006/09/21/nyregion/21bloomberg.html (accessed January 4, 2008); J. Hernandez, "Klein Promotes School Initiatives in Australia," *New York Times*, November 26, 2008, http://cityroom.blogs.nytimes.com/2008/klein-promotes-school-initiatives-in-ustralia (accessed December 2, 2008).
52. S. Dorn and J. Jennings, "The Proficiency Trap: New York City's Achievement Gap Revisited," *Teachers College Record*, 2008, http://www.tcrecord.org/content.asap?contenid=15366 (accessed January 2, 2009).
53. David Hursh has found that NCLB (No Child Left Behind) has worsened the quality of education for poor children and has spawned more privatization. See D. Hursh, "Undermining Democratic Education in the USA: The Consequences of Global Capitalism and Neoliberal Policies for Education at the Local, State, and Federal Levels," *Policy Futures in Education* 2, no. 3/4 (2004): 607–20. Pauline Lipman argues that in Renaissance 2010 the small schools paired with a plan for gentrification of Chicago neighborhoods are isolating poor people of color and relegating them to low-quality school options. See P. Lipman, *High-Stakes Education*.

54. M. Carnoy et al., *The Charter School Dust-Up: Examining the Evidence on Enrollment and Achievement* (Washington, D.C.: Economic Policy Institute, 2005).
55. L. Dingerson et al., *Keeping the Promise: The Debate Over Charter Schools* (Milwaukee, WI: Rethinking Schools, 2007).
56. K. Saltman, "Schooling in Disaster Capitalism," 131–56.
57. M. Klonsky and S. Klonsky, *Small Schools.*
58. T. Pedroni, *Market Movements: African-American Involvement in School Voucher Reform* (New York: Routledge, 2007), 29–32.
59. D. Herszenhorn, "In New York's Smaller Schools, a Good Year and a Tough Year." NY Times 8/8/05 p. A1.
60. Teachers and principals at small schools founded under earlier initiatives had explicit connections to progressive education models and social justice. NCSI has defined small schools much differently than they had originally envisioned them.
61. Several progressive small-school leaders expressed dissatisfaction with how NCSI was put into practice in interviews and informal conversations I had with them.
62. Pseudonyms.
63. S. Stern, "Grading Mayoral Control," *City Journal,* 2007, http://www.city-journal.org/html/17_3_mayoral_control.html (accessed January 13, 2009).
64. J. Hatch, *Doing Qualitative Research in Educational Settings* (Albany: State University of New York Press, 1990), 154–61.
65. J. Shiller, field notes, December 12, 2005.
66. Ibid., November 2, 2005.
67. Policy Studies Associates, "Evaluation of New Century High Schools: Profile of an Initiative to Create and Sustain Small, Successful High Schools," October 2007, http://www.policystudies.com/school/NCHS%20Evaluation%20Final%20Report%2010-07.pdf (accessed November 15, 2007).
68. E. Garan, *In Defense of Our Children: When Politics, Profit and Education Collide* (Portsmouth, NH: Heinemann, 2004), 53.
69. The Teaching Fellows program recruits and hires second-career teachers. They are placed immediately in high-need schools and are mandated to take courses after school to complete a master's degree while they are working full time.
70. Some individual educational management organizations (EMOs) that now oversee the schools did provide some support to individual schools, but reports from teachers indicated that it was sporadic and insufficient.
71. L. Powell, "The Achievement (K)not: Whiteness and 'Black Underachievement,' " in *Off White: Readings on Race, Power, and Society*, ed. M. Fine (New York: Routledge, 1997), 3–12.
72. J. Shiller, field notes, March 10, 2006.
73. Ibid., December 19, 2006.
74. M. Weinstein et al., *Stability in Student and Teacher Characteristics*, 9.
75. J. Shiller, field notes, January 18, 2006.
76. For reports by the city's Department of Education see their website, http://schools.nyc.gov/default.htm.
77. J. Jennings and S. Dorn, "The Proficiency Trap," 2008.
78. Team Academy, Vision High, and City Prep each opened in 2002 with a cohort of ninth graders. The student populations at the three schools were mainly poor students of color. Over 90 percent of students at each school were African American or Latino, and over 70 percent of them qualified for free lunch (at one school over 90 percent qualified). Although this demographic of students often perform poorly on academic indicators, the three

schools managed to have a very high attendance rate for the 2005–2006 school year: over 80 percent students attending on average (data collected from Columbia University's Teachers College National Center for Excellent Teaching).

79. A grade of 65 is passing in New York and the report cards follow in 5 point increments. The next possible grade is a 70.
80. Problems with the validity of these standardized exams have been documented. See D. Hursh, *High-Stakes Testing*; D. Hoff, "Flaws Could Spell Trouble for New York Regents Exams," November 5, 2003 www.edweekly.org/login.html?source=http://www.edweekly.org/ew/articles/2003/11/05/10.regents.n23.htm/8levelID=2100 (accessed January 4, 2004); M. Winerip, "Moving Quickly Through History" June 18, 2003 www.nytimes.com/2003/06/18/nyregion/on-education-moving-quickly-through-history.html (accessed July 30, 2004).
81. Students were required to pass five exams with a 65 or better to receive a Regents diploma. The passing rate for the exams has been 55 since the requirement was phased in during the 2001–2002 school year.
82. Policy Studies Associates, "Evaluation of New Century High Schools: Profile of an Initiative to Create and Sustain Small, Successful High Schools."
83. D. Abromoski, "What Happens Next? Class of 2006 in Their First Year after High School" (paper presented at New York City Teachers Network, 2006).
84. Policy Studies Associates, "Evaluation of New Century High Schools: Profile of an Initiative to Create and Suatain Small, Successful High Schools," 7.
85. S. Dorn and J. Jennings, "The Proficiency Trap: New York City's Achievement Gap Revisited," *Teachers College Record,* 2008, http://www.tcrecord.org/content.asap?contenid=15366 (accessed January 2, 2009). The following report warns that gaps in achievement are stark and need to be addressed: New York City Coalition for Educational Justice, *Looming Crisis or Historic Opportunity: Meeting the Challenge of the Regents Graduation Standards* (New York: Annenberg Institute, 2009), 11.
86. Gates Foundation, "2009 Annual Letter from Bill Gates: US Education" (2009), http://www.gatesfoundation.org/annual-letter/Pages/2009-united-states-education.aspx (accessed February 19, 2009).
87. Ibid.
88. L. Darling-Hammond and N. Richardson, "Teacher Learning: What Matters?" *Educational Leadership* 66, no. 5 (2009): 46–53.
89. D. Ravitch, *The Great School Wars: A History of New York City Schools* (Baltimore: John Hopkins Press, 2000), 397.

5 Corporatism, KIPP, and Cultural Eugenics

Jim Horn

Corporatism is about crushing the capacity for moral choice.

—Chris Hedges

In a 2009 report entitled *Parsing the Achievement Gap II*, researchers[1] recalibrated the achievement gaps[2] that Barton had first documented in *Parsing the Achievement Gap: Baselines for Tracking Progress.*[3] The updated report once again examined sixteen factors, or "correlates of achievement," that researchers have identified as affecting the academic achievement of children: curriculum rigor, teacher preparation, teacher experience, teacher attendance and turnover, class size, availability of instructional technology, fear and safety at school, parent participation, birth weight, exposure to lead and mercury, hunger and nutrition, talking and reading to babies and young children, excessive television watching, parent-pupil ratio, frequent changing of schools, and summer achievement gain/loss.[4] Many of these factors are the same ones that other researchers[5] have identified as contributing to the achievement gap, or "education debt," as Gloria Ladson-Billings[6] has labeled the canyon of inequity between rich and poor.

Parsing II glumly concludes that "although a few of the gaps in the correlates of achievement have become a bit narrower in some instances and a bit wider in others, overall the gaps identified in the earlier report remain apparent and disturbing.[7] Overall, there is little change."[8] In the final chapter of the report, Barton and Coley offer the following frank insight regarding the blame-the-schools excuse used by politicians and their corporate patrons to avoid effective (and expensive) public policy decisions to address poverty:

> There is fear that looking outside school will provide schools with excuses. And there is fear that a focus entirely on the schools will foster neglect of other matters important to children's well-being and learning, and may result in unrealistic expectations of the role that schools can play. Nothing in a child's development or environment should result in lower expectations for that child, nor minimize what teachers and schools can accomplish. Yet ignoring the impact of a student's home circumstances will do nothing to help teachers and schools narrow

> achievement gaps. Unrealistic expectations for schools may be used to provide excuses for public policy, and thus ignore policies that might prevent learning gaps from opening. Schools are where we institutionalize learning; they are also where we tend to institutionalize blame.[9]

A corrosive social and economic system that perpetuates the conditions for achievement gaps to continue is strategically ignored by the philanthrocorporate community, even as the education debt to the poor piles up and despite the heroics-on-demand that corporate school-reformers seem to expect from the urban public schools.

Even more prominent, however, is a third fear that the ETS researchers have missed: the fear that acknowledging the real effects of poverty on children in America will leave us with no moral alternatives other than to (1) actually do something about poverty and its effects on children in particular, or (2) admit that we as a society are willing to discard the bottom quintile of children who are not needed to insure the societal well-being of those of us who are accustomed to being well. Either of these alternatives is difficult to acknowledge, the former due to the economic cost of taking action against the real problem of poverty, and the latter due to the inherent threat against our political ideology that espouses equality and opportunity, even as classism and racism rage. Regardless of which alternative our market-based culture chooses (or does not choose), the continuing self-imposed blindness to poverty meanwhile pushes public policy makers and the corporate reform-schoolers toward a new generation of reforms based on doing more of the same, with even harsher school interventions called for to compensate for the plague of poverty that public education, or any other education, will never solve alone. Never.

Interestingly, the advocates for revamping (again) the twenty-year-old test-and-punish school reforms that have left the achievement gaps gaping find themselves increasingly squeezed by two other questions for which convincing responses appear more distant with each subsequent season of test scores: (1) how do reform-schoolers advocate for more concentrated doses of the same reform treatment based on tougher testing and tougher consequences while they claim the mantle of change agents and disruptors[10] of the status quo; and (2) how do reform-schoolers convincingly portray the growing chorus of high-stakes testing skeptics and critics as mossbacks and protectors of a status quo that these same critics would gladly jettison if they could? Answering these questions within the demands of simple logic is no small task for the reform-schoolers, for *their own reforms now comprise the status quo*, a status quo whose continued repackaging has not altered the repeated failed results that reform critics would gladly deposit to the dustbin of educational history if it were not for the continued imposition of the same reform strategy, though labeled 'new and improved,' that has had two decades now to prove itself inadequate to the purported task of closing the achievement gap.

Fortunately for the reform-schoolers, who more and more resemble antiquarians turned so they face in the opposite direction,[11] the media and its public have proven more susceptible to powerful public relations and advertising than to reasoned arguments or research findings that have nothing to recommend them other than common sense and unadorned facts. But as is required of all good product advertising over time, an improved packaging is regularly called for in order to rekindle interest. So even as the current reform label has grown toxic to our taste, nonetheless, the next generation of test-and-punish products is prepared with a new logo and jingle for launch by the new party in power.[12] Indeed, it would seem that the new political party of 'change you can believe in' will not allow their predecessors' education reform failures to get in the way of themselves embracing the same rank judgments, particularly if it means an uninterrupted flow of support from the same corporate coffers and philanthro-capitalist foundations whose agendas remain immune to the intermittent trading of good and bad fortunes between the national political parties.

If threats, punitive measures, or wishful thinking (in any combination applied by liberals *or* conservatives) would have worked in the public schools to bring about the closing of the achievement gap between Black and White, or rich and poor, then the children of the poor over the past twenty years might have been spared, perhaps, the continuing steroidal remedies and monstrous ministrations[13] that are now accepted practice in many urban schools trying to keep pace with the demands of No Child Left Behind's Adequate Yearly Progress decree. And even as sanity insists that poor children will find the more rigorous national tests (now on the drawing board) even harder to pass than the less rigorous state ones that they now fail in droves, the next likely tough-love chapter in the reform-schooling of urban America appears to be moving into alignment, explicably borne forward by willful ignorance, political hubris, moneyed arrogance, and a national advertising campaign to publicize a new secret weapon in the continuing crusade to raise test scores and close the achievement gap. The reformers' new secret weapon is a nonprofit corporate chain of charter schools known as the Knowledge Is Power Program (KIPP).

Since being embraced by George W. Bush in 2000, KIPP has become the new miracle (or mirage) choice model that promises to finally fix the children in neighborhoods where poverty is left unchecked and in a viral state. With a new administration now in Washington even more keen than the last one on accelerating the number of charter schools in urban areas where a psychological 'no excuses' rehab seems to be in order, we could see the fruition of an ideological commitment to privatization, antiunionism, and social efficiency control that, heretofore, has constituted the education agenda of political conservatives only. The seamless replacement of urban public schools by corporate-run charter schools could depend, sadly, on the ability of cash-starved states and cities to withstand takeover bids from corporations and their foundations, which now effectively exert their power through the federal education establishment. With the latest Secretary of Education, Arne Duncan, publicly supportive of the CEO-powered urban model, from the mayor's office down to the principal's office, resistance may prove futile among economically hard-pressed state and city governments.

In their history of twentieth-century education reforms, David Tyack and Larry Cuban point out that the most persistent and influential reforms have been those functional add-ons that satisfy multiple political constituencies without challenging the basic "grammar of schooling."[14] Based on these criteria, KIPP's influence should be wide ranging and long lasting. For even as KIPP resembles a steroidal version of the traditional schools that John Dewey railed against as "chain gangs" during the early days of the last century,[15] KIPP does not depart too far from the conventional structures that our parents and our parents' parents would recognize as school. On the constituencies count, KIPP has been embraced by conservatives as the poster school for the 'no excuses' bare-knuckled, test-driven approach to schooling, while it has also received accolades from 'liberal' organizations such as the Education Trust,[16] who laud KIPP as proof that high expectations, or wishful thinking at least, can be enough to allow all children to learn, rich or poor, Black or White. Also notably on board the KIPP corporate charter bus is leading philanthro-capitalist Bill Gates, whose enthusiasm is reported by Jonathan Alter with a matched enthusiasm: "Gates argues that rigorous accountability is the only option, from mayoral control (elected school boards are mostly a menace) to principal control (teacher tenure and onerous work rules are quality-killers) to data control (IT systems that closely track performance are a must)."[17]

On February 4, 2009, Bill Gates was a featured speaker at a Technology, Entertainment, and Design (TED) conference[18] where he considered four world problems that must be dealt with for twenty-first century humanity to have a chance to thrive: malaria, AIDS, pneumonia, and teachers. At the close of his speech, Gates promised everyone in his audience a copy of Jay Mathews' celebratory chronicle of KIPP's young founding fathers, David Levin and Mike Feinberg.[19] Gates had only good things to say about KIPP teachers and students alike, but he offered the following comparison[20] that may help to explain why teachers in general would be discussed alongside malaria, AIDS, and pneumonia:

> How does that [KIPP school] compare to a normal school? Well, in a normal school teachers aren't told how good they are. The data isn't gathered. In the teacher's contract, it will limit the number of times the principal can come into the classroom—sometimes to once per year. And they need advanced [*sic*] notice to do that. So imagine running a factory where you've got these workers, some of them just making crap, and the management is told, "Hey, you can only come down here once a year, but you need to let us know, because we might actually fool you, and try and do a good job in that one brief moment."

It probably doesn't take an educator or even a PTA dad to guess that Gates was stretching the truth beyond recognition, perhaps to better serve his earthy implied comparison that portrays his imagined factory workers and their products with the same obvious hostility and disgust that he views "normal" teachers and "normal" students. For whatever his personal motives may be, some very concrete ideological commitments become clarified that are usually shrouded in the gauzy, technocratic rhetoric of urban education reform movements funded by billionaires whose philanthropic hobbies just happen to be good for business at the same time.

KIPP RESEARCH

Begun as a single middle school in 1994 by two ambitious Teach for America alums in Houston, Texas, the KIPP chain now has 99 locations and the financial backing of America's most active corporate givers to K–12 education. Since 2000, when a simulated KIPP classroom skit was presented as part of the program for the Republican National Convention, the growing list of benefactors has grown impressively. With many deep pockets at the ready to assist, KIPP has emerged as the poster school for urban education reform.

Here is a partial list of benefactors, available on the KIPP Foundation website:

- $25,000,000 and above
    - Doris and Donald Fisher
- $10,000,000 to $24,999,999
    - The Atlantic Philanthropies
    - The Broad Family Foundation
    - The Walton Family Foundation
- $5,000,000 to $9,999,999
    - Bill and Melinda Gates Foundation
    - Robertson Foundation
- $1,000,000 to $4,999,999
    - John and Laura Arnold
    - Reed Hastings and Patty Quillin
    - Jack Kent Cooke Foundation
    - Marcus Foundation
    - Michael and Susan Dell Foundation
    - Miles Family Foundation
    - New Profit
- $500,000 to $999,999
    - Ewing Marion Kauffman Foundation
- $100,000 to $499,000
    - All Stars Helping Kids

- o The Annie E. Casey Foundation
- o Anonymous
- o CityBridge Foundation
- o Thomas and Susan Dunn
- o John and Laura Fisher
- o Goldman Sachs Foundation
- o Goldsbury Foundation
- o Kinder Foundation
- o Koret Foundation
- o Steve Mandel
- o National Geographic Education Foundation
- o SAP
- o State Farm Companies Foundation[21]

Along with politicians of all stripes, the news media is also eager to see the KIPP model adopted in urban schools as the next promised solution to the achievement gap. Jonathan Alter typifies the view presented within the news media, which continues to target the "Paleolithic teachers [*sic*] unions" as the real reason the achievement gap has not been closed:

> The irony is, we know what works to close the achievement gap. At the 60 KIPP (Knowledge Is Power Program) schools, more than 80 percent of 16,000 randomly selected low-income students go to college, four times the national average for poor kids. While KIPP isn't fully replicable (not enough effective teachers to go around), every low-income school should be measured by how close it gets to that model, where kids go to school from 7:30 a.m. to 5 p.m. and part of the summer, and teachers are held strictly accountable for showing student improvement.[22]

Not entirely convinced that these figures could be accurate, San Francisco reporter Caroline Grannan contacted the KIPP home office to find out if their numbers matched those offered in Jonathan Alter's *Newsweek* piece. She found, in fact, that "the actual number of KIPP alumni who had started college [by 2008], KIPP spokesman Steve Mancini said at that time, was 447."[23] And even though Alter is no less falsely convinced that KIPP offers the solution to the achievement gap, he at least offers a refreshing admission that Gates and others are unwilling to make as they hawk the idea of KIPP charters as the urban education solution: KIPP cannot be scaled up to fill the bill for which it is advertised. Here's why.

Until the first longitudinal research study was published by SRI International, an impressive public relations apparatus from within the KIPP Foundation closely controlled the KIPP narrative and product image, with rising test scores and the percentage of KIPP students going on to college as that part of the KIPP story cited as evidence of KIPP's ability to close the achievement gap.[24] If we accept KIPP's own numbers that 80 percent of students who complete eighth grade at KIPP go on to college,[25] what does that really say or not say? In the SRI study of five KIPP schools in the Bay Area, researchers found that 60 percent of fifth-grade students in five Oakland KIPP schools who began KIPP in fifth grade did not finish eighth grade:

> Together, the four schools began with a combined total of 312 fifth graders in 2003–04, and ended with 173 eighth graders in 2006–07 (see Exhibit 2–3). The number of eighth graders includes new students who entered KIPP after fifth grade.[26]

If the 40 percent of children who survive KIPP from grades five through eight all finish high school, that would mean that 30 to 35 percent of children who began KIPP in fifth grade eventually go on to college. That would still be an impressive statistic, if we were to accept Alter's claim that, nationally, 20 percent of poor kids go to college. According to more reliable sources, however, the percentage of 'poor kids' who attend college soon after high school is in fact 52 percent,[27] rather than 20 percent, as Alter claims:

> In terms of family income, 91% of high school students from families in the highest income group (above $100,000) enroll in college. The enrollment rate for student from middle-income families (from $50,001 to $100,000) is 78% and for those in the lowest income group ($20,000 and below) the rate is 52%.[28]

These numbers indicate KIPP is less of a miracle than supporters claim.

Given the winnowing of KIPP students between grades five and eight, and given the fact that KIPPsters spend 65 to 70 percent more time in school than their public school counterparts, KIPP's college attendance rate begins to appear less miraculous. Also important in the college attendance rate is the self-selection process[29] among parents who are keen on having their children become participants in the unique kind of academic lockdown that characterizes the total compliance regime of KIPP. When these factors are considered, KIPP's potential as the next silver bullet for urban education achievement gaps appears less of a certainty than the mainstream media might believe—or would have readers to believe.

As long as it remains a small charter boutique chain with eighty-two schools in nineteen states, plus the District of Columbia, KIPP can continue to emphasize the fact that it is a school of choice that encourages those who disagree with its philosophy and methods to go elsewhere. If KIPP were indeed to become the model that Bill Gates would like all urban schools to emulate, we must wonder what would happen to the other 50 to 60 percent of middle schoolers in the Bay Area (and in other urban communities, we may assume) who leave KIPP, the ones who are unable or unwilling, or whose parents are unwilling, to be subjected to the kind of boot camp educational intervention that KIPP provides without exception. Where would they go? So far, KIPP's wide and thin dispersal across nineteen states makes KIPP a scarce commodity with a very effective public relations machine that cannot, however, conceal the odds that KIPP's "best chance at success is to be the exception rather than the rule in any city where it operates."[30]

Another significant finding of the SRI report involves the predominance of low achievers within that 60 percent of students who leave KIPP between grades five and eight. Even Jay Mathews, the mainstream media's self-acknowledged cheerleader for KIPP, admitted in the *Washington Post* that "60 percent of Bay Area fifth-graders entering KIPP in 2003 left before completing eighth grade, and they were usually low achievers."[31] It should come as no surprise, then, that sizable increases in test scores would result over time among the surviving higher achievers, since low performers or those who are too far behind to keep up are lost by the wayside, without the unpleasant publicity associated with involuntary expulsion:

> We found that students who remained at KIPP had higher incoming scores in both reading and mathematics than did their peers who entered KIPP in fifth grade but exited before completing the program . . . We also considered the question from another perspective: Are students with lower scores more likely to exit KIPP? We used fall fifth-grade SAT10 scores to predict those exiting KIPP and found that the probability of a student's leaving KIPP before completing eighth grade is higher for those with lower entering scores.[32]

KIPP's low-flying students, then, 'choose' their way out to other schools, thus reducing the drag on organizational performance in regards to test scores. The KIPPsters' reputation for impressive test performance is based largely on the winnowing of those who 'choose' to go elsewhere, thus leaving the KIPP brand unscathed by low test-score performance.

If public schools had the luxury or lack of conscience required to lose most of the lower performers, public school test results surely would be more in line with these results that Mathews is glad to report for KIPP: "Since 2001, middle school students who completed four years at KIPP increased their average math achievement level on average from the 40th to the 82nd percentile and their reading level from the 32nd to the 60th percentile—gains not seen anywhere else."[33] And with almost half the school day spent on math and reading test prep—a school day that runs from 7:30 to 5:00 (plus a half day on Saturdays and three extra weeks during the summer)—we might, indeed, expect significant gains among the fittest survivors.

Student attrition, then, is a real problem, to say the least—but one that does nothing to dampen the heat of enthusiasm among those looking to 'rigor' as a means to close the achievement gaps. The idea of 'scaling up' a system that leaves over half the students to give up may be a laudable model for philanthro-capitalists like Don Fisher who believed "that education is a business" and that a school is "not much different from a Gap store,"[34] but such a system would throw gasoline on the failure fire that, under NCLB, is already consuming public schools in poor communities. The big gains in the testing bottom line among the KIPP survivors only ignores the retail brutality of a system that treats children like dry goods that can be culled and sorted, within a compliance model based on pressure-cooker pedagogy and a pervasive application of psychological interventions aimed at cultural displacement.

Assured by other means of holding only the better test performers, the denial among KIPP proponents and the KIPP Foundation of 'creaming' the best test performers through selective recruitment remains technically true. The high selectivity that KIPP maintains, rather, is achieved by an unceasing recruiting process to replace those low performers and resistors who 'choose' to go elsewhere, and by a strict and unwavering socialization process that depends upon a stringent behavioral catechism and psychological realignment. Sometimes referred to as 'KIPP-notizing,'[35] the psychological induction and maintenance regimen is effective in quickly weeding out those who threaten the compliance structure of the organization or the results upon which KIPP's marketing strategy is based. The persistent admonition to students, parents, and teachers alike that KIPP is a school of choice (see Pillar 2 of the Five Pillars)[36] is not just an empty element of a mission statement: it is the method used to distinguish between a cult and a sect on the continuum of selectivity, if KIPP were a religious organization.[37]

TEACHER ATTRITION

An attendant problem to the 60 percent attrition rate among KIPP students is the attrition rate among KIPP teachers, a rate that would be unsustainable if KIPP did not depend upon large numbers of recruits from Teach for America (TFA), another favorite nonprofit educational organization among philanthro-capitalists.[38] When David Levin and Mike Feinberg created KIPP in 1994, they were in fact fresh TFA[39] alums, and it is clear that they envisioned TFA, with its two-year service contract for inexperienced teacher candidates who are heavily recruited from Ivy League schools, as a source for a ready supply of fresh blood that would be required to sustain the martyrly commitment and performance standards that KIPP demands from teachers.

Even though TFA has seen a recent surge in recruits with the current economic decline and its ramped-up advertising campaign that spends more each year on recruitment than it does on preservice training,[40] it is inconceivable, however, that TFA could offer the hundreds of thousands of teachers that would be required to sustain such a model as KIPP on a scale that would serve all or most of the schools of urban America. Interestingly, TFA recruits who score high during their KIPP teaching missions are subsequently recruited into KIPP leadership positions.[41] These new leaders, in turn, are given CEO power in the principal's office to make decisions that were once the responsibility of publicly elected school boards, now relics in an era of publicly funded schools that are planned and managed by corporations without oversight or regulation. As we shall see, such a singular, unmonitored focus on the new bottom line opens the door to unethical and abusive practices.

The teacher turnover issues at the Bay Area KIPP schools are made clear in the SRI report,[42] which found the teacher turnover rate ranged from 18 percent to 49 percent at the five KIPP schools studied:

> Since 2003–04, the five Bay Area KIPP school leaders have hired a total of 121 teachers. Of these, 43 remained in the classroom at the start of the 2007–08 school year. Among teachers who left the classroom, at four of the schools they spent a median of 1 year in the classroom before leaving; at one school, the typical teacher spent 2 years in the classroom before leaving.[43]

SRI researchers found teachers committed but clearly doubtful of their capacity to continue under the stress of sixty-five hours of school-related work per week (which includes two hours per night for telephone homework assistance). One veteran teacher told researchers, "The consequence is I can't do this job very much longer. It is too much. I don't see any solution with our structure and our nonnegotiables. No one has really presented any way to solve that problem."[44]

Meanwhile, TFA continues to ramp up its advertising to include national buys on television, as many of the same corporate benefactors from KIPP's impressive list of givers pour in more edu-preneurial investments through nonprofit and tax-sheltered foundations and social entrepreneurial investment funds such as the Gates' supported NewSchools Venture Fund. With the average KIPP teacher leaving after three years' service[45] and with new KIPP locations planned, the $18 million to $20 million that TFA now annually spends on recruiting will likely fall short of the amount needed to sustain the teacher induction effort.

KIPP CRUSADERS

In an interview posted at the blog Open Education on December 11, 2008, David Socol makes the case that KIPP and TFA embody the zeal of well-heeled colonialist missionaries on a crusade to save the souls of indigenous urban poor children by converting them to middle-class values and middle-class mindsets.[46] The history of missionary efforts is of course replete with examples that good intentions offer no immunity from very bad results, as the conversion process often lapsed into indoctrination, exploitation, cultural genocide, or other bad outcomes that would never be accepted in more civilized settings with less primitive souls to save. Socol makes the same point when he angrily suggests that we should

> go to those 'best schools in America' in the wealthiest suburbs of New York, Boston, Chicago, Los Angeles. Why aren't they run like KIPP Academies? Always ask this when rich people offer 'solutions' for poor people which [*sic*] those rich people would never accept for themselves . . . So, sure, convert Scarsdale High into a KIPP Academy, show me how it works there, and then offer it to those 'less fortunate.'[47]

Socol's rhetorical question confronts head on the fact that KIPP, as secular sect, provides a path to socioeconomic salvation that would never be acceptable in Scarsdale because those children already display the signs required of having been saved, or elected, by the grace, shall we say, of market forces.

The salvation of the children of the poor, however, depends upon deliverance from the bad habits and traits derived from cultural deficits for which society has too long offered excuses that are no longer acceptable to the tough-love missionaries. This mission becomes clear, if we follow our analogy a tiny bit further, to the 'no excuses' ideology[48] handed down first in Thernstrom and Thernstrom's inspirational text, *No Excuses: Closing the Racial Gap in Learning.* The solemn and difficult crusade to educate Black urban children is laid out plainly:

> The process of connecting black students to the world of academic achievement isn't easy in the best of educational settings—and such settings are today few and far between. But that only means that in order to "counter and transform" African-American "cultural patterns," . . . fundamental change in American education will be necessary—change much more radical than that contemplated by the most visionary of today's public school officials. Recognizing the problem is the first step down that long and difficult road.[49]

The Thernstroms view race as defined by culture, which they claim exerts twice as much influence on academic achievement than does family income, accumulated wealth, and skin color. Culture defines race, then, for good or bad, in much the same way that genetic inheritance was believed to define race by eugenicists at the beginning of the twentieth century. Cultural characteristics, according to the 'no excuses' creed, are racial characteristics, and they can be separated out from economic or class characteristics. The Thernstroms preach that two-thirds of the achievement gap between Black and White children is attributable to culture, whereas one-third is shaped largely by poverty, parental education, and the environment.[50]

Richard Rothstein's research, however, clearly demonstrates how social class functions as the primary contributor to achievement differences, with family income, accumulated wealth, skin color, and culture comprising the elements that make up social class. Rothstein concludes "the debate about whether the low achievement of black students is rooted in culture or economics is largely fruitless because socioeconomic status and culture cannot be separated."[51] According to Rothstein, then, the neat separation of elements that is achieved by the Thernstroms, with the larger chunk of achievement influence reserved for the role of culture, misses the larger point that culture, too, cannot escape the systemic influence of poverty, or lack thereof, in the formation and activity of culture.

In the KIPP schools and the charter school knockoffs that continue to be inspired by KIPP, this forced separation between culture and socioeconomic class is required in order to draw attention away from the effects of poverty, which in turn exacerbates the kinds of callous cruelty enacted by KIPP personnel who act with little oversight and while under unrelenting pressure to achieve the unsustainable. The 'no excuses' ideology, then, not only ignores the documented and substantive effects of poverty on the poor, but it becomes the all-pervasive, blinding excuse for justifying dangerous, damaging, and morally repugnant acts that would not otherwise be entertained in a society grounded by humane values and ethical rules of conduct. This pervasive 'no excuses' mentality results in an authoritarian organizational model that spawns a dark "moral nihilism"[52] that gets played out against the most vulnerable children in schools that operate from public funds but without the benefit of any credible public oversight:

> This moral nihilism would have terrified Adorno. He knew that radical evil was possible only with the collaboration of a timid, cowed and confused population . . . He feared a culture that banished the anxieties and complexities of moral choice and embraced a childish hyper-masculinity.
>
> [Hedges quoting Adorno:] "This educational ideal of hardness, in which many may believe without reflecting about it, is utterly wrong . . . The idea that virility consists in the maximum degree of endurance long ago became a screen-image for masochism that, as psychology has demonstrated, aligns itself all too easily with sadism."[53]

Jay Mathews' book *Work Hard, Be Nice* offers a friendlier gloss on the "hyper-masculinity" exhibited by KIPP founders Dave Levin and Mike Feinberg, whose exploits and excesses are presented as the overexuberance of two irrepressible young übereducators who drive through any roadblock on their road to prove that poverty is no obstacle to learning the 'no excuses' way.[54] And despite the fact that Feinberg and Levin have created a corporate organization whose ethos of total compliance is often described as harsh, cruel, and abusive, the documented moral lapses, ethical breaches, and other excesses by the poster boys for "No Excuses" are simply shrugged off by Mathews as the cost of not letting anything stand in the way of achieving a mission that, in the end, requires the psychological alteration of children to achieve the organizational goals that mirror its oppressive ideology. Yet even through the soft-focus lens of smitten reporters like Mathews,[55] the applicability of Adorno's observation nonetheless stands out in the recounting of the KIPP story. The exhausting commitment, for instance, of Levin and Feinberg in the early years in Houston has become the benchmark for all KIPP teachers since, as alluded to earlier in KIPP teacher comments documented by SRI researchers.[56]

During the early days of KIPP Houston, in fact, an infantilized form of contested endurance was played out quite literally in a legendary one-on-one basketball game that ended only after both Levin and Feinberg succumbed to utter exhaustion. Beyond the macho schoolyard exhibitions of endurance that border on masochism is the pervasive and perverse expression of hardness in the classroom that sometimes careens over into sadistic excess, as is documented in many cases of screaming at children, unsupervised segregation of children, and explosive tantrums. See, for example, an enraged Mike Feinberg who, with children present in the room, threw a chair through a large plate glass window because of an unsatisfactory apology for a minor disciplinary infraction.[57]

More recently, other disturbing events have been reported by parents at the Fulton County KIPP;[58] and still other, more serious allegations involve excessive punishment, child endangerment, and violations of state and federal laws[59] by school officials at KIPP Fresno, a school that was shut down within a few months after Fresno Unified School District filed a detailed report with the State of California. Fresno Unified's sixty-three-page "Notice to Cure" alleged legal and ethical lapses at the school by the principal and staff that involved abusive treatment, risks to student safety, breaches in test security, copyright infringement, teacher credentialing irregularities, and mishandling of school funds. Among the long list of allegations in the "Notice to Cure" are these, published by Grannan:

> Student (name deleted) said that in December of 2007, Mr. Tschang [the school principal] told him to get on his hands and knees and bark like a dog. (Name deleted) said it was a metaphor to get him to stop joking around in class.
>
> It was reported by Kim Kutzner that students who were late to school would not be allowed to eat their meals provided by the state. Student (name deleted) stated that Mr. Tschang told her, "People who are late don't get to eat."
>
> Parent (name deleted) reported that Mr. Tschang took student (name deleted) glasses away from him because (name deleted) was constantly

> adjusting his glasses. (Name deleted) is totally dependent on his glasses and cannot see without them. Mr. Tschang admitted to taking [the student's] glasses away.
>
> Several students stated that students are not allowed to talk or socialize at all during school hours. When asked about this policy, Mr. Tschang stated, "If parents are not happy with the school program, it is a school of choice. They are free (and indeed encouraged) to remove their kids from the school. There are plenty of other public school options for their children."[60]

However, with a robust public relations apparatus that effectively contains incidents like these within the local media, and with the national media consistently uninterested in stories like these, the bipartisan party of 'No Excuses' continues to move forward (or backward, as one may argue) to open new KIPP charters and KIPP imitators, each intended to expand the mission of transforming children of the urban poor into pliable future assets schooled in positivity and age-appropriate versions of corporate groupthink.[61]

The near-religious zeal of reform-schoolers like the Thernstroms and philanthro-capitalists like Bill Gates becomes eerily reminiscent of the social reform crusade fueled by the pseudoscience of eugenics that was loosed during the first half of the previous century. It is beyond the scope of this chapter to tease out all the similarities, but there are disturbing overlaps that are too apparent to ignore.

The ministrations, for instance, that reform-schoolers require to save Black and brown urban children today from their defective cultural traits provide reminders of the ways that the disabled, the petty criminals, and those otherwise disadvantaged by poverty of the early twentieth century were treated. Deemed to be saddled at birth with what was believed to be defective, inheritable germ plasm,[62] the urban and rural poor of the early twentieth century were targeted by both conservative and liberal eugenics enthusiasts for containment, segregation, remediation, and even involuntary sterilization.[63] Elite reformers, from Harvard dons to clergymen and philanthropists, embraced eugenics techniques as entirely respectable measures to protect society from the spread of crime, feeblemindedness, and negative habits and attitudes that were thought to be inheritable traits among the dispossessed.

Today's behavioral and character training at KIPP is a thinly-veiled effort to impose a new variety of cultural eugenics by those who view the transmission of urban cultural traits as a threat to White middle-class values and economic prosperity. As such, KIPP constitutes a widely lauded special treatment by both conservatives and liberals for this generation's delineation of the depraved, and it is built, too, upon conditions of segregation, containment, remediation, and an attempt to impose a form of cultural sterilization that purportedly will allow children who receive the treatment to enter, at some future date, the middle-class corporate world without threat of perpetuating their own kinds of defective cultural memes into the world of privilege to which they desperately aspire. The transplantation of new cultural values to replace those that the KIPP regimen negates requires children to transfer their loyalty from community and family to a new loyalty to the KIPP family and its group values.

As previously noted, the same blame-the-poor mindset thrives among less conservative supporters of KIPP, as evidenced in Malcolm Gladwell's mega–best seller, *Outliers*. Gladwell blindly attributes the educational achievement disadvantages of the poor to the failure of poor families to provide the cultural perks that poverty, in fact, has made impossible for them to provide. As sad evidence of his myopia, Gladwell offers us the example of twelve-year-old Marita, whose "community does not give her what she needs," and thus is placed into the KIPP crucible:

> Marita's life is not the life of a typical twelve-year-old. Nor is it what we would necessarily wish for a twelve-year-old. Children, we like to believe, should have time to play and dream and sleep. Marita has responsibilities. What is being asked of her is the same thing that was asked of the Korean pilots. To become a success at what they did, they had to shed some part of their own identity, because the deep respect for authority that runs throughout Korean culture simply does not work in the cockpit. Marita has had to do the same because the cultural legacy she had been given does not match her circumstances either—not when middle- and upper-middle-class families are using weekends and summer vacation to push their children ahead. Her community does not give her what she needs. So what does she have to do? Give up her evenings and weekends and friends—all the elements of her old world—and replace them with KIPP.[64]

It is, then, the sacrifice of childhood and family that becomes the price demanded of poor children for the ultimate shortcomings of a well-heeled society that, in the most basic ways, has turned its back on the plight of minority children trapped by poverty and racism. The education, or miseducation, of the urban poor must be driven, then, by a draconian psychological and sociocultural intervention that leaves to fester the socioeconomic contexts whose attempted alteration by a more caring and less cavalier society would have offered the kinds of humane pedagogical, health, housing, and job treatments preferred by the middle and upper classes.

Gladwell's modern-day version of blaming the poor for the effects of their poverty is widespread, and it is not so far as it may seem from our Puritan forefathers' preferred explanation of poverty as the result of moral depravity and sin. Today's public punishment of the poor comes, however, not in physical humiliations on the public square, but in the pedagogical interventions grounded in an economic-behavioral catechism enforced in segregated neighborhood schoolrooms by mostly White and inexperienced teachers. These missionary-minded teacher recruits are supplied from among the members of the Economic Elect, teachers who most often share neither cultural nor ethnic likeness to those they would save, and whose concern for poor children's cultural salvation is neatly contained within a covenant that, in the case of Teach for America, expires at the end of two years.[65]

For KIPPsters (as students are referred to by their teachers), the "long and difficult road" that the Thernstroms envision starts during the first week of KIPP-notizing.[66] Children are introduced to KIPP's organizational compliance demands through exposure to KIPP's system for communicating and embedding power relations, a system that conforms to Amitai Etzioni's threefold typology: coercive power, remunerative power, and normative power. In the remaining space, I will briefly outline the dimensions of KIPP life that embody these three modes of control.[67]

KIPP'S ORGANIZATIONAL COMPLIANCE MODEL

In response to an extensive *New York Times* article by Paul Tough that lavishly praised KIPP and its methods, researcher Howard Berlak reported at the online discussion group Assessment Reform Network (ARN) regarding his own visit to a KIPP school in San Francisco:

> When I was there children who followed all the rules were given points that could be exchanged for goodies at the school store. Those who resisted the rules or were slackers wore a large sign pinned to their clothes labeled 'miscreant.' Miscreants sat apart from the others at all times including lunch, were denied recess and participation in all other school projects and events . . . I've spent many years in schools. This one felt like a humane, low security prison or something resembling a locked-down drug rehab program for adolescents run on reward and punishments by well-meaning people. Maybe a case can be made for such places, but I cannot imagine anyone (including the *Times* reporter) sending their kids there unless they have no other acceptable options. What is most disturbing is the apparent universal belief by KIPP staff and partisans that standardized tests scores are the singular and most important measure of a truly good education. [68]

While reporters like Paul Tough and Jay Mathew would no doubt balk at Berlak's comparison to a prison, low security though it may be, their own descriptions of KIPP's harshness are not inconsistent with what Berlak found, and the documentary reports of others[69] offer evidence that supports Berlak's observations. As noted in the following, even researchers supportive of the KIPP cause have found this picture to be accurate as well.

KIPP-NOTIZING

The three weeks that KIPP students spend in summer school is devoted to an intensive socialization and enculturation process for new students soon to begin fifth grade and for other students who are learning the compliance demands of the next grade level. New students must learn the SLANT rules, which is an acronym for "sit up straight, look and listen, ask and answer questions, nod to show understanding, [and] track the speaker."[70] They must learn that any rule infraction will bring an instant corrective response, and they must learn that the smallest misdeed will be no more tolerated than the most egregious offense. New recruits practice walking, getting off the bus, sitting in the cafeteria, and going to the bathroom the KIPP way. Students must learn that KIPP rules apply inside and outside of school. 'Miscreants' must learn, for instance, that isolation and ostracism from the KIPP family is total as long as the punishment lasts, and children who talk to 'miscreants' at or away from school risk the same punishment if apprehended. In fact, it becomes the duty of other students to report offenders who associate in any way with 'miscreants.' If they do not, they, too, risk the same punishment. New recruits, then, learn compliance through the exercise of coercive power and constant surveillance.

New students must also learn by the remunerative power of the 'paycheck'; at KIPP, the 'paycheck' accompanies the student at all times and thus offers any teacher a handy way to keep track of a student's academic and behavioral performance in other classes, which may cause dollars to be added to or subtracted from the student's paycheck.[71] At the end of each week, students may use accumulated KIPP dollars to buy KIPP gear or candy in the school store, or they may apply earnings toward future 'field lesson'[72] participation. At the completion of the three weeks of intense KIPP-notizing, students are properly tuned for the culminating normative power exercise embodied in the ritual to grant the KIPP uniform shirt.[73] This symbolic reward and acknowledgement of new students' becoming part of the KIPP team or KIPP family marks the conclusion of the initial indoctrination into a new school life that will be characterized by 'choosing' total compliance or else an abbreviated enrollment. Some uniform shirts will carry the message "Work Hard, Be Nice," and others will read "No Shortcuts, No Excuses."

As reported in the *New York Times*, Dr. Martin Seligman's influence has been and continues to be central in shaping the 'noncognitive' behaviors described by the KIPP compliance model as self-control, adaptability, and patience:

> Toll and Levin are influenced by the writings of a psychology professor from the University of Pennsylvania named Martin Seligman, the author of a series of books about positive psychology. Seligman, one of the first modern psychologists to study happiness, promotes a

technique he calls learned optimism, and Toll and Levin consider it an essential part of the attitude they are trying to instill in their students. Last year, a graduate student of Seligman's named Angela Duckworth published with Seligman a research paper that demonstrated a guiding principle of these charter schools: in many situations, attitude is just as important as ability.[74]

Not mentioned in Tough's laudatory piece on KIPP and the bold reformers who back KIPP are the historic experiments conducted by Dr. Martin Seligman in the 1960s and 1970s that demonstrated "animals receiving electric shocks, which they had no ability to prevent or avoid, were unable to act in subsequent situations where avoidance or escape was possible."[75] Dr. Seligman's unexpected finding brought behavioral assumptions in psychology face-to-face with a phenomenon that behaviorism could not explain, a phenomenon Seligman termed 'learned helplessness.' Seligman's role in developing the KIPP instructional model surely deserves further investigation, and central to that research should be this question: how does one tell the difference between a manifestation of learned helplessness and a display of self-control, or self-regulation, particularly when the depressive effects of learned helplessness could be masked by continual ministrations of its antidote, 'learned optimism,' through the happiness training[76] of positive psychology?

And so it is, then, that KIPP children are initiated into a state that may easily be mistaken for learned helplessness if it were not for the KIPP promotional literature[77] that labels it 'self-control.' However we choose to characterize the resulting submissive detachment these KIPP children exhibit, it is achieved by unrelenting and constant surveillance, harsh and sure verbal castigation, public humiliation and labeling, manipulative reinforcement, and ostracizing isolation. From this depressive state of total dependency, KIPP then applies ample and ongoing doses of Dr. Seligman's 'learned optimism' techniques that aim to instill resilience and to temper reactions to the unalterable compliance mechanisms by encouraging the illusion of individual choice.[78] By doing so, any anger or resentment among students arising out of punishments becomes internalized and accepted as the resultant consequences of improper individual choices and actions, rather than being directed outward toward questioning the organizational structure of total control and constant surveillance.

Students are converted, then, from potentially bad actors to good audiences, from recalcitrant resistors to eager and hard workers, from a former state of victimization to a kind of delusional empowerment that masks the full embrace of total submission to KIPP compliance demands. And if things don't work out for these children in terms of not working hard enough or not being nice enough to survive in KIPP, as is the case for over half the children in the Bay Area KIPP schools, then perhaps they will at least have learned along the way that they can blame no one but themselves for their own shortcomings and failure. No excuses. No shortcuts. Work hard, be nice. Hedges sums it up this way for those whose efforts fail to attract the best things in life, which is the promise that positive psychology makes to those who try hard enough or wish hard enough to earn that attraction: "for those who run into the hard walls of reality, the ideology has the pernicious effect of forcing the victim to blame him or herself for his or her pain or suffering."[79]

As long as the focus remains on fixing the insides of children's heads while ignoring the conditions these kids must return to after their ten-hour days of working hard and being nice in their apartheid schools, all manner of indoctrination and extraordinary educational renditions may be deemed necessary and appropriate to achieve KIPP goals. At its unacknowledged core, KIPP remains an intervention aimed at cognitive and behavioral control that occurs when we use the happy-talk manipulations of corporate psychology as a means to turn poor minority children into the White Ivy League teachers' version of middle-class children. In the meantime, poor children are taught to turn away from their communities, rather than learning to change them by challenging the system of privilege that now proclaims their liberation while embracing a renewed form of segregated confinement. The KIPP charter phenomenon and its imitators represent the corporate colonization[80] of urban America, with all the zeal that we might expect from missionaries looking to save souls by shaping their converts to openly accept the omnipotent forces emanating from the Market's invisible hand.

Even though our history should save us from shock, it remains, nonetheless, a breathtaking expression of blind hubris and Orwellian irony that the wealthiest in our society should come to embrace KIPP's self-serving educational shortcut as the preferred way to pay down our vast educational debt to those oppressed by poverty and discrimination for the past 400 years. The longer KIPP's abusive and extreme measures are allowed to function as a palliative, or excuse, for our society's refusal to act against urban poverty, apartheid schools, and racism, the closer this dominant culture comes to the forced moral bankruptcy that awaits those societies that proclaim equality while they practice torturous interventions against the children of its least equal citizens as an inexpensive shortcut to preserving the façade of equal opportunity.

For White philanthro-capitalists such as Bill Gates, the KIPP charter schools offer an urban reform solution based on nonstop behavioral control, cultural sterilization, and psychological character interventions aimed at producing compliant, delusional, and hardworking children who will offer 'proof' that the effects of poverty can be overcome by interventions less expensive[81] and easier to control than the public schools. KIPP, then, remains the billionaire philanthropist version of social and education reform on the cheap, wherein a dubious economy of scale is more important than the children who are sacrificed through the unethical and experimental excesses that are imposed under the shredded banner of equal access to quality education. There are humane ways to run schools and increase academic achievement at the same time.[82] KIPP is not one of them. In fact, KIPP and its imitators represent the antithesis to education reform based on caring and fairness, quality and equality. As such, KIPP offers us a policy version of social justice in blackface, an institutionalized caricature whose legacy and ultimate cost we cannot yet begin to fathom.

NOTES

1. P. Barton and R. Coley, *Parsing the Achievement Gap II* (Princeton, NJ: Educational Testing Service, 2009).
2. Similar findings related to the unaffected nature of achievement gaps can be found in the *NAEP Trends in Academic Progress* (NCES 2008). Between 2004 and 2008, for instance, the Black-White gap in math showed a two-point increase between nine-year-olds, a two-point decrease between thirteen-year-olds, and a one-point decrease between seventeen-year-old Black and White students (34–35). In reading, nine-year-olds showed a three-point decrease in the gap, with a four-point decrease in the gap for thirteen-year-olds and a two-point increase in the gap for seventeen-year-olds (14–15).
3. P. Barton, *Parsing the Achievement Gap: Baselines for Tracking Progress* (Princeton, NJ: Educational Testing Services, 2003).
4. Ibid., 7.
5. D. Berliner, "Our Impoverished View of Educational Reform," *Teachers College Record*, 2005, http://www.educationanddemocracy.org/Resources/Berliner.pdf (accessed January 30, 2009); R. Rothstein, *The Way We Were: The Myths and Realities of America's Student Achievement* (New York: Century Foundation Press, 1998); R. Rothstein, *Class and Schools: Using Social, Economic, and Educational Reform to Close the Black-White Achievement Gap* (New York: Teachers College Press, 2004); J. Anyon, *Radical Possibilities: Public Policy, Urban Education, and a New Social Movement* (New York: RoutledgeFalmer, 2005); J. Kozol, *The Shame of the Nation: The Restoration of Apartheid Schooling in America* (New York: Crown Publishers, 2005).
6. G. Ladson-Billings, "From the Achievement Gap to the Education Debt: Understanding Achievement in U.S. Schools," *Educational Review* 35, no. 7 (2006): 3–12, http://aera.net/uploadedFiles/Publications/Journals/Educational_Researcher/3507/02ERv35n7_Ladson-Billings.pdf (accessed June 1, 2009).
7. The most recent state-by-state analysis of 2007 NAEP data (Vanneman, Hamilton, Anderson, and Rahman, 2009) shows a similar picture, with the gap actually widening in more states than it is closing in others.
8. P. Barton and R. Coley, *Parsing II*, 3.
9. Ibid., 33.
10. In a *Newsweek* article, J. Alter (2008) put Bill Gates among the "bomb throwers" or "disruptors" who obviously view their own attempts to hasten the previous administration's education policies as something new and radical. In the same article, influential Congressman George Miller noted that " 'the debate is between incrementalists and disrupters, and I'm with the disrupters.' So is Bill Gates." None of the disruptors' priorities, however, appear to challenge policy initiatives that would have easily been waved through by Ronald Reagan.

11. A beautiful allusion used in a different context by O. Marquard in *Farewell to Matters of Principle: Philosophical Studies* (New York: Oxford University Press, 1987).
12. In an *Associated Press* story by L. Quaid in March 2009, Secretary Duncan indicated that he would like "hold a contest for school kids to come up with a new name" for the No Child Left Behind Act (NCLBA).
13. See, for instance, L. Perlstein's *Tested: One American School Struggles to Make the Grade* (New York: Henry Holt, 2007), an unforgettable chronicle of the teachers, principal, and students of Tyler Heights Elementary School in Anne Arundel County, MD. For a qualitative case study (Horn 2003), see *LEAP-ing Toward Accountability: Ideology, Practice, and the Voices of Louisiana Educators.*
14. D. Tyack and L. Cuban, *Tinkering Toward Utopia: A Century of Public School Reform* (Cambridge, MA: Harvard University Press, 1995).
15. J. Dewey, *Experience and Education*, 60th anniversary ed. (orig. published 1938; reprint, Indianapolis: Kappa Delta Pi Publications, 1998).
16. The Gates Foundation is listed fourth among funders of Education Trust. The Broad Foundation is listed first.
17. J. Alter, "Bill Gates Goes to School," *Newsweek*, December 6, 2008, http://www.newsweek.com/id/172572 (accessed July 3, 2009).
18. C. Burrell, "Framing Teachers: Bill Gates' Disturbing TED Rhetoric," *Change.org*, 2009, http://education.change.org/blog/view/framing_teachers_bill_gates_disturbing_ted_rhetoric (accessed June 1, 2009).
19. J. Matthews, *Word Hard, Be Nice: How Two Inspired Teachers Created the Most Promising Schools in America* (New York: Algonquin Books, 2009).
20. C. Burrell, "Framing Teachers."
21. KIPP Foundation, "Five Pillars," 2009, http://www.kipp.org/01/fivepillars.cfm (accessed June 1, 2009).
22. J. Alter, "Bill Gates Goes to School."
23. C. Grannan, "Debunking Yet Another False Claim about KIPP Alumni and College," *Examiner.com*, October 7, 2009, http://www.examiner.com/x-356--SF-Education-Examiner%7Ey2009m2d21-Excerts-from-report-on-Fresno-KIPP-school-Abuse-cheating-alleged (accessed March 23, 2009).
24. K. Woodworth and others, *San Francisco Bay Area KIPP Schools: A Study of Early Implementation and Achievement* (Menlo Park, CA: SRI International, 2008), http://policyweb.sri.com/cep/publications/SRI_ReportBayAreaKIPPSchools_Final.pdf (accessed March 23, 2009).
25. J. Alter, "Bill Gates Goes to School."
26. K. Woodworth et al., *San Francisco Bay Area KIPP Schools*, 12.
27. National Center for Public Policy and Higher Education, *Measuring up 2008: The National Report Card on Higher Education*, 2008, http://measuringup2008.highereducation.org/print/NCPPHEMUNationalRpt.pdf (accessed July 11, 2009).
28. Ibid., 7.
29. R. Rothstein, *Class and Schools.*
30. S. Mosle, "The Educational Experiment We Really Need: What the Knowledge Is Power Program Has Yet to Prove," *Slate*, March 23, 2009, http://www.slate.com/id/ 2214253/pagenum/all/#p2 (accessed April 20, 2009).
31. J. Matthews, "Inside the Bay Area KIPP Schools," *Washington Post*, September 19, 2008, http://www.washingtonpost.com/wpdyn/content/article/2008/09/19/AR2008091900978.html (accessed March 1, 2009).
32. K. Woodworth et al., *San Francisco Bay Area KIPP Schools*, 15–16.
33. J. Matthews, "Inside the Bay Area KIPP Schools."

34. S. Duxbury, "Businesses Invest in Charter School Innovation," *San Francisco Business Times*, July 2008, 18–24, http://www.kippbayarea.org/files/2008_07_18_ SF%20Business%20Times.pdf (accessed March 9, 2009).
35. H. Smith, *Making Schools Work: KIPP* (New York: Public Broadcasting System, 2005), http://www.pbs.org/makingschoolswork/atp/transcript.html (accessed January 23, 2009).
36. KIPP schools share a core set of operating principles known as the Five Pillars:
    1. High Expectations. KIPP schools have clearly defined and measurable high expectations for academic achievement and conduct that make no excuses based on the students' backgrounds. Students, parents, teachers, and staff create and reinforce a culture of achievement and support through a range of formal and informal rewards and consequences for academic performance and behavior.
    2. Choice and Commitment. Students, their parents, and the faculty of each KIPP school choose to participate in the program. No one is assigned or forced to attend a KIPP school. Everyone must make and uphold a commitment to the school and to each other to put in the time and effort required to achieve success.
    3. More Time. KIPP schools know that there are no shortcuts when it comes to success in academics and life. With an extended school day, week, and year, students have more time in the classroom to acquire the academic knowledge and skills that will prepare them for competitive high schools and colleges, as well as more opportunities to engage in diverse extracurricular experiences.
    4. Power to Lead. The principals of KIPP schools are effective academic and organizational leaders who understand that great schools require great school leaders. They have control over their school budget and personnel. They are free to swiftly move dollars or make staffing changes, allowing them maximum effectiveness in helping students learn.
    5. Focus on Results. KIPP schools relentlessly focus on high student performance on standardized tests and other objective measures. Just as there are no shortcuts, there are no excuses. Students are expected to achieve a level of academic performance that will enable them to succeed at the nation's best high schools and colleges. (KIPP Foundation, 2009)
37. A. Etzioni, *A Comparative Analysis of Complex Organizations: On Power, Involvement, and Their Correlates* (New York: Free Press, 1961), 156.
38. S. Mosle, "The Educational Experiment We Really Need."
39. Its critics often refer to TFA as Teach for Awhile, since most of the Ivy League recruits do not teach beyond the two-year commitment required in the contract.
40. Teach for America, *2007 Annual Report: Teach for America*, http://www.teachforamerica.org/assets/documents/TeachForAmerica_Annual_Report_2007_000.pdf (accessed January 2, 2009), 29.
41. The relationship between TFA and KIPP is even more than cozy—it is familial. Wendy Kopp, CEO and founder of TFA, is married to KIPP CEO Richard Barth.
42. K. Woodworth and others, *San Francisco Bay Area KIPP Schools*.
43. Ibid., 32.
44. Ibid., 35.
45. L. W. Browne, "A Character Education Approach to Founding a KIPP College Preparatory Charter School" (EdD executive position paper, University of Delaware, 2008), 174.

46. See "Ira David Socol on Teach for America, KIPP Schools, and Reforming Education," Open Education blog, http://www.openeducation.net/2008/12/11/ira-david-socol-on-teach-for-america-kipp-schools-and-reforming-education/ (accessed May 20, 2010).
47. Ibid.
48. See Pillar 2 in note 36.
49. A. Thernstrom and S. Thernstrom, *No Excuses: Closing the Racial Gap in Learning* (New York: Simon and Schuster, 2003), 147.
50. Ibid.
51. R. Rothstein, *Class and Schools*, 51.
52. C. Hedges, "America Is in Need of a Moral Bailout," *Truthdig: A Progressive Journal of News and Opinion*, 2009, http://www.truthdig.com/report/print/20090323_america_is_in_need_of_a_moral_bailout/ (accessed June 20, 2009).
53. Ibid.
54. J. Matthews, *Work Hard, Be Nice.*
55. Ibid.
56. J. Matthews, "Inside the Bay Area KIPP Schools."
57. J. Matthews, *Work Hard, Be Nice*, 235–39.
58. H. Vogell, "Charter School Faces Withdrawals over Punishment," *Atlanta Journal-Constitution*, March 22, 2009, http://www.ajc.com/metro/content/metro/atlanta/stories/ 2009/03/22/kipp_school_withdrawals.html (accessed July 2, 2009).
59. C. Grannan, "Excerpts from Report on Fresno KIPP School: Abuse, Cheating Alleged," *Examiner.com*, February 21, 2009, http://www.examiner.com/x-356-SF-Education-Examiner%7Ey2009m2d21-Excerts-from-report-on-Fresno-KIPP-school-Abuse-cheating-alleged (accessed March 23, 2009).
60. C. Grannan, "Excerpts from Report on Fresno KIPP School."
61. C. Hedges, *Empire of Illusion: The End of Literacy and the Triumph of Spectacle* (New York: Nation Books, 2009), 115–39.
62. E. Black, *War against the Weak: Eugenics and America's Campaign to Create a Master Race* (New York: Dialog Press, 2003); C. Rosen, *Preaching Eugenics: Religious Leaders and the American Eugenics Movement* (New York: Oxford University Press, 2004).
63. During the last century, thirty-three states (Lombardo, n.d.) had, at one time or another, statutes that required involuntary sterilizations of more than 60,000 citizens across the nation that did not end until the mid-1970s.
64. M. Gladwell, *Outliers: The Story of Success* (New York: Little, Brown, 2008), 266.
65. Those TFA alums who do well during their two-year stints as teachers are often recruited into leadership CEO, CFO, and COO positions at KIPP schools, thus maintaining an organizational purity that is untainted by outside practices.
66. A. Thernstrom and S. Thernstrom, *No Excuses.*
67. A. Etzioni, *A Comparative Analysis of Complex Organizations.*
68. P. Tough, "What It Takes to Make a Student," *New York Times*, November 26, 2006, http://www.nytimes.com/2006/11/26/magazine/26tough.html (accessed June 1, 2009).
69. H. Smith, *Making Schools Work*; D. Branacaccio, "The Report Card and Lending a Hand," *NOW with David Branacaccio* (New York: Public Broadcasting System,2007), http://www.pbs.org/now/transcript/325.html (accessed February 15, 2009).
70. L. W. Browne, "A Character Education Approach," 58.

71. S. Jones, "Studying 'Success' at an 'Effective' School: How a Nationally Recognized Public School Overcomes Racial, Ethnic and Social Boundaries and Creates a Culture of Success" (PhD diss., University of California, Santa Barbara, 2004), 38–39.
72. KIPP prefers 'field lesson' (Mathews 2009) to 'field trip,' as field lesson conveys to students the fact that the larger world is an extension of the KIPP classroom and thus reinforces the bubble effect that helps to sustain the total control that the KIPP organization demands of its charges.
73. L. W. Browne, "A Character Education Approach," 58.
74. P. Tough, "What It Takes to Make a Student."
75. Gale Research, "Learned Helplessness," *Encyclopedia of Childhood and Adolescence* (Farmington, MI: Gale Research, 1998), http://findarticles.com/p/articles/ mi_g2602/is_0003/ai_2602000349/ (accessed July 30, 2009).
76. C. Hedges, *Empire of Illusion.*
77. P. Tough, "What It Takes to Make a Student."
78. M. Seligman, *Learned Optimism: How to Change Your Mind and Your Life* (New York: Vintage, 2007).
79. C. Hedges, *Empire of Illusion*, 119.
80. Whereas KIPP and most of its 'no excuses' knockoffs limit their direct indoctrination to character building and psychological control, the American Indian Public Charter School (AIPCS) in Oakland openly disparages multiculturalism and openly advances the philosophy of Milton Friedman. Consider this teacher recruitment ad from the AIPCS website that became part of a story (Landsberg 2009) in the *Los Angeles Times*: "We are looking for hardworking people who believe in free market capitalism . . . Multicultural specialists, ultra liberal zealots and college-tainted oppression liberators need not apply." And this ad is not intended as a self-parody.
81. An AFT report (2008) found that charter schools in the forty states that have charter laws pay teachers 20 percent less on average than public schools. This is a rarely acknowledged reason that politicians of both parties find charters so attractive, especially for the urban poor.
82. R. Berger, *An Ethic of Excellence: Building a Culture of Craftsmanship in Schools* (Boston: Heinemann, 2003); M. Benitez and others, *Big Ideas: The Essential Guide to Successful School Transformation* (San Francisco: Jossey-Bass, 2009); D. Meier, *In Schools We Trust: Creating Communities of Learning in an Era of Testing and Standardization* (Boston: Beacon Press, 2003).

6 Disabusing Small-Schools Reformism

An Alternative Outlook on Scaling Up and Down[1]

Craig B. Howley and Aimee Howley

This chapter provides a retrospective analysis of the 'small-schools' reform package supported by the Gates Foundation. In particular we examine the origins of the initiative; the rhetoric surrounding it, including its 'theory of action'; its distinctly urban focus; and its likely influence on the fate of small high schools in the United States. Our unusual standpoint ensues from our long involvement with small schools in rural communities, especially in Appalachia.

Claims about the limited efficacy of the Gates Foundation's programs have been widely publicized of late, and detailed findings from a five-year evaluation are also available for inspection,[2] so our analysis will not primarily review that information. Rather, we are most concerned to understand how the foundation's initiative transformed knowledge about small schools—both the quantitative literature on school size and the more anecdotal case study literature—into a philanthropic agenda and a public rhetoric about 'small-schools' reform. The analysis equally speaks to the possibilities of philanthropy and of the evolving constructions and reconstructions of what we call *school reformism*. This analysis, and our standpoint itself, lead us to speculate about features of small-scale schooling that exist beyond the line of vision of reformers and that will be predictably damaged by the fallout from the Gates Foundation's 'small-schools' initiative.

WHERE THE SMALL-SCHOOL INITIATIVE CAME FROM

Certainly before and even after James B. Conant[3] called for larger, more comprehensive high schools in all communities, school size tended to vary by locale, with smaller schools more prevalent in small towns and rural communities and larger ones in cities and suburbs.[4] The overall trend in most locales, however, was toward enrollment growth.[5] In rural communities, in fact, Conant's recommendations merely added fuel to consolidation efforts that had been underway since early in the century. In general, then, efforts to consolidate schools intensified in rural communities, and efforts to build megaschools enrolling 1,500 or more students in grades ten through twelve or nine through twelve persisted in urban and suburban communities.[6]

Even in the 1940s, however, some urban educators saw high-school size as an issue of concern, as the following passage attests:

> Recent years have seen the big high schools reach their peak, and decline. A New York City high school with 10,000 pupils has been shorn to about 5,000. And look what happened to Forest Hills, NY, High School, which two years ago had about 3,300 pupils. The new principal noticed that the building was three stories high. Believing . . . that a small school of 1,000 has many advantages over a school three times as big, he made a separate high school of each floor.[7]

Subsequently, however, the perspective of school reformers began to change as the century unfolded. According to Tom Gregory,[8] for example, the last scholarly report to endorse the construction of large schools was written in 1970 by Robert Meeker and Daniel Weiler, working under the sponsorship of the Ford Foundation.[9] From that point forward, reformers began to give more attention to the arguments that larger schools contributed to students' alienation and unrest,[10] fostered unhealthy school climates,[11] and detracted from teachers' feelings of efficacy.[12] By this time Conant's agenda had not only been achieved but surpassed, with very large and megasized 'comprehensive' high schools providing secondary schooling for a majority of American youth.[13]

Because school climate and its influence on students' emotional well-being, behavior, and engagement were major concerns of scholars and advocates in the late 1960s through the early 1980s, the size of the school became less of a focus than the size of the so-called 'learning community.' Early on, therefore, reformers began to conflate "small schools" with "small learning communities,"[14] and they saw the 'school-within-a-school' as an innovation positioned to address the characteristic depersonalization of the very large high school. These reformers did not imagine that the 'school-within-a-school' would merely *simulate* the smallness of smaller extant schools. Instead, some saw it as a way to combine the presumptive *best* features of smaller *and* larger schools, as the passage below illustrates:

> Depersonalization usually accompanies bigness, and there is no doubt that today's schools are getting bigger. This is necessarily so, since small high schools with limited enrollments and inadequate staffs can only be considered as 20th century anachronisms. The efficient *transfer of knowledge* today requires highly diversified curricular offerings and well-trained staff members that only schools of adequate size can provide. The problem lies in finding ways for the staff in a large school to relate in meaningful fashion with individual students. Only so can each student enrolled profit from the curricular and instructional advantages such a school offers. At the same time each student will not be deprived of the advantages of the more intimate atmosphere of a smaller school.[15]

Ernest Boyer, a liberal reformer whose work purportedly influenced the Gates Foundation,[16] was also an early advocate of the 'school-within-a-school' and positioned it as a way for smaller high schools to connect to communities as well as to colleges.[17] In an interview during his tenure as U.S. Commissioner of Education, Boyer illustrated his recommendation with brief descriptions of four distinctive smaller high schools:

> A *high school art center connection* might be made, offering apprenticeships at community theatre groups, and internships in galleries and museums and orchestras;
>
> A *school-business* partnership, in which local business and industry adopt a school, and provide on-the-job training for students who are eager to be out working and honing their skills;
>
> A *social service school* with ties to community institutions so that young people could work with retirees and in hospitals and old age homes and parks.
>
> A *university in the schools* concept in which a local college would offer advanced academic work to high school students, both on the grounds of the high school, and on the college campus.[18]

Like Boyer, other liberal writers of the late 1970s and the 1980s began to link the concept of personalization with the idea of school choice. Prior to that time, however, the focus on 'personalization' and 'individualization' fell more in line with the version of progressive education articulated during the mid-1960s and early 1970s, which served as an arguable corrective to the essentialist focus that prevailed at the time.[19] Connecting 'humanist' perspectives on education with the need to create learning environments for those high school students who did not take to traditional schooling, urban educators in particular began to experiment with small 'alternative' schools.[20] Some of the earliest of these efforts were private-school ventures modeled on Summerhill and other 'free schools.'[21] The emphasis was what might be termed 'liberatory learning' if not always liberation per se—a concern very different from 'rigor,' which would, at least in official discourse, characterize some of the later efforts, especially those operating under the Gates imprimatur.[22]

An initiative in District 4, one of New York City's newly restructured school districts,[23] was one of the first concerted efforts by a public school system to create small schools with distinct missions and improved attentiveness to students' needs.[24] During this early phase of small-school reform—between 1974 and 1984—District 4 restructured many of its larger schools and, by the end of the ten-year period, had created twenty new small schools.[25] Forty additional small schools in NY were established as part of a system-wide initiative in the 1990s.[26] By that time, however, low graduation rates and poor academic performance had replaced 'depersonalization' as the primary motive for small-school reform. Many small-school reformers held the belief that reducing a school's size would enable other changes (e.g., teacher collaboration, individualization of instruction) that would in turn improve students' engagement and, ultimately, it was hoped, their achievement.[27] But policy analysts from some quarters[28] attributed the hoped-for improvements to the fact that New York's small schools were organized as schools of choice: choice, on this view, would prove a more robust sponsor of improvement than size.

In addition to efforts in New York City, other city systems started 'small-schools' programs in the 1980s and 1990s—well before large-scale funding from the Gates Foundation and other sources became briefly but munificently available. According to Pat Ford and Michael Klonsky, for example, the small-schools movement in Chicago started in grassroots fashion through the separate (and sometimes collaborative) efforts of principals, teachers, and advocates.[29] The Small Schools Workshop, founded in 1991 at the University of Illinois at Chicago, played an important role. These well-known efforts continued through the arrival of the Gates Foundation money. One must observe that both the New York and Chicago efforts were actual political and class *struggles* according to both Klonsky and Meier.[30] Social justice, too, is a motive far different from rigor, though as we shall see, the Gates Foundation also expressed concern for equality of educational outcomes and opportunity.

In Oakland, California, a faith-based network of community organizations, Oakland Community Organizations (OCO), lobbied for small autonomous schools at about the same time that the foundation was beginning to fund such initiatives; support primarily for high school reorganization came from the foundation. The OCO, however, also proceeded with efforts to revitalize Oakland neighborhoods through a variety of strategies, including the creation of small autonomous *elementary* schools.[31]

Some—but certainly not all—of the early 'small-schools' initiatives seem to have had an influence on the Gates Foundation. In a 2003 article, for instance, executive director Vander Ark identified three "pockets of excellence"[32] as the inspiration for small-school reform: urban Catholic schools, small schools in NYC, and charter schools. He also attributed the success of these exemplars to a set of shared features: small size, rigorous academic focus, accountability tied to school improvement, adequate funding based on needs, and opportunities for families to choose from among a set of coherent school programs. In framing the argument, moreover, Vander Ark drew on the research literature from the late 1960s forward in which small schools were purported to be responsible for positive outcomes such as increased student engagement, improved academic achievement, and greater achievement equity.[33]

Arguably, some research and commentary on the benefits of small schools seemed more salient to the foundation than other work; and a group of high-profile writers such as John Goodlad, Ernest Boyer, Deb Meier, and Ted Sizer appear to have been influential.[34] Less persuasive, perhaps, was research that focused on the generally salutary effects of smaller schools on student outcomes irrespective of either locale or the schools' implementation of particular reform practices.[35] The foundation's support, in any case, went almost exclusively to urban schools and to those promising to implement a particular set of reforms.

The foregoing retrospective shows that action to make high schools smaller than the evolving twentieth-century norm began almost as soon as educators (and students, families, and communities) experienced megaschools, at least by the 1940s. Most of these efforts were initiated by educators who were often acting, as they claimed, with teacher unions, communities, and progressive allies in the big-city bureaucracies. In particular, the roots of the effort in New York City stretch back much further than is generally thought. New York in fact had a long history of this activity, and this history might help explain why the New York effort proved more comparatively successful than those in the other sites evaluated by Evan and colleagues.[36]

When was the Gates effort? Based on our review of press releases, most of the grant-making activity took place in 2003; new grant making in 2004 was much more meager; and by 2005, we discovered no relevant press releases. Why? By 2005 early evaluation results (see note 2) may have suggested the difficulty of breaking large-city megaschools (which warehouse the urban poor) into improved 'small learning communities'; and even the new 'small-schools' effort did not seem (yet) to have been yielding the achievement outcomes (except in New York City) that had been so impatiently anticipated. Indeed, the judgment of failure was such that the Gates Foundation terminated its sweeping evaluation of the 'small-schools' effort early.[37] In doing so, it argued in a stunning non sequitur that the evaluation no longer represented the effort being conducted.[38] By 2008, Bill Gates himself had declared the 'small-schools' strategy a failure.[39]

Considering how much, how rapidly, and how briefly it supported 'small-schools' activity, we wanted to understand what the foundation itself claimed as it undertook to disburse its substantial funds (reportedly about $1.5 billion for related projects). We summarize our examination of the foundation's rhetoric next.

CHARACTERIZING THE GATES FOUNDATION'S SMALL-SCHOOLS RHETORIC

We examined only the foundation's public statements about 'small schools,' most of which consisted of an anonymous organizational discourse, with some offered by identifiable individuals. These documents offer many claims and few real warrants, as one can well imagine, but they nonetheless describe events and circumscribe positions.

The press releases announcing grants for the foundation's high school reform effort were one, perhaps key, source. We also examined the views articulated coevally by the Gates Foundation's founding education director,[40]

Tom Vander Ark,[41] and we accepted as authoritative the description of the foundation's "theory of action" given by the foundation-sponsored evaluation report.[42] Finally, the foundation has recently issued a retrospective of its education effort for the period 2000–8, in which Vander Ark's name is not even mentioned, and the 'small-schools' strategy is presented as having limited value at best.[43]

Press Releases

We examined Gates Foundation press releases[44] for those that substantively referenced funding for new projects on 'small schools.' These sources applied the terms 'small' or 'smaller' to high schools 165 times, and usage of the terms varied from one instance (December 7, 2004) to eighteen instances (September 17, 2003). Although some mentions were purely intended to identify the character of the initiatives, other mentions suggested *warrants* (references to authoritative research or experience), *instrumentalities* (projections of future benefit), *local attributions* (warrants stated or benefits claimed by local partners), and *policy desiderata* (explicit indications of what the foundation would prefer). We describe these substantive mentions in the following paragraphs.

Warrants supply justification. No particular studies were cited in any of these press releases, except for one press release concerning a study funded by the Gates Foundation. Vague references were made in several cases to studies issued, not by scholars, but by corporate entities—a Harvard study, a Manhattan Institute study, a Jobs for the Future study—or associated with particular jurisdictions (namely, a Chicago study and a New York study).

Instrumentalities position 'small-schools reform' to accomplish certain good deeds: one creates small or smaller schools as a means, not an end.[45] The promise of benefits, of course, must be made in press releases: 'hype' is a quality that marks the genre (examples follow):

> The new schools will use technology and strong relationships—teacher-student, teacher-staff and student-work relationships—to help create small, personalized learning environments that help all students achieve. (Napa, November 14, 2000)

> This grant will transform some of Oregon's ineffective schools into smaller results-oriented learning communities. (Portland, April 22, 2003)

> The goal of these small schools will be to close the achievement gap between under-performing students and their higher-achieving counterparts, while improving students' post-secondary options—whether college, technical training or the working world. (Indianapolis, May 15, 2003)

Vander Ark summed up the relevant instrumentalities as the Three Rs: rigor, relevance, and relationships.[46]

Local attribution refers to a press-release technique of attributing supportive statements to representatives of local partners (or beneficiaries). These attributed statements function both as warrants (local authority) and as instrumentalities (statements of local purpose). These statements are more wide ranging, and sometimes strange seeming, at least in the context of the lean line taken by the Gates Foundation:

> "Small schools offer our students an opportunity to be part of a smaller learning environment that will cater to those students that function academically best in those surroundings," said Michael Scott, Chicago Board of Education president. (Chicago, April 21, 2003)

> "The current high school model was created for rural learners . . . we believe that we need smaller, relationship-based high schools, a rigorous and relevant curriculum, and successful instructional models." [attributed to Grand Rapids' superintendent Bert Bleke] (Grand Rapids, August 18, 2003)

Policy desiderata are comparatively rarely stated by the foundation in these press releases, though of course the overall structure and manner of presentation of the documents indicate a concern for policy and for politics; that is, mayors, chief state school officers, city chancellors, and others take predictable cheerleading roles in these documents. These statements primarily characterize the schools that policies ought to support. They are not simply small, but something additional—additional even to 'good.' Five of the twenty-five press releases mention charter schools, for instance:

> Like all good small schools, good charter schools are focused and rigorous and foster strong relationships between students and adults who support and guide them. (Los Angeles, May 28, 2003)

> Typically much smaller than traditional public schools and freed from bureaucratic constraints, many charters allow for a level of innovation and personalization needed to help students being left behind. (San Francisco, June 30, 2003)

Despite the normative intent of these statements, only one explicitly phrased 'should' statement crops up in the twenty-five press releases:

> All students should be able to choose from an array of small, focused high schools designed to give them a solid, personalized education and the promise of a bright future [attributed to Vander Ark]. (Chicago, May 21, 2003)

Overall in these press releases, the Gates Foundation expressed concern with (1) achievement equity; (2) preparation for college; (3) school 'goodness,' a set of characteristics relating to the *process* of schooling; and (4) choice (particularly as illustrated by its engagement with 'charter' schools). 'Small schools' were a means and the 'small-schools' effort was a *strategy*. Seeking improvement in both the processes (curriculum, instruction, assessment) *and* the outcomes of schooling (attendance, course taking and passing, graduation rate, and achievement), the foundation quickly disbursed a very large sum to partner organizations (generally private local foundations) in mid- to large-size cities to accomplish the designated instrumentalities. One must wonder about the source of optimism: was it the strategy, the charisma of the education director, or the money?

Other Sources

Vander Ark published three brief pieces in the *Education Week* commentary section.[47] Appearing at the outset of the Gates Foundation's initiative, the earliest commentary may offer an insight into the foundation's original view of high-school reform. Briefly, the piece argues the obsolescence of the comprehensive high school and identifies the challenge of reform as structural ("architectural"); and it champions smaller schools—with particular reference to those then existing in New York City, which the authors had visited. The end of the essay announces the Foundation's plans: "In the coming months and years, the . . . Foundation will be exploring ways to create, support, and link more closely 'reinvented' high schools like the ones described above."[48]

The second commentary, "A Critical Fork in the Road," argues for a performance-based accountability system to assess learning more important than that measured by "cheap" standardized tests. Reference to small schools appears in a list of conditions allegedly needed to ensure that students "perform at very high levels," that is, "much smaller schools, teacher teamwork, a personalized learning environment, and many more opportunities for applied and hands-on learning." The warrant provided for this list is that it emerged from a conference sponsored by the foundation. The commentary also argues that school districts need a "*portfolio* of schools" [emphasis added]:[49] alternative, small, magnet, charter, and so forth.[50] This policy desideratum is consistent, of course, with the support for charter schools evident among the press releases examined.

Vander Ark's 2003 commentary asserts that high schools "are the least effective part of the American education system." He makes five recommendations: (1) focus standards on college admissions; (2) improve accountability so it serves a formative purpose; (3) provide funding adequacy based on the "real costs" of educating particular sorts of students; (4) offer parental choice among small schools of differing character and purpose; and (5) increase "access" to college.[51] With a plea for teacher support, including a workload proportional to the instructional mission, faculty collegiality designed to build instructional skill, and "strong in-house leadership," this commentary concludes:

> The decisions we make—or fail to make—in the next few years will help dictate the social, civic, and economic health for generations to come. If we keep building impersonal tracked high schools, we'll need to expand our prison system. Education is the best investment a state can make.[52]

Of the three commentaries, this last is arguably more coherent and perhaps both bolder and more nuanced than its predecessors. The recommendations take extant mainstream practices and argue for substantial redirection; the positions—and the final prediction—resemble those made by progressive school reformers.[53]

The officially sponsored evaluation report describes the Foundation's "theory of action," which the authors of the report would have been under contract to take seriously. Here's the description:

> Although the small size the foundation recommended for high schools . . . was what attracted the attention of outside observers, the foundation's education initiative was *never about small size per se*. Foundation staff identified a set of characteristics—or 'attributes'—commonly found in high schools that successfully retained students from historically underserved populations and helped them attend and graduate from institutions of higher education. The essence of the foundation's theory of change was that the creation of high schools *with these attributes* would lead not only to better outcomes for the students attending the schools but also to increased demand for more such schools [emphasis added].[54]

The valued attributes were (1) common focus, (2) high expectations, (3) personalization, (4) respect and responsibility, (5) time to collaborate, (6) performance based [*sic*], and (7) technology as a tool. Though *human scale* was one of the thirteen concepts articulated by Sizer,[55] the attribute under which 'small schools' figures in the list given by Evan and colleagues is *personalization*:[56]

> The school is designed to promote sustained student relationships with adults where every student has an adult advocate and a personal plan for progress. Schools are small: no more than 600 students (less than 400 strongly recommended)[57]

'Curtains' for Small Schools

The Gates Foundation's retrospective on its high-school initiative observes:

> We have learned that a focus on structural change at the school level, including the creation of new schools and small learning communities,

> is not sufficient to ensure that all students are ready for college, career, and life.[58]

Instead, the foundation now believes that a focus on content, pedagogy, and standards *will* realize the desiderata.[59] Vander Ark's replacement at the foundation claimed, "This is an evolution. It's not a 360-degree turn by any means."[60]

To many observers, of course, it does seem to be a 180-degree turn. It seems that if 'personalization' could be achieved by means other than small size, then small size would not be necessary.[61] This juncture is precisely where we personally part company with the thinking of many of our esteemed urban confreres *and* with the foundation, and we consider the related issues next.

NATURALLY OCCURRING AND FABRICATED SMALL SCHOOLS

We make here an unusual argument about small schools, both naturally occurring (already small) and fabricated (newly small: 'small schools'). Our standpoint is that of the rural communities in which and with which we have worked and lived since 1973.[62]

The argument is quite simple in outline: in the rural circumstance, *small* really is valuable in itself; that is, as an already-existing reality and not as an imagined, designed, planned, or hoped-for one. In short, many schools are 'naturally' small.[63] They *already* have value for the community, for families, and *thus* for children and youth.[64] Their small enrollments are neither an accident nor an oversight. But these already-existing small schools are continually threatened with closure, usually as a way of dealing with a state-level crisis of legitimacy.[65] In rural places, then, school closure is usually understood as an attack on the community itself.[66] Being rural and already small not only does not exempt a school and its community from struggle—educational, political, cultural, racial, and class struggle—but it arguably intensifies such struggles. Being rural, in fact, invites patronizing from state and federal officialdom, from foundation actors, and especially from cosmopolitan school reformers.

The rural outlook is widely dismissed in writing not only about 'small-school' fabrications but in writing about school size in general. For instance, one prominent school-size researcher, Valerie Lee, and her colleague Douglas Ready opine:

> Some high schools are small because they want to be small, and others are small because they just don't have many students. These two types of small schools should not be confused. The 'small by design' high schools share many advantages not shared by the 'small by default' high schools. This has led us to be somewhat skeptical about 'smallness' as an inherently valuable characteristic of high school design.[67]

In a seriously flawed study (see Howley and Howley 2004 for the specifics), Lee has famously found that the universally best size for an American high school, wherever it might be located, is 600 to 900 (Lee and Smith 1997).[68] The fact that no high schools in rural Montana, for instance, enroll nearly so many as 600 students is not apparently taken as harboring any practical or theoretical significance.[69] Lee and Ready don't see the rural circumstance and don't care about it.

But conservative versions of the 'one best way' with respect to school size are not the only ones to put rural circumstances out of mind. Klonsky and Klonsky begin their recent book about the recent history of the 'small-schools' movement with this passage:

> The small-schools movement was probably misnamed. It was never really *just* about 'small.' Some social theorists, such as economist E. F. Schumacher, saw great value in small things. However, what captured the vision of many urban educators . . . were the traditional democratic values of Deweyan progressivism.[70]

The nod to Schumacher (1911–1977) is apt. Schumacher's 1973 book, *Small Is Beautiful*, did indeed articulate a valuable principle about the inhuman scale of human institutions in the twentieth century, and the rural alternative *was* visible to him.[71] The current global economic crisis is very much an issue of scale, as is the environmental crisis. The book is perhaps even more salient today than it was four decades ago.

For Schumacher, the human (i.e., small and small*er*) scaling of institutions does not merely *facilitate* quality of life but is the only way to enact it decently—and responsibly. On this view, *small* is not simply an issue of 'personalization,' but constitutes the fabric and apparatus of human relationships and meaningfulness. The educational implications (meaningfulness and the good), then, are at least as profound as the economic implications. Dismissing the issue of scale as 'merely' or 'just' about small is a predictable misstep for neoliberal conservatives, but it is a distinct oversight among urban progressive educators.

World-cities such as New York, Chicago, and Los Angeles not only present to the eye an immense scale, but the cosmopolitan cultural apparatus lodged in such places promotes immensity as the global norm via, in Raymond Williams' phrase, the "persistent intellectual hegemony of the metropolis."[72] Impoverished urban and rural people are every bit the victims; immense scale prevents us from knowing how the apparatus works or even seeing it. More recently—and ominously—we have learned that immensity means 'too big to fail.' Some critics,[73] of course, have always seen schooling as both a passive and active enabler of such deception.[74] So do we; but we see alternatives, notable among which is a smaller scale for nearly everything: banks, factories, farms, cities . . . and ambitions, notably including those of school improvers.

REFORMISM AS A COSMOPOLITAN RUSE

We observe that the *design* of reformist 'small schools'[75] inevitably entails the lionization of certain features of such *to-be-reformed* schools, features that are positioned to trump smaller scale as a reality in its own right. The features vary, but the lionization of hoped-for practices to be contained by the to-be-reformed schools does not. All parties have particular instrumentalities in mind, and these quite varied instrumentalities must be guided, facilitated, funded, and struggled toward. The significance of the initial insight (i.e., that smaller scale is a necessary condition for reform) is lost, and eventually discredited, especially under the influence of peremptory megafunding with private monies. The reformation *must* be fast and complete (as the Gates Foundation's withdrawal so well shows). Because it can never be so—reform being what it is—the discrediting is inevitable.

Why? Because of the ontology: the goal is so grand and the means (rapid spending of money) so ethically—even *morally*—suspect. Recall Gates' formula cited previously: "The creation of new schools and small learning communities is not sufficient to ensure that all students are ready for college, career, and life." Traditional reform of public schooling is exceedingly—excruciatingly—difficult, precisely because it requires the cooperation of so many parties with such conflicting interests and commitments.[76] Money might be a lubricant, but drowning the effort in grease suffocates all actors. Hubris and impatience cannot change the reality either.

Establishing a few hundred smaller schools is the easy stretch on this doomed path to utopia. The difficult—impossible—part is the dubious attempt to accommodate the requisites of hubris and impatience. Those are the terms of a very bad bargain, and on those terms anything else is failure, no matter the impossibility of success. This point, however, is where extant research about school size might have exerted a moderating influence on the Gates Foundation's planning and expectations.

In the present era, the most compelling instrumentality is 'higher test scores,' and the best improvements are, of course, statistically significant higher scores. This longed-for result did not materialize with sufficient speed or incidence, it seems, even if the New York results looked promising.[77] Of course, absent a randomized controlled experiment in which hapless subjects are sorted into schools of various sizes and held there for a long time, the best evidence for the achievement costs of large school size comes from correlational studies. And these exist, some of them widely replicated, and known among 'small-schools' reformers of all stripes. Like Lee and colleagues, we have conducted some of the relevant studies.[78] In general, this body of evidence suggests that smaller high schools, as a feature of entire *then-extant* educational systems, did benefit (were associated with) the achievement of impoverished students.[79]

The point is that these findings are not about *reformist* schools (of any size) with complex and contested agendas for 'improvement,' but concern (precisely because they proceed from the analysis of) *schools of all size with warts and all.* Overall, the influence of size is not huge, but small to moderate; though of course in some jurisdictions (states and regions), the observable effects would be substantial, whereas in others they would be negligible or even opposite. But overall, small to moderate effects could be predicted—quite apart from the difficult struggle to facilitate inquiry learning, multicultural sensitivity, authentic assessment, rigor, and relevance.

One key part of this work about scale concerned district size. The beneficial effects of smaller size applied not just to schools, but to districts—and the Gates Foundation's 'small-schools' effort was being enacted in some of the nation's *largest* school districts. The only researcher-author of a specified study in the foundation's press releases, Jay Green, had himself conducted work that demonstrated such benefits of smaller district size.[80]

Knowing the relevant research on school and district size, why any educator, philanthropist, or commonsensical thinker would expect not just *robust* effect sizes, but a sort of *wonderland* of quick accomplishment (rapid and notable improvement in all major processes and outcomes of schooling, as with the Gates Foundation) escapes us. Perhaps the answer lies in the immensity of the funding provided or in the seductive qualities of one's own hyperbole or in a combination thereof. It is clear, though, that no one, including Vander Ark, believed that small size was the proverbial 'silver bullet.'

We speculate, however, that the trouble goes deeper, to the bad habit of *reformism*, which has become such an entrenched norm in the management of American schooling. Under the operant logic of the reformist norm, the best effort has become the *best-funded effort*, and great things can be predicted for it in disregard of all common sense and common decency. The previously extant 'small-schools' effort, which had been conducted with suitable modesty and humility, became overwhelmed with the Gates Foundation's quite different approach and demands.[81] Unfortunately, the money was the prime mover, and the larger the sum, the more moving the experience.

In this thinking, we're not being too original or outrageous. James Scott's 1998 work *Seeing Like a State* is our inspiration. Scott studies grand schemes for human betterment and finds them wanting on a number of grounds, including hubris, impatience, remoteness, blindness to grassroots resistance, and most critically, the overall tendency to discredit the human agency of lowly subjects (e.g., struggling teachers, students, families, and communities). Social engineering—which is by definition a top-down operation—misconstrues the subjects to whom it relates and the nature of the actions it undertakes with them, and so it inevitably proves itself inept, according to Scott. The grander the scheme, the more extreme must be the subsequent denials. The ineptness is always denied, always blamed on whatever will serve best in the circumstances: bad strategy, ignorant peasants and workers, enemies, human nature, or even bad genes.[82]

After the blaming, what will happen next under reformism? *Different* reforms will be called for: the reformist cycling and recycling must continue, since reformism constitutes an economic system through its cycles, its familiar pendulums. Although it may be true that the instrumentalities to be inserted in schools that will be 'small by design' exhibit arguable merit, depending on one's standpoint, all these simultaneous instrumentalities are themselves the problem and not the solution. What they do best, though, is to reinforce constant disappointment, as so many astute critics of school reform have noted.

Ironically, but predictably, the Gates Foundation's current strategy (to focus on curriculum, instruction, and leadership) is a much more traditional reformist strategy than the 'architectural' one commended by Wagner and Vander Ark.[83] Arguably, one can make schools smaller with predictable, very long-term results[84] from the *statistically likely* (not certain in every case) accumulation of small associated benefits. On one hand, the fashions of curriculum and pedagogy and management are so changeable that one can hardly ever gauge the benefits and losses. On the other hand, one is assured of indefinite tinkering and the associated spending. The Gates Foundation may indeed tire of supplying funds to such endless and bootless efforts.

'SMALL-SCHOOLS' FALLOUT

Claims abound in the Gates Foundation's press releases; warrants are vague and cheerleading is loud. The real stories of the agonized struggles in schools and districts escape nearly everyone except the lowliest of local actors. The official evaluations do a credible synoptic job, but they cannot capture the grit and exhaustion at the grassroots. Worse, the publicized hyperbole not only outstrips but outlives the ineffable realities. The public's association of small schools (no scare quotes) with the Gates Foundation will tragically outlive the foundation's support for 'small schools,' perhaps for a long time, together with the oversimplified conclusion that 'small schools don't *work*.'[85] This is how reformism turns successes into failures and vice versa: the scheme and scale must be huge, the hubris sufficient to silence both reason and caution, and the power concentrated at the top and deployed impatiently and insistently downward. Others have probably also observed that it's taken a billion and a half dollars to prove that 'small schools don't work.'

We can't judge if this is tragedy or farce, but in fact, of course, nothing of the sort has been proven empirically. The proof is of a very different order. The 'proof' is rhetorical or even *performative*:[86] saying so with a lot of money makes it so. The associated discourse renders it not only *as if so*, but *as good as so*. But to the contrary, the official evaluation found that some portions of the funded initiative, in a short time, in some places, and to some extent, seemed to have accomplished some of the intentions, at most to a modest extent. It's exactly the result that could have been predicted based on the extant correlational research.

PROBABLE CONSEQUENCES FOR SMALL SCHOOLS IN RURAL PLACES

Although one possibility is that the large-scale and well-publicized failure of the Gates Foundation 'small-schools' initiative will have little impact on existing small schools, historical precedents suggest otherwise. First, efforts to close small schools in rural locales have been persistent for decades, even throughout the heyday of 'small-schools' reform.[87] Second, the trajectory of initiatives positioned as 'reforms' seems almost always to move outward from cities to the countryside.[88] Finally, despite the rhetoric of 'distinctiveness' that accompanies the push for charter schools, the general thrust of the standards movement is toward increased uniformity across schools throughout the nation and, indeed, throughout the world.[89]

For more than 100 years, policy makers have viewed consolidation and closure of small rural schools as a method of improving them.[90] Proponents of reform-through-closure have argued that small schools provide inadequate curricula, employ teachers with lesser credentials, and lack resources for offering needed programs and support services. Furthermore, they often identify substandard buildings as a rationale for consolidation.[91] Despite advocates' claims that consolidation represents an improvement, however, many rural parents and community members actively resist this putative reform[92]—a stance for which they are often maligned as backward, negligent, and 'romantic.' On this view, educators and policy makers are the ones best positioned to act on behalf of children's interests, whereas parents and community members simply get in the way.

That professional educators routinely see this construction of what's going on as a perspective that makes sense demonstrates the extent to which *reformism* has become a well-entrenched norm. Reformism, in fact, places knowledge of what's best beyond the reach not only of parents and community members, but ultimately beyond the reach of professional educators as well. Whereas reform issues from a powerful center,[93] implementation must inevitably occur in each local place.[94] Each locale, then, requires the services of functionaries who exercise uniform practices—practices in line with the latest reform—supposedly crafted and disseminated for the betterment of the populace.[95] Reformers, however, find the practice of such functionaries (in this case, teachers and principals) difficult to control; and when particular reform efforts fail, central reformers typically blame the functionaries.

These dynamics have certainly been at play with the Gates Foundation 'small-schools' initiative: when the reform package did not work, the foundation attributed the failure to teachers and school administrators. Because it was an urban initiative, these particular culprits were urban teachers and administrators. Nevertheless, the general consensus that rural educators tend to be less competent than urban educators[96] suggests that reformers might conclude as a corollary that small schools in rural places are even less likely to succeed than small schools in cities. Indeed, the rhetorical positioning of 'small by design' as salutary and 'small by default' as deficient already embeds this hallowed distinction.[97] Rural schools, on this view, might turn out to be too inept to handle their own smallness. This analysis is speculative, of course, but it does provide a way to understand the persistence with which centralized reforms (even when their content ostensibly engages 'smallness' and 'distinctiveness') in fact require scalability and compliance to a uniform code.

At the same time, much of the public rhetoric about schooling has now moved away from 'personalization' and 'engagement' and even, to some extent, from the imperative to redress the 'achievement gap.' Formulating education in terms of a race for economic supremacy, a new coalition of foundations, businesses, and state education agencies is cutting a swath so broad that the goals of the Gates Foundation's initiative appear quaint and its largesse paltry:

> The nature of education is changing internationally. The United States is falling behind on critical international comparisons of educational performance, particularly when it comes to higher-level thinking and problem-solving skills . . . Recent initiatives by the U.S. Department of Education, the National Governors Association, the Bill and Melinda Gates Foundation, the U.S. Conference of Mayors and other prominent organizations have focused attention on the nation's high schools—and the urgent national priority of making a high school education rigorous, meaningful and relevant in our changing global context. The Partnership applauds these efforts. At the same time, we believe that unless high school redesign initiatives anticipate the 21st century knowledge and skills that all students need to succeed and function ethically in civic life, higher education and the workforce, they will miss their mark . . . High schools cannot begin to take on the work of redesigning expectations, buildings or schedules without first determining the results that matter. This should be the first step—not an afterthought—in the high school reform movement. The results that matter should shape every aspect of modern high schools.[98]

Meanwhile, the Gates Foundation has moved on to other work. Perhaps the problems of high schools were too large, perhaps the aspirations of being a giant in the effort to commandeer 'high-school reform' too grandiose. Whatever the actual case, all of it seems to fit the logic of *reformism* and none of it to be particularly attentive to the magnitude of the problems facing urban students in large dysfunctional schools and districts or the challenges confronting rural communities whose naturally small schools are nearly always under attack.

NOTES

1. Like some of the other authors in this book, one of us (Craig) has been involved in Gates Foundation work. He is a coauthor of the *Dollars and Sense* volumes (Lawrence et al. 2002; Lawrence et al. 2005), partly funded by the foundation. That involvement also resulted in an empirical study of size-related high-school construction costs (Howley 2008). Craig was also employed on a contract from a Gates-funded partner foundation that evaluated several early college high schools. C. Howley. "Don't Supersize Me: Relationship Of Construction Costs To School Enrollment In The US." *Educational Planning* 17, no. 2 (2008): 23-40. B.K. Lawrence, P. Abramson, V. Bergsagel, S. Bingler, B. Daimond, T. Greene, B. Hill, C. Howley, D. Stephen, and E. Washor. *Dollars And Sense II: Lessons From Good, Cost-Effective Small Schools* (Cincinnati, OH: KnowledgeWorks Foundation, 2005). B. K. Lawrence, S. Bingler, B. Diamond, B. Hill, J. Hoffman, C. Howley, S. Mitchell, D. Rudolph, and E. Washor. *Dollars And Sense: The Cost Effectiveness of Small Schools* (Cincinnati, OH: KnowledgeWorks Foundation, 2003).
2. A. Evan et al., *Evaluation of the Bill & Melinda Gates Foundation's High School Grants Initiative: 2001–2005 Final Report* (Washington, D.C., and Menlo Park, CA: American Institutes for Research / SRI International, 2006); L. Shear et al., "Contrasting Paths to Small-School Reform: Results of a 5-year Evaluation of the Bill & Melinda Gates Foundation's National High Schools Initiative," *Teachers College Record* 110, no. 9 (2008): 1986–2039.
3. J. B. Conant, *The American High School Today: A First Report to Interested Citizens* (New York: McGraw Hill, 1959): 41–76.
4. J. Lay, *Building Good Citizens: The Roles of School Size and Community Context in the Development of Democratic Values* (PhD diss., University of Maryland, 2004), 30; B. L. Schneider, *America's Small Schools* (Austin, TX: National Educational Laboratory Publishers, 1980), ERIC no. ED187508, http://www.eric.ed.gov (accessed July 30, 2010).
5. H. Adams, *The Education of Henry Adams* (Boston: Houghton Mifflin, 1918), http://www.bartleby.com/159/5.html (accessed May 10, 2010).
6. Lee and Smith ("High School Size,"1997) report that schools with more than 900 students impose achievement costs for all students. In light of this finding, an enrollment of 1,500 in grades nine through twelve seems a *conservative* lower limit for the construct of megaschool. Enrollment in such schools is increasing, not declining: the National Center for Education Statistics reported in 2008 that the proportional enrollment of U.S. students in regular high schools at least this large *rose* from 43.21 percent in 2004 to 44.36 percent just two years later. Recall that Conant's enrollment minimum was just 400 students in grades nine through twelve. V. E. Lee and J. B. Smith, "High School Size: Which Works Best and for Whom?" *Educational Evaluation and Policy Analysis* 19, no. 3 (1997): 205–27. National Center for Education Statistics. *Number and Percentage Distribution of Public Elementary and Secondary Schools and Enrollment, by Type and Enrollment Size of School: 2004–05, 2005–06, and 2006–07* (Washington, D.C: Author, 2008), http://nces.ed.gov/programs/digest/d08/tables/dt08_095.asp (accessed August 9, 2009).
7. Anonymous, "Making Little Ones out of Big Ones," *Education Digest* 9, no. 4 (December 1943): 54.
8. T. Gregory, *School Reform and the No-Man's-Land of High School Size* (2000), ERIC no. ED451981, http://www.lcsc.us/userfiles/file/Referendum%20Info/costs_of_school_size.pdf (accessed May 10, 2010).

9. A design for a K–12 school planned to enroll 2,600 students appears in R. J. Meeker and D. M. Weiler, "A New School for the Cities," *Education and Urban Society*, no. 3, (1971): 129–243.
10. See, for example, S. Leggett et al., "The Case for a Small High School," *Education Digest* 36, no. 3 (1970): 15–18; E. A. Wynne, "Behind the Discipline Problem: Youth Suicide As a Measure of Alienation," *Phi Delta Kappan* 59, no. 5 (1978): 307–15.
11. T. B. Gregory and G. R. Smith, "Differences between Alternative and Conventional Schools in Meeting Students' Needs" (paper presented at the annual meeting of the American Educational Research Association, Montreal, Quebec, Canada, April 11–15, 1983).
12. T. B. Gregory and G. R. Smith, *High Schools as Communities: The Small School Reconsidered* (Bloomington, IN: Phi Delta Kappa, 1987).
13. See note 6.
14. S. Hawke, "The School of Urban Studies: A School Within a School," *Profiles of Promise* 34, 1974, ERIC no. ED100732, http://www.eric.ed.gov/ERICWebPortal/contentdelivery/servlet/ERICServlet?accno=ED100732 (accessed May 10, 2010).
15. C. H. Peterson, "When Staff Members Relate to the Pupil," *Educational Leadership* 23, no. 4 (1966): 307.
16. T. Toch, C. D. Jerald, and E. Dillon, "Surprise—High School Reform Is Working," *Phi Delta Kappan* 88, no. 6 (2007): 433–37.
17. E. L. Boyer and J. L. Burdin, "Access and Excellence—Key Words in Education Commissioner's Program," *Journal of Teacher Education*, 1978: 20–22, ERIC no. EJ189474, http://www.eric.ed.gov/ERICWebPortal/recordDetail?accno=EJ189474 (accessed May 10, 2010).
18. Page 22 (same source as n17). Note the similarity between this recommendation and the early college high schools later supported by the Gates Foundation.
19. H. Kliebard, *The Struggle for the American Curriculum, 1893–1958*, 2nd ed. (New York: Routledge, 1995).
20. R. Neumann, *Sixties Legacy: A History of the Public Alternative Schools Movement, 1967–2001* (New York: Peter Lang, 2003); S. F. Semel and A. R. Sadovnik, "The Contemporary Small-School Movement: Lessons from the History of Progressive Education," *Teachers College Record* 110, no. 9 (2008): 1744–71.
21. R. Neumann, *Sixties Legacy.*
22. One might, in fact, argue that 'rigor' is the reformist word of the day. It continues to be used to justify most of the Gates' initiatives, for example.
23. In response to pressure for greater community involvement in school governance, the New York State Legislature divided the NYC district into thirty-one smaller community districts (New York State, Senate, 1981). New York State Senate. *An Act to Amend the Education Law, the New York City Charter and the New York City Administrative Code, in Relation to Establishing a Community School System* (Albany: NY, 1968). ERIC No. ED024730, http://eric.ed.gov/ERICWebPortal/contentdelivery/servlet/ERICServlet?accno=ED024730 (accessed August 1, 2010).
24. R. Neumann, *Sixties Legacy.*
25. A. Hartocollis, "Choosing Schools Betters Students In East Harlem," *New York Times*, February 24, 1998, http://www.nytimes.com/1998/02/24/nyregion/choosing-schools-betters-students-in-east-harlem.html (accessed May 10, 2010).
26. Amy Ellen Schwartz et al., "Small Schools, Large Districts: Small-School Reform and New York City's Students," *Teachers College Record* 110, no. 9 (2008): 1837–78.

27. See, for example, L. Darling-Hammond, J. Ancess, and S. Ort, "Reinventing High School: Outcomes of the Coalition Campus Schools Project," *American Educational Research Journal* 39, no. 3 (2002): 639–73.
28. See, for example, M. Schneider, P. Teske, and M. Marschall, *Choosing Schools* (Princeton, NJ: Princeton University Press, 2002).
29. P. Ford and M. Klonsky, "One Urban Solution: Small Schools," *Educational Leadership* 51, no. 8 (1994): 64–67.
30. M. Klonsky, *Small Schools and Teacher Professional Development* (Charleston, WV: Appalachia Educational Laboratory, 2002); D. Meier, *The Power of Their Ideas: Lessons for America from a Small School in Harlem* (Boston: Beacon Press, 1995).
31. E. Gold, E. Simon, and C. Brown, *Case Study: OCO, Oakland Community Organizations; Strong Neighborhoods, Strong Schools: The Indicators Project on Education Organizing*, (Chicago: Cross City Campaign for Urban School Reform, 2002), ERIC no. ED469255, http://www.eric.ed.gov/ERICWebPortal/contentdelivery/servlet/ERICServlet?accno=ED469255 (accessed May 10, 2010).
32. T. Vander Ark, "America's High School Crisis: Policy Reforms that Will Make a Difference," *Education Week* 22, no. 29 (2003): 52, 41.
33. T. Vander Ark, "The Case for Small High Schools," *Educational Leadership* 59, no. 5 (2002): 55; T. Vander Ark, "America's High School Crisis," 52, 41.
34. T. Toch, C. D. Jerald, and E. Dillon, "Surprise—High School Reform Is Working."
35. See, for example, C. B. Howley and A. A. Howley, "School Size and the Influence of Socioeconomic Status on Student Achievement: Confronting the Threat of Size Bias in National Data Sets," *Educational Policy Analysis Archives* 12, no. 52 (2004): 1–33; V. E. Lee and J. B. Smith, "High School Size: Which Works Best and for Whom?" *Educational Evaluation and Policy Analysis* 19, no. 3 (1997): 205–27.
36. Gates Foundation, *All Students Ready for College, Career, and Life: Reflections on the Foundation's Education Investments 2000–2008* (Seattle, WA: Author, 2009), http://www.gatesfoundation.org/learning/Documents/reflections-foundations-education-investments.pdf (accessed May 20, 2010); A. Evan et al., *Evaluation of the Bill & Melinda Gates Foundation's High School Grants Initiative.*
37. The final report by A. Evan and colleagues bears a 2006 publication date.
38. If this assertion is more than an excuse, it arguably represents an assumption that disables systematic inquiry. See D. Viadero, "Foundation Shifts Tack on Studies," *Education Week* 26, no. 9 (October 25, 2008): 1–25.
39. E. Weiss, *Gates Foundation Turns to New Strategies,* Michigan Policy Network, November 19, 2008. http://www.michiganpolicy.com/index.php?option=com_content&view=category&layout=blog&id=37&Itemid=121 (accessed August 1, 2010).
40. Vander Ark left the foundation in 2006 (Shaw 2006), and his leadership is not acknowledged in the foundation's 2009 retrospective (Gates Foundation 2009). Shaw, L. "Foundation's Small Schools Experiment Has Yet to Yield Big Results," *Seattle Times*, November 5, 2006, http://seattletimes.nwsource.com/html/education/2003348701 _gates05m.html (accessed August 1, 2010). Gates Foundation. *All students ready for college, career, and life: Reflections on the Foundation's education investments 2000-2008.* (Seattle, WA: Author, 2009), http://www.gatesfoundation.org/learning/Documents/reflections-foundations-education-investments.pdf (accessed August 1, 2010).
41. T. Vander Ark, "America's High School Crisis," 52, 41; T. Vander Ark and T. Wagner, "Between Hope and Despair: The Case for Smaller High Schools,"

Education Week 19, no. 41 (2000): 76; T. Wagner and T. Vander Ark, "A Critical Fork in the Road," *Education Week* 20, no. 30 (2001): 56.

42. A. Evan et al., *Evaluation of the Bill & Melinda Gates Foundation's High School Grants Initiative.*
43. Gates Foundation, *All Students Ready for College, Career, and Life.*
44. We examined twenty-five press releases issued November 14, 2000 through December 7, 2004, all taken from the Gates Foundation's website. The releases we have quoted are identified by city/region and date and are available at the "Press Room" page of the website at http://www.gatesfoundation.org/press-room/Pages/overview.aspx (accessed May 10, 2010).
45. Elsewhere in this chapter we will argue that this sort of instrumentalism is the key conceptual misstep in the Gates Foundation's 'small schools' work and in the big-city 'small-schools' movement generally—a point difficult for city-based 'small-schools' actors to hear. This critique proceeds from our own experience with rural schools and districts, and with school closure and district consolidation.
46. K. Kinsella, "Tom Vander Ark, Executive Director, Education, Bill & Melinda Gates Foundation," *Philanthropy News Digest* (October 2003): 1.
47. See note 41 for information about the *Education Week* pieces. Also note that the Gates Foundation provides funding to the newspaper's publisher, Editorial Projects in Education. http://www.edweek.org/ew/index.html
48. T. Vander Ark and T. Wagner, "Between Hope and Despair," 76.
49. T. Wagner and T. Vander Ark, "A Critical Fork in the Road," 56.
50. See, for example, R. Chalusian, B. Donohue, and I. Zucker, *New Visions for Public Schools (New York City)–New Century High Schools* (New York: New Visions, 2009), http://www.annenberginstitute.org/pdf/EKF06_NewVision.pdf (accessed May 10, 2010).
51. See T. Vander Ark, "America's High School Crisis," 52, 41. 'Access' here means college preparation as the main purpose of high school, and it is arguably redundant with the first recommendation.
52. T. Vander Ark, "America's High School Crisis," 41.
53. M. Klonsky and S. Klonsky, *Small Schools: Public School Reform Meets the Ownership Society* (New York and London: Routledge, 2008); D. Meier, *The Power of Their Ideas*; T. Sizer, *Horace's Hope: What Works for the American High School* (Boston: Houghton Mifflin, 1996).
54. A. Evan et al., *Evaluation of the Bill & Melinda Gates Foundation's High School Grants Initiative.*
55. T. Sizer, *Horace's Hope*, 76–109.
56. We realize that some of Sizer's principles over the years have also included personalization.
57. A. Evan et al., *Evaluation of the Bill & Melinda Gates Foundation's High School Grants Initiative*, 3, table 1.
58. Gates Foundation, *All Students Ready for College, Career, and Life*, 4.
59. See note 56.
60. E. Robelen, "Strategy Retooled at Gates," *Education Week* 28, no. 13 (November 19, 2008): 1.
61. Our experience includes work in special education. The construct *personalization* is a small-schools shibboleth akin to *individualization*, long a byword in special education. The terms strike us as ontologically strange: the reality they suggest is one in which anomie has become the norm *among children.* On this view, the grassroots outrage at megaschools ought to be comprehensible even to those who credit these strange constructs.
62. This standpoint, evident in our empirical work and our advocacy pieces, perhaps explains why we are so seldom contacted by professional educators and so very often contacted by rural community members and advocates.

63. S. A. Swidler, "Conversation and Control: Emergent Progressive Pedagogy in the Last of Nebraska's One-Teacher Schools," *Journal of Research in Rural Education* 20, no. 4 (2005), http://www.jrre.psu.edu/articles/20-4.pdf (accessed May 10, 2010).
64. Because such schools already have value for communities and families, we accept them as having value for children and youth. This logic will be regarded as 'unprofessional' by some colleagues. So be it.
65. See, for example, A. DeYoung and C. Howley, "The Political Economy of Rural School Consolidation," *Peabody Journal of Education* 67, no. 4 (1992): 63–89.
66. Rural sociologist Tom Lyson (2002) has in fact demonstrated the association between school closure and community well-being. T. Lyson. "What Does a School Mean to a Community? Assessing the Social and Economic Benefits of Schools to Rural Villages in New York," *Journal of Research in Rural Education* 17, no. 3 (Winter 2002): 131-137.
67. See page 198 in V. Lee and D. Ready, "The Schools-Within-Schools Reform," in *Educating Adolescents*, ed. F. Pajares and T. Urdan (Greenwich, CT: Information Age, 2004), 179–206.
68. Briefly: the study uses a database intended to represent individuals to draw conclusions about schools, which feature underrepresents small schools since comparatively fewer students attend smaller as compared to larger schools; it does not measure the academic growth of students who drop out before grade twelve; and in judging the findings, the interpretation privileges 'excellence' criteria over equity criteria. If the authors gave their equity findings equal weight with their 'excellence' findings, the ideal high school size would vary from 300 to 900 students. Instead the authors conclude that a considerably narrower range is 'best.' C. B. Howley and A. A. Howley, "School Size and the Influence of Socioeconomic Status on Student Achievement: Confronting the Threat of Size Bias in National Data Sets," *Educational Policy Analysis Archives* 12, no. 52 (2004): 1–33; V. E. Lee and J. B. Smith, "High School Size: Which Works Best and for Whom?" *Educational Evaluation and Policy Analysis* 19, no. 3 (1997): 205–27.
69. In 2003–2004 the mean enrollment of high schools in rural Montana was 135; the minimum was 30 and the maximum 371. One megaschool in Billings that enrolled 1,653 students was misclassified by NCES as rural (computation with 2003–2004 CCD file; confirmation of error via inspection of school address through Google Earth).
70. M. Klonsky and S. Klonsky, *Small Schools*, 15.
71. See, for example, the videos of his talks posted on the Schumacher Society's YouTube site, http://www.youtube.com/user/Efssociety. Schumacher was an influential thinker; in 1995 the *London Times Literary Supplement* put *Small is Beautiful* on its list of the 100 most influential books published since 1945.
72. R. Williams, *The Politics of Modernism* (London: Verso, 1989), 38.
73. H. Adams, *The Education of Henry Adams*, http://www.bartleby.com/159/5.html; S. Aronowitz, *Against Schooling: And for an Education that Matters* (Boulder and London: Paradigm Publishers, 2008); P. Goodman, *Compulsory Miseducation* (New York: Horizon Press, 1962); N. Postman, *The End of Education* (New York: Knopf, 1996).
74. This insight motivates progressive reform, of course.
75. Cf. "small by design" in V. Lee and D. Ready, "The Schools-Within-Schools Reform."
76. See, for example, D. Cohen, *Teaching Practice: Plus ça Change*, (East Lansing, MI: National Center for Research on Teacher Education, 1988), ERIC no. ED299257; H. Kliebard, *The Struggle for the American Curriculum, 1893–1958*, 2nd ed. (New York: Routledge, 1995).
77. Gates Foundation, *All Students Ready for College, Career, and Life.*

78. Contact the authors for a full list and consult Howley (2002) for a synthesis of well-grounded empirical findings related to school size. C. Howley. "Small Schools." In *School Reform Proposals: The Research Evidence*, 49–77. Greenwich, CT: Information Age Publishing, 2002.
79. For one synthesis, see Howley (2002). C. Howley. "Small Schools." In *School Reform Proposals: The Research Evidence*, 49–77. Greenwich, CT: Information Age Publishing, 2002.
80. J. Greene, "The Effect of Residential School Choice on Public High School Graduation Rate," *Peabody Journal of Education* 18, no. 1 (2006): 203–16.
81. M. Klonsky and S. Klonsky, *Small Schools*.
82. J. Scott, *Seeing Like a State: How Certain Schemes to Improve the Human Condition Have Failed* (New Haven, CT: Yale University Press, 1998).
83. T. Wagner and T. Vander Ark, "A Critical Fork in the Road," 56.
84. Berry and West, using data on generations of American students, show substantial achievement and economic benefits accruing to students who, all else equal, attended smaller schools. Again, this is a correlational study. See C. Berry and M. West, *Growing Pains: The School Consolidation Movement and Student Outcomes* (Chicago: Harris School, University of Chicago, 2007).
85. We suspect that, especially in places like New York and Chicago—and maybe elsewhere—interest in 'small schools' (the reform package) will fade following the withdrawal of Gates Foundation money, but that interest in *smaller schools* will nonetheless endure for decades, since such interest is logically connected to the desire for humanly scaled institutions.
86. J.-F. Lyotard, *The Postmodern Condition: A Report on Knowledge* (Minneapolis, MN: University of Minnesota Press, 1979).
87. A. Howley and C. Howley, "Small Schools and the Pressure to Consolidate," *Education Policy Analysis Archives* 14, no. 10 (2006): 1–31.
88. See, for example, A. Howley and C. Howley, "The Transformative Challenge of Rural Context," *Educational Foundations* 14, no. 4 (2000): 73–85; T. E. Moriarty, "State Educational Policies and the Mission of Rural Community Schools" (paper presented at the Annual Northern Rocky Mountain Educational Research Association Meeting, Jackson Hole, WY, October 4–6, 1984); F. Yeo, "Thoughts on Rural Education: Reconstructing the Invisible and the Myths of Country Schooling," *Educational Foundations* 12, no. 2 (1998): 31–44.
89. See, for example, A. T. Roach and J. Frank, "Large-Scale Assessment, Rationality, and Scientific Management: The Case of No Child Left Behind," *Journal of Applied School Psychology* 23, no. 2 (2007): 7–25.
90. J. Bard, C. Gardener, and R. Wieland. "Rural School Consolidation: History, Research Summary, Conclusions, and Recommendations," *Rural Educator* 27, no. 2 (2006): 40–48.
91. B. Kent Lawrence, *Effects of State Policies on Facilities Planning and Construction in Rural Districts* (2001), ERIC no. ED459970, http://www.eric.ed.gov/ERICWebPortal/recordDetail?accno=ED459970 (accessed May 10, 2010).
92. J. Bard, C. Gardener, and R. Wieland. "Rural School Consolidation."
93. J. Scott, *Seeing Like a State*.
94. See, for example, M. Foucault, *Discipline and Punish: The Birth of the Prison* (New York: Pantheon Books, 1977).
95. See note 91.
96. See, for example, D. H. Monk, "Recruiting and Retaining High-Quality Teachers in Rural Areas," *Future of Children* 17, no. 1 (2007): 155–74.
97. See, for example, V. Lee and D. Ready, "The Schools-Within-Schools Reform."
98. Partnership for 21st Century Skills, *Results that Matter: 21st Century Skills and High School Reform* (Tucson, AZ: Author, 2006), 6, 9, http://www.21stcenturyskills.org/documents/RTM2006.pdf (accessed May 10, 2010).

7 Governing Identity through Neoliberal Education Initiatives

'Get[ting] Schooled' in the Marketplace

Leslee Grey

> Get Schooled is founded on the belief that our nation can be made stronger by educating the minds and improving the skills of every American.
>
> —Get Schooled[1]

INTRODUCTION

As the above quote from the Bill and Melinda Gates Foundation's website for one of its main educational initiative illustrates, business stakeholders and policy makers consider education to be a key space for engineering and maintaining public spheres, and as such are "central to the production of citizens."[2] Market-sponsored educational reform movements are but one of many everyday experiences that reflect the workings of techniques of neoliberal governing.[3] Under neoliberalism, educational goals, which were once understood as social and/or political, "are re-positioned within the domain of self-governance, often through techniques imposed by private institutions."[4] As Baez and Talburt posit, "techniques seeking to create self-government are the distinguishing feature of liberal governmental rationalities."[5]

In this chapter, I examine two of the Gates Foundation-funded education initiatives, the College-Ready Education Plan and Get Schooled, and analyze these initiatives as neoliberal projects that aim to direct the conduct of individuals. As Ong contends, neoliberalism is a technology[6] of governing that "relies on calculative choices and techniques in the domains of citizenship and of governing."[7] Situating educational initiatives within a framework of Foucault's notion of governmentality,[8] I foreground the ways in which market-sponsored programs such as the Gates Foundation's educational initiatives work to infuse market values into nearly every aspect of social life, which shifts the responsibility from the state or federal government onto the individual.[9] The foundation utilizes rationalities of neoliberal governance such as 'expert knowledge' to incite individuals to work on themselves and become certain types of citizens—specifically, self-reliant, self-governing, and entrepreneurial individuals whose rational choices and investments determine their citizenship.

QUALIFYING EDUCATION INITIATIVES AS GOVERNMENTAL

Clashes over education policy are not simply disputes over the most effective means to educate young people; they are disagreements over the shape and direction of society itself. The way that policy makers and community and business stakeholders battle over United States education is indicative of larger beliefs about what it means to be a responsible citizen, moral agent, and free and happy person. In other words, these narratives are not neutral. Conversations about education initiatives are rife with values that are unarticulated, ideology that is taken for granted, and rationalities that rely heavily on moralized assumptions. As Apple reminds us, behind all educational proposals are particular visions of which practices and policies best contribute to the making of a "just society and a good student."[10] Likewise, Popkewitz describes reform movements as embodying "salvation narratives about the moral sensibility, self-responsibility and self-motivation that enables the child to act as the democratic citizen-of-the-future."[11] Cruikshank contends that these narratives are governmental in that they "foreclose the ways in which is it possible to be a citizen." In other words, "citizens are not born; they are made"[12] in specific ways to serve specific interests.

Indeed, the logic and rationalities of educational reform movements "have a *moral* form," as Rose puts it, "insofar as they concern such issues as the . . . ideals or principles to which government should be addressed."[13] Apple posits that the "hidden effects . . . in the rhetoric and metaphors" of educational initiatives should be made visible.[14] The goal of this chapter is to highlight the underlying rationalities of the Gates Foundation's initiatives and to address the ways in which various *regimes of truth*[15] act as "mechanisms of governance" that work to "form identities, create political subjects, and produce knowledge and truths."[16] In Foucauldian terms, a regime of truth, for example, *the* official way to characterize the goals of education, becomes a "done deal"[17] that represses other possibilities. Following Ball, neoliberal education initiatives are justified through already established truths such as the regime of standards, accountability, entrepreneurial culture, and privatization.[18] Analyzing neoliberal discourse through the lens of governmentality clarifies the connections between the use of such truths and the exercise of power that is used to control public discourses. Therefore, what is taken as common sense can and should be scrutinized in order to discover how discourses are shaped, enacted, and accepted.

Apple writes, "In neoliberalism the *state* seeks to create an individual who is an enterprising and competitive entrepreneur [my emphasis]."[19] Under the theory of governmentality, the concept of governing is not simply top-down control by the state. Rather, governing is concerned with "strategies whereby norms, designed to regulate populations and individuals, are discursively generated through 'expert knowledges' and deployed through multiple institutions."[20] In this view, governing power does not originate from a centralized state; rather, it is "comprised of a broad repertoire of technologies"[21] or rationalities that operate across the boundaries of public and private, state and market. Thus, *government* refers not solely to policies and practices of the state but to, as Baez and Talburt posit, "the ways in which not only the state (formal or political government) but myriad institutions . . . seek to guide, shape, or affect the conduct of individuals . . . *and* the ways individuals govern themselves and their actions."[22]

The lens of governmentality clarifies the ways in which neoliberal policies and practices regulate the behavior of individuals. Ong describes governmentality as "the array of knowledges and techniques that are concerned with the systematic and pragmatic guidance and regulation of everyday conduct."[23] As such, it is the 'art of government' or the "conduct of conduct."[24] Through this "governing mentality," institutionally appointed experts create regimes of truth that regulate individuals' identities in a normative process of becoming good global citizens. As Marshall puts it, governmentality is "a form of activity which attempts or aims at the conduct of persons . . . to affect not only the conduct of people but also the attempt to constitute people in such ways that they can be governed."[25] Furthermore, this governance is accomplished through particular rationalities that "address themselves specifically to the shaping of conduct, and are directed at making particular forms of reality thinkable and practicable."[26]

I examine the specific political rationalities or 'technologies' these initiatives use and show how they are deployed through particular tactics that forge links between schooling, youth culture, and the marketplace. "Technologies of the self," according to Foucault, are the tools by which individuals constitute themselves. Attention to these technologies foregrounds the ways in which "everyday routines" are "linked up with major political objectives,"[27] thereby "solidifying what is possible to think, say, do, and be."[28] Technologies of the self allow individuals to work on themselves by regulating their bodies, behavior, and thoughts; they are the practices by which subjects constitute themselves. After briefly introducing two of the Gates Foundation's initiatives, I analyze several of the technologies employed by these programs to "conduct the conduct" of young people, allowing them to become empowered, self-reliant, entrepreneurial and "responsible future citizens."[29] I analyze the initiatives of the Gates Foundation as governmental[30] projects that direct behavior in particular ways and through specific techniques and rationalities; namely, by appealing to expert knowledge to circulate commonsense notions of responsibility, freedom, and citizenship that entice the individual to govern his or her 'self.'

THE GATES FOUNDATION'S GOVERNMENTAL INITIATIVES

As chairman of Microsoft and one of the world's wealthiest people, Bill Gates has become the face of the new era of knowledge-based global economics. Thus, it is no surprise that Gates applies the same marketplace logic responsible for Microsoft's near-monopolist success to his philanthropic endeavors. As one of the largest private foundations in the world, the Gates Foundation is involved in a multitude of international philanthropic activities. For example, in Africa and Latin America, the foundation is working to bring banks and ATMs to underserved populations, thereby creating new markets for its products and investors.[31] Couched in terms of economic development and even human rights, the introduction of banking technology is said to help "the poor" "climb out of poverty."[32] The presence of banks encourages individuals to develop good habits by saving and depositing money. Moreover, if these new customers deposit money on a fixed schedule, the diligent savers will receive higher interest rates on their savings accounts than those who only sporadically make deposits.[33] The message here is to encourage individuals to adopt the good habit of regular saving. Such behavior will allow individuals to take charge of their own well-being and to make rational decisions, to transform themselves into responsible, modern citizens. This example illuminates how the rational choices of the individual become connected to the welfare of the population and to the improvement of its condition in such areas as modernization and accumulation of wealth.[34] The Gates Foundation provides the *opportunity* or the *choice* for the individual to build wealth; it is up to the individual to make the correct choices (or adopt the good habits) to do so.

In the United States, the Gates Foundation focuses almost exclusively on public school reform. Just a few years ago, guided by the notion that public schools were 'failing' because they were too large and unmanageable, Gates turned his attention to breaking large secondary schools into smaller, more manageable and more easily controlled units. This reform, Gates argued at the time, would correct the failures of public education and result in more 'effective' schools, better workers, and a more robust economy. Doing its part to help downsize schools, the Gates Foundation pledged to contribute $375 million toward small-school reform. Only when Gates abandoned this initiative because it failed to raise test scores[35] did the foundation turn its focus to postsecondary education. In the following section, I outline the College-Ready Education Plan and Get Schooled, two of the Gates Foundation's main initiatives for secondary and postsecondary schooling, respectively. I foreground the ways in which these initiatives use certain governmental techniques of neoliberalism to forge links with political objectives and direct the behavior of individuals.

THE COLLEGE-READY EDUCATION PLAN AND GET SCHOOLED

As of late 2009, the Gates Foundation's website features two main education initiatives: the College-Ready Education Plan,[36] with a mission of "ensuring that a high school education should result in *college readiness* [my emphasis]";[37] and the Get Schooled[38] program, which focuses on postsecondary education (college and vocational training). Both of these programs claim that "postsecondary education should result in a degree or certificate with *genuine economic value* [my emphasis]."[39] It is important to note that the phrases *college readiness* and *genuine economic value* are intentionally left unexplained and unqualified. Such vague catchphrases as these are repeated so often that they are taken as commonsense "truths," a tactic that hides the overarching ideologies beneath them. In the following sections, I identify several of the techniques that the Gates Foundation's initiatives use to constitute the identities of teachers and young people and then to govern themselves. The concept of governmentality prompts critical reflection of not only overarching policies but also the everyday choices that individuals make and the behaviors in which they engage. Using the Foucauldian notion of governmentality, I identify the techniques or rationalities these initiatives mobilize in order to direct the conduct of individuals to specific ends. These techniques direct the attitudes and behaviors that individuals must adopt for themselves in order for neoliberalism to 'work.'

GOVERNING THE CLASSROOM

The Gates Foundation's College-Ready Education Plan utilizes several governing techniques or strategies such as evidence, standards, accountability, partnerships, and empowerment to govern teachers and classroom practices. In the following section, I summarize the online materials for the College-Ready program and highlight the logic that underlies this initiative, then discuss how these rationalities are mobilized for specific ends.

The Technique of Expertise and Evidence

The Gates Foundation describes its initiative for secondary education, the College-Ready Education Plan, as striving to increase high-school graduation rates and to prepare young people for postsecondary training. Couched in terms of "rais[ing] expectations and achievement of all students nationwide," this plan supports "public-private partnerships with school districts and state governments" with the intention of "working to ensure that schools and government define and measure graduation and college-readiness rates in similar ways." In other words, the Gates Foundation supports national standards "so that students in Massachusetts will learn the same key skills as students in Mississippi." The Gates Foundation website states that "alignment from state houses to schoolhouses" is necessary to "ensure that the work teachers and students do is totally focused on what is required" for students to pass tests, graduate, and then move on to the next step: postsecondary training in the form of college or vocational schooling. In order to "measure progress accurately," states the Gates Foundation website, a standardized, national curriculum would provide a "universal way" to keep track of achievements and failures (measured in standardized test scores), as well as a way to hold teachers accountable for student achievement and matriculation.

As market ideology has increased its stranglehold on public policy over the past few decades, parents, politicians, and business leaders have increasingly demanded accountability from teachers in schools; they want to be assured that they are getting their 'money's worth' from publicly funded education. Learning is focused on outcomes, as education is measured in inputs and outputs and standardized via test scores so that each school and each student can be ranked.[40] Market-influenced reforms use the tools for which the private sector can take credit; namely, the strategic use of data through technology and standards.[41] The Gates Foundation describes its strategy "to define more clearly the skills that lead to college readiness," thereby deciding what makes a young person successful, self-reliant, and worthy. The end goal is greater accountability to parents, taxpayers, and ultimately, to the marketplace.

As the Gates Foundation's online materials state, "we need better data," and "we need evidence" to "measure teacher effectiveness" and to "fairly and accurately identify effective teaching" that will allow the creation of "a profession centered on evidence."[42] Reading more like an advertisement for a database management system than an education initiative, the Gates Foundation states that it will "support the design and roll-out of better data systems to measure progress in each classroom, so teachers and students know whether classroom practices are working and so we can evaluate our investments."

These initiatives utilize expert knowledge "to manage the choices of individual citizens."[43] The foundation claims to have come to these initiatives empirically after having "studied and evaluated research in the field." For all its emphasis on evidence, the foundation only references research from the Manhattan Institute for Public Policy (a conservative, market-oriented think tank),[44] ACT (formerly American College Testing, creators of the standardized college-entry exam of the same name), Achieve (which receives funding from the Gates Foundation), and other private institutions such as the international accounting and consulting firm Deloitte.[45] Using this "evidence" and "data" (processed with "new technology products and platforms" created, in all probability, by Microsoft) will allow the foundation to "go deeper in our investments," "accelerate our investments," and identify "clearer standards that define a ladder to college readiness," according to the Gates Foundation website.

The Logic of Empowerment: Choice and Freedom

The language the Gates Foundation employs frames 'accountability' in the classroom and school in terms of 'partnering' with or 'empowering' teachers and students with data-gathering programs. The rhetoric of a partnership implies equality among colleagues, when the reality here is that teachers and students under constant surveillance by panoptic[46] technology end up policing their own behavior. As Baez and Talburt posit, "neoliberal rationality positions subjects as actors who are 'free to' and 'responsible for' the administration of their own lives."[47] These initiatives construct the idea of 'choice' as though it gives teachers and administrators more freedom and autonomy. However, what are considered acceptable classroom practices will have already been decided (standardization) and enforced through evaluation (surveillance) of teachers' performances through Microsoft data systems. Thus, what counts as knowledge and effective teaching and learning in the classroom is already being defined and governed in particular ways.

Governmentality involves regulation and administration of individual behavior, enforcing rules that are backed up through punishment, such as the firing of teachers whose classes fail to meet 'standards.' In other words, while these initiatives carry the pretense of freedom and partnerships, they are actually quite coercive, as teachers bear the responsibility for the successes or failures of their students. In fact, the Gates Foundation aims to take professional freedom away from teachers, as these initiatives do not recognize teachers as experts in their own fields. For example, the foundation calls for "putting" teachers on a "positive career path." As the foundation's website states, "We spend billions of dollars paying teachers for earning masters [*sic*] degrees that, except in the case of math and science, have shown no positive relationship with student-learning gains." The foundation supplies no specific reference or link to any study that would provide evidence for this conclusion. The meaning is obvious; because the foundation sees no direct return on investment, as measured by test scores, taxpayers should not be responsible for paying for teachers' academic and professional development.

To summarize, the high school initiative College-Readiness utilizes governmental techniques such as expertise and accountability to direct the behavior of teachers, going so far as to define for them which professional development (i.e., master's degrees) should and should not be supported by the public. By controlling the discourse of what makes an effective teacher, these initiatives are essentially controlling what it means to be a teacher. In the following section, I turn my focus onto initiatives that aim to govern the behavior and identities of students.

GOVERNING THE STUDENT: THE ENTREPRENEURIAL SELF

According to the Gates Foundation's online materials, "less than 25 percent of minority young people are prepared for college, at tremendous cost to themselves and to society." The site states that the foundation "believes that every life has equal value and each individual should have the opportunity to live up to his or her potential."[48] Indeed, as Hamann makes clear, "all neoliberal subjects are presumed 'equal' and 'free.' "[49] With this commonsense notion of equality—a level playing field—neoliberalism attributes economic disparity to "failures of *individual* choice and responsibility."[50] If the individual does not succeed, it is due to her own moral failure. The Gates Foundation contends that "education is the great equalizer." The foundation's online text reads: "It enriches our lives, informs our choices, and prepares us for meaningful employment and to contribute to the communities in which we live." Evoking equality, freedom, choice, and responsibility, such discourse instills a paradoxical notion of a 'community of individuals,' the idea that we are all in this together, but we each take care of ourselves.

The Logic of Good Habits

The logic of the Gates Foundation's initiatives stresses individualism and an enterprising self, whereby the self is constructed much like a business with an inherent tendency toward constant self-improvement and increasing success. For example, as the foundation's website states, "Transforming the motivation and engagement of students is essential to accelerating their academic performance." This transformation takes place by encouraging young people to see themselves as free and responsible to act on their own well-being.[51] Responsibility and success are framed in terms of taking control of one's life and defining and achieving one's goals. An array of knowledges and expert systems act on individuals so that they will optimize their choice and more efficiently compete in ever-changing market conditions. "Such techniques of optimization" writes Ong, "include the adherence to health regimes, acquisition of skills, development of entrepreneurial ventures, and other techniques of self-engineering and capital accumulation."[52]

Through the strategic use of expert knowledge, the Gates Foundation initiatives control the forms of knowledge that are valuable; such knowledges are then passed to individuals, encouraging/enabling them to govern themselves. Neoliberalism privileges self-regulation, rationality, enlightenment, and individualism. As Sharland puts it, "The individual is invested with moral responsibility, guided by experts to make rational choices over lifestyle, body and mind."[53] The foundation's site states, "We will invest in helping students develop the *habits* that research has found are tied to improved academic performance and greater college readiness [my emphasis]." Individuals then constitute themselves by "inculcating desires for self-development that expertise itself can guide."[54] In order to reduce direct responsibility for its citizens, neoliberal governing entities develop indirect techniques to control individuals without actually being responsible for them. By using the truth claims of expertise,[55] individuals learn the dangers of such social risks as unemployment or undereducation. With knowledge of risks, young people are then empowered to choose other options.

In other words, we need experts to help us accomplish what we cannot achieve on our own. Again, because this research was funded and/or conducted by the Gates Foundation, the foundation controls what is considered expert knowledge and thus controls the definition of good habits, although none of these habits is specified on the website.

The Logic of Freedom

The use of the term 'opportunity' carries with it notions of freedom, as these initiatives appear to foster individual freedom rather than coerce via force. However, as Baez and Talburt argue, the concept of "freedom" has no "essential content." Rather, "its meanings and manifestations are outcomes of their enactment of techniques and rationalities" meant to guide conduct. In other words, they write, " 'freedom' is constantly being rewritten to reflect the complementary and contradictory objectives among and between political, civic, and self-government."[56] Subjects "come to understand their actions as based on autonomous choice and freedom to act."[57] The notion of choices and freedoms entice the individual so that "all subjects govern themselves effectively," forging a seamless "continuity between the ideals of the state and the actions of citizens."[58] Consequently, all "individuals will, in turn, behave as they should."[59]

A rationality of an autonomous and responsible agent underlies the adoption of good habits, as it is the task of the individual student to buy into the American dream of the rugged individual making his or her own way. Neoliberal logic creates a "national citizen to embody an American narrative"[60] of self-reliance, individualism, and entrepreneurship. It is then the responsibility of the individual to conduct herself accordingly. After all, if all students were equal and all have been given every opportunity to succeed—and if education is the "great equalizer" that the Gates Foundation argues it is—then the individual student is solely responsible for her own choices and success. She must pull herself up by her bootstraps and shape her own destiny. If the student fails, it is no one's fault but her own because she has simply made bad choices. Thus, individuals learn the 'logic' that their decisions and choices help them reach their goals. Couched in terms of individualism is the 'challenge' for individuals to take charge of their bodies and lives. Such discourse reflects the notion that if individuals are just determined enough, they can accomplish anything. As Sharland argues, "the culture of individualism is an expression of the technology of governance that leaves young people feeling accountable for their own fates."[61]

Thus, central to these initiatives is a notion of responsibility. Schooling is a technique of neoliberal governance for creating independent and responsible future citizens, as these initiatives use the rhetoric, discourses, and practices that motivate individuals to "act on their own accord."[62] This is why neoliberalism can be described as a mode of 'governing through freedom.' Writes Ong, "neoliberal logic requires populations to be free, self-managing, and self-enterprising individuals" in various spheres of life.[63] Rather than being viewed as a citizen with claim on the state, the neoliberal subject is a "self-enterprising citizen-subject who is obligated to become an 'entrepreneur of himself or herself.'"[64]

TECHNIQUES OF YOUTH CULTURE: RIGHTS, CHOICES, AND RESPONSIBILITIES

Another powerful technique the Gates Foundation employs in its vision of education reform is its appeal to youth culture. In partnership with entertainment conglomerate Viacom, the Gates Foundation has produced a short film entitled *Get Schooled: You Have the Right* and its accompanying website.[65] According to the website, Get Schooled is a five-year initiative that "creates a platform for corporate and community stakeholders to address the challenges facing America's public schools."[66] It is important to note that no input is solicited from teachers here. The "Get Schooled national initiative aims to help find effective solutions to the problems facing America's education system" through, again, the power of expertise—the "foundation's deep knowledge of education reform" coupled with the "power of Viacom's diverse brands" to "provide information and solutions for students and their families." Linking together Viacom's brands with young people and education, the film *Get Schooled: You Have the Right* profiles young people who work for American Idol Kelly Clarkson, professional basketball player LeBron James, and President Obama in various capacities. The film highlights the educational paths that enabled these workers to attain their jobs. Although these celebrities surely appeal to young people, their success stories bear little resemblance to those of most students. Furthermore, it is rather ironic that *Get Schooled* features Clarkson and James in its film as neither celebrity received any postsecondary education, and in high school, James unsuccessfully petitioned to drop out to become a professional basketball player. These are hardly role models for postsecondary education. This technique, however, is not about appealing to role models; rather, it involves appealing to youth culture to direct behavior toward particular ends. By forging links between entertainment and education (after all, the conglomerate Viacom is the parent company of television networks MTV, VH1, Comedy Central, and CMT, as well as Paramount Studios), the initiative constructs its young audience, the target of these programs, not only as consumers but as *entitled* consumers: *You Have the Right*, reads the film's subtitle. It may as well read You Have the Right to All This Stuff. Airing on September 9, 2009 on all of Viacom's twenty-two networks simultaneously, "Get Schooled" is considered "the first programming 'roadblock' of any kind across of Viacom networks,"[67] meaning that the program had a nearly captive audience of cable viewers.

Get Schooled: You Have the Right conditions young people to desire goods, experiences, and lifestyles that mimic those of highly paid celebrities in the sports and entertainment industries. In order to be able to afford such a lifestyle, an individual must acquire 'credentials' and 'marketable skills' through postsecondary training. The Gates Foundation's education initiatives serve as *texts* that shape young people as *particular* kinds of self-regulating subjects who are able to 'choose' only particular identities in particular sorts of ways. Young peoples' identities are being shaped by limiting representations and 'choices' that serve other interests, which I will discuss further in the next section.

While the previously discussed high-school initiative claims that secondary education "should result in college readiness," this second initiative states that college (or postsecondary training) should result in a degree or certification or "credentials"[68] with "genuine economic value," equipping its owner with "skills" and "knowledge" to succeed in the twenty-first century. Other than a form letter by which to "Write Your Governor," the Get Schooled website offers little more than slogans, a contest for making and submitting your own "I Am What I Learn" video, and lists of jobs and the educational paths to those jobs. For instance, one may click on the job title "canned good inspector" and learn that "no high school diploma [is] necessary" and that the salary for such a job is minimum wage. One can only assume that this job listing and others like it (e.g., cashier) are only listed on the site to direct young people to more lucrative, higher-skilled career paths in the entertainment industry (e.g., cosmetologist or video game designer).

When young people are defined primarily as consumers and the only choices presented to them are consumeristic, they take up this subjectivity and choose subsequent consumer-oriented actions accordingly.[69] Sharland argues, "the culture of individualism is an expression of the technology of governance that leaves young people feeling accountable for their own fates."[70] The focus is squarely on the individual chooser. Focusing on youth as a target market for such programs discursively constitutes young people, meaning that through ideas, language, and behaviors, identities are assigned and assumptions are made about young people's responsibilities and the paths toward their 'future' citizenship.

I perused the Get Schooled website looking for ways that parents and students can get involved in their communities besides writing their governors with the handy form letter is supplied on the website. When I visited the link entitled "Get Involved," no ways to get involved were listed. I emailed the program inquiring about ways to get involved and received the following reply:

> Dear Leslee—
>
> Thank you for your interest in Get Schooled—an initiative, co-founded by the Bill & Melinda Gates Foundation and Viacom, to engage our

government and communities in rethinking and restructuring public education in the United States.

Get Schooled aims to build a national platform that connects, inspires and mobilizes people—from policymakers and corporate leaders to educators and kids. Over the next five years, we will be counting on individuals like you to take action and help find effective solutions to the challenges facing our education system.

Activities and ways to get involved will be featured on GetSchooled.com, the online gateway we are developing to help engage people and connect resources. Please check back in the next couple of months to find ways you can make a difference in your local community.

Sincerely,

Get Schooled[71]

The Gates Foundation's reliance on individuals like me (rather than a centralized state or federal government) to "restructure public schools" echoes a technique of neoliberal governance "that centers on the capacity and potential of individuals and the population as living resources that may be harnessed and managed by governing regimes."[72] The Gates Foundation views me and other individuals who peruse its website as resources to further its cause. The request that I check back in the next couple of months to find ways that I can make a difference in my community places the responsibility back on me to continue my active citizenship.

GOVERNING CITIZENSHIP: NATION BUILDING AND THE MARKET

I return to the quote at the beginning of this essay: "Get Schooled is founded on the belief that our nation can be made stronger by educating the minds and improving the skills of every American."[73] The links between public education and the state of the nation are nothing new. The 1983 report *A Nation at Risk*[74] claims that U.S. public education compares unfavorably with schools from other advanced countries, which threatens not only the U.S. economy but the nation at large. Like the Gates Foundation's education initiatives, this report is not backed by substantiated research although its claims continue to influence policy.[75] Thus, the general public, including parents as well as school leaders, accept this link between education and the economy as fact, so much so that proof of such a crisis has not been necessary because it has become a "naturalized" way of thinking.[76] There is little questioning of these ideas by mainstream news media, national leaders, or by a significant portion of the public. Like "A Nation at Risk," the Gates Foundation links the "failures" of public education to the United States' economic performance in the global marketplace: "In the near and long term, this situation compromises our ability to compete effectively in a global economy—to produce young adults capable of taking on the demands of and succeeding in a twenty-first century workplace and democracy," the foundation's online materials read. Thus, successful education is linked to successful nation building. Failing at school is framed as a bad choice, linked with failing oneself, one's school, and one's country. The shame of failing is a significant motivating technique of governance, as the United States' success or failure in the global marketplace is shifted onto the individual citizen. Because the "nation-state" can no longer protect its currency or "generate real economic activity," as Torres points out, it is up to the "individual consumer" to become entrepreneurial and self-reliant to "drive the expansion and operation of the global economy."[77] Hamann refers to this kind of citizen as a "Neoliberal *Homo economicus*," a "free and autonomous 'atom' of self-interest who is fully responsible for . . . using rational choice and cost-benefit calculation *to the express exclusion* of all other values and interests."[78] Business rhetoric redefines citizenship and freedom as the widening of opportunity to enter into global economic competition. The Gates Foundation presents its initiatives 'commonsensically' as simply meeting the challenges of a contemporary, high-tech world with global business practices.

While all education initiatives are governmental in the sense that they aim to direct the conduct of individuals, neoliberal educational initiatives construct the citizen-subject as "an individual who is morally responsible for navigating the social realm using rational choice and cost-benefit calculations grounded on market-based principles to the exclusion of all other ethical values and social interests."[79] Equality has been redefined as the right to enter into free competition. (However, as Bill Gates' involvement in numerous antitrust litigations attests, the social, economic, and cultural advantage of some means that the competition can never be absolutely 'fair.') These governing technologies work not through force but by encouraging the individual to align her personal goals with those of the nation. As these techniques become understood as common sense, "individuals volunteer themselves to them."[80]

Again, the application of neoliberal technologies of governance to schooling is not a new development in education initiatives. During the 2004 presidential debates, George W. Bush exposed what a number of scholars argue is the economic impetus of the reform when he stated that "No Child Left Behind is really a jobs act, when you think about it."[81] And as then Secretary of Education Rod Paige remarked: "If we can improve the educational system, we can improve the corporate bottom line."[82] More recently, President Obama agreed that students should be trained with the skills necessary to join the workforce. On the U.S. Department of Education's website, Obama's education talking points include: "After graduating high school, all Americans should be prepared to attend at least one year of job training or higher education to better equip our workforce for the twenty-first century economy."[83] The guiding logic behind President Obama's education initiative, the Race to the Top Fund, is clear: "Adopting standards and assessments that prepare students to succeed in college and the workplace and to compete in the global economy" and "building data systems that measure student growth and success, and inform teachers and principals about how they can improve instruction"[84] are his top priorities. This language could have just as likely been lifted directly from the Gates Foundation website. The assumption is that there are numerous jobs just waiting for the right (highly skilled) graduate. Unemployment, goes the commonsense thinking, is really just a problem with the individual worker/student; if only schools did a better job educating children to be better prepared for the workplace, then the economy would work itself out. Following a business model, the way to make education better is through assessment, or standardized testing, which increases responsibility, accountability, and governance of teachers and administrators.

CONCLUSION

Corporate philanthropies such as the Gates Foundation have long adopted education reform and applied market-influenced solutions such as standards and accountability initiatives to identify and fix what, in their view, is wrong with public schools. Some analysts hold that reforms based on market ideology support an agenda to end all government participation in education.[85] Spring argues that the preparation of students for the ever-changing workplace has emerged as public education's single most important goal. Education is evaluated purely as an economic investment. He explains that, differing from the laissez-faire traditions of the nineteenth century, neoliberalism "calls for government intervention to promote and protect free markets."[86] These ideas coincide with the free market's self-promotional campaign to "establish itself as the true provider of equity and opportunity in the 'objective' realm of capital, and to provide so-called objective 'proof' of public sector failure."[87] Schools exist for market purposes.

Using the lens of governmentality, we can explore the technologies through which power is exercised, question the foundations on which neoliberal policies are based,[88] and understand the techniques by which citizens are made governable. I have highlighted the ways in which governing forces work on young people through expert knowledges that constitute not only what is considered normal and desirable behavior, but also what are considered reasonable choices, good citizenship, and rational and responsible citizens. Because they are devised and implemented by so-called experts, such educational initiatives embody structures that define and order what counts as 'normal.' They reflect social practices of dominant, normalizing groups and can be read as guides to success. As Popkewitz argues, the subject assumed and created through neoliberal strategies "embodies and normalizes particular characteristics and dispositions" that qualify some for and disqualify others from civic action and participation.[89] Likewise, Pykett points out that governmental power shapes particular regimes of truth by allowing particular behaviors in forbidding others.[90] In other words, certain people, those who are normatively rational and reasonable, are able to participate while others are excluded. In this way "obligations of citizenship are established."[91] The lens of governmentality illuminates the power of language and demonstrates the ways in which forces enacting power (various societal forces and state agendas) control the conversation to construct, package, and sell commonsense understandings of education and citizenship. Neoliberal education initiatives, such as those of the Gates Foundation, presuppose certain truths by structuring the possibilities for citizenship. Pykett contends, "*de jure* freedoms within liberal democracies do not translate automatically into practical citizenship rights."[92]

Within a framework of Foucault's work on governmentality, lifestyle choices must be regulated by experts in a normative process. Neoliberal education initiatives can be read as texts that shape readers as *particular* kinds of self-regulating subjects who are able to 'choose' only particular identities in particular sorts of ways. The individual is invested with moral responsibility to make choices that benefit the economy and the nation. Gates Foundation initiatives discursively constitute individuals, as identities are assigned and assumptions are made not only about individuals but also about larger social and political responsibilities and behaviors.

NOTES

1. Get Schooled website, http://www.getschooled.com/about (accessed December 20, 2009).
2. R. Lukose, "Empty Citizenship: Protesting Politics in the Era of Globalization," *Cultural Anthropology* 20, no. 4 (2005): 506.
3. See also C. Vander Schee, "The Politics of Health as a School-Sponsored Ethnic," *Educational Policy* 22, no. 6 (2008); B. Baez and S. Talburt, "Governing for Responsibility and with Love: Parents and Children between Home and School," *Educational Theory* 58, no. 1 (2008); K. Mitchell, "Educating the National Citizen in Neoliberal Times: From the Multicultural Self to the Strategic Cosmopolitan," *Transactions of the Institute of British Geographers* 28, 2003.
4. T. H. Hamann, "Neoliberalism, Governmentality, and Ethics," *Foucault Studies* 6 (2009): 40.
5. B. Baez and S. Talburt, "Governing for Responsibility and with Love," 39.
6. Following Olssen, I use 'technology' or 'technique' to refer to the means by which policies are devised and implemented. See M. Olssen, *Michel Foucault: Materialism and Education* (Westport, CT: Bergin and Garvey, 2006).
7. A. Ong, *Neoliberalism as Exception: Mutations in Citizenship and Sovereignty* (Durham, NC: Duke University Press, 2006), 4.
8. For the purposes of this chapter, I use the term 'governmentality' to stand for the 'conduct of conduct.' For an extensive explanation of Foucault's

notion of governmentality, see N. Rose, *Governing the Soul: The Shaping of the Private Self* (London: Routledge, 1990); A. Barry, T. Osborne, and N. Rose, eds., *Foucault and Political Reason: Liberalism, Neo-Liberalism, and Rationalities of Government* (Chicago: University of Chicago Press, 1996); C. Gordon, "Governmental Rationality: An Introduction," in *The Foucault Effect: Studies in Governmentality*, ed. G. Burchell, C. Gordon, and P. Miller (Chicago: University of Chicago Press, 1991).
9. T. Hamann, "Neoliberalism, Governmentality, and Ethics," 41.
10. M. Apple, "Comparing Neo-Liberal Projects and Inequality in Education," *Comparative Education* 37, no. 4 (2001): 414.
11. T. Popkewitz, "Pacts/Partnerships and Governing the Parent and Child," *Current Issues in Comparative Education* 3, no. 2 (2002): 122.
12. B. Cruikshank, *The Will to Power* (Ithaca, NY: Cornell Press, 1999), 5.
13. N. Rose, "Governing 'Advanced' Liberal Democracies," in *Foucault and Political Reason: Liberalism, Neo-Liberalism and Rationalities of Government* (see note 8), 40.
14. M. Apple, "Comparing Neo-Liberal Projects and Inequality in Education," 413.
15. M. Foucault, *Power/Knowledge*, ed. C. Gordon, (New York: Pantheon Books, 1980), 131.
16. C. Vander Schee, "The Politics of Health As a School-Sponsored Ethnic," 857.
17. J. Pykett, "Making Citizens Governable? The Crick Report as Governmental Technology," *Journal of Education Policy* 22, no. 3 (2007): 316.
18. S. Ball, *Education Reform: A Critical and Post-Structrual Approach* (Buckingham: Open University Press, 1994), 22.
19. M. Apple, "Comparing Neo-Liberal Projects and Inequality in Education," 414.
20. E. Sharland, "Young People, Risk Taking, and Risk Making: Some Thoughts for Social Work," *Forum: Qualitative Social Research* 7, no. 1 (2006).
21. M. Dahlstedt, "Democratic Governmentality: National Imagination, Popular Movements and Governing the Citizen," *Journal for Critical Education Policy Studies* 7, no. 2 (2009): 3. www.jceps.com. Accessed December 19, 2009.
22. B. Baez and S. Talburt, "Governing for Responsibility and with Love," 28.
23. A. Ong, *Neoliberalism as Exception*, 4.
24. C. Gordon, "Governmental Rationality."
25. J. Marshall, "Foucault and Neo-Liberalism: Biopower and Busno-Power," http://www.ed.uiuc.edu/EPS/PES-Yearbook/95_docs/marshall.html (accessed November 12, 2009).
26. B. Baez and S. Talburt, "Governing for Responsibility and with Love," 28.
27. Ibid., 30.
28. B. Cruikshank, *The Will to Power*, 2.
29. B. Baez and S. Talburt, "Governing for Responsibility and with Love," 32.
30. When referring to state government in the traditional sense, I will use the phrases 'federal government' or 'state government.' Otherwise I will use 'government' in the Foucauldian sense.
31. See http://www.gatesfoundation.org/financialservicesforthepoor/Pages/default.aspx (accessed August 16, 2010).
32. K. Kuehner-Hebert, "Gates Foundation Grants Spur Savings by the Poor," *American Banker* 2009. Despite Gates' humanitarian focus on "the poor," Hamann points out that "neoliberal rationality allows for the avoidance of any kind of collective, structural, or [state] governmental responsibility" for lives. "Instead," he writes, "impoverished populations, when recognized

at all, are often treated as 'opportunities' for investment." See T. Hamann, "Neoliberalism, Governmentality, and Ethics," 44.

33. K. Kuehner-Hebert, "Gates Foundation Grants Spur Savings by the Poor."
34. J. Joseph, "Governmentality of What? Populations, States and International Organisations," *Global Society* 23, no. 4 (2009).
35. See the full text of Gates' November 11, 2008 speech at the Gates Foundation website, http://www.gatesfoundation.org/speeches-commentary/Pages/bill-gates-2008-education-forum-speech.aspx (accessed May 5, 2009).
36. Gates Foundation, http://www.gatesfoundation.org/learning/Pages/college-ready-education-plan.aspx (last accessed December 20, 2009).
37. Gates Foundation, http://www.gatesfoundation.org/topics/Pages/high-schools.aspx# (accessed May 9, 2009).
38. Get Schooled, http://www.getschooled.com/ (last accessed December 20, 2009).
39. Gates Foundation, http://www.gatesfoundation.org/united-states/pages/program-overview.aspx (last accessed December 20, 2009).
40. L. Trammell, "Measuring, Fixing, Filling and Drilling: The ExxonMobil Agenda for Education," in *Schools or Markets? Commercialism, Privatization, and School-Business Partnerships*, ed. Deron R. Boyles (Mahwah, NJ: Lawrence Erlbaum Associates, Inc, 2005).
41. E. Shaker, "Privatizing Schools: Democratic Choice or Market Demand," *Education, Limited* 1, no. 3: ii, http://www.policyalternatives.ca/sites/default/files/uploads/publications/National_Office_Pubs/edultd3.pdf (accessed December 20, 2009).
42. The appeal to 'evidence' and 'scientifically-based' research gained momentum in the sweeping education reform initiative the No Child Left Behind Act (NCLB), which George W. Bush signed into law with bipartisan support in January 2002. NCLB set into place national standards of accountability by which public schools would be measured as a condition of receiving federal funds.
43. G. Tait, *Youth, Sex, and Government* (New York: Peter Lang, 2000), 68.
44. As Kovacs and Christie point out, the Gates Foundation and the think tanks it supports are responsible for marketing policy reports to politicians. Though underresearched, these reports are circulated and cited to the extent that they become commonsense understanding of the workings of public schools. See, for example, P. Kovacs and H.K. Christie, "The Gates' Foundation and the Future of U.S. Public Education: A Call for Scholars to Counter Misinformation Campaigns," *Journal for Critical Education Policy Studies* 6, no. 2 (2008).
45. The Deloitte 2009 Education Survey can be accessed at http://www.deloitte.com (accessed August 16, 2010).
46. See M. Foucault, *Discipline and Punish: The Birth of the Prison* (New York: Vintage Books, 1995), 195–228.
47. B. Baez and S. Talburt, "Governing for Responsibility and with Love," 40.
48. Gates Foundation, http://www.gatesfoundation.org/learning/Documents/postsecondary-education-success-plan-executive-summary.pdf (accessed December 19, 2009).
49. T. Hamann, "Neoliberalism, Governmentality, and Ethics," 50.
50. Ibid.
51. W. Larner, "Neo-Liberalism: Policy, Ideology, Governmentality," *Studies in Political Economy* 63 (2000).
52. A. Ong, *Neoliberalism as Exception*, 6.
53. E. Sharland, "Young People, Risk Taking, and Risk Making," 255.
54. N. Rose, *Powers of Freedom: Reframing Political Thought* (Cambridge: Cambridge University Press, 1999), 88.

55. N. Rose, "Government, Authority and Expertise in Advanced Liberalism," *Economy and Society* 22, no. 3 (1993): 285.
56. B. Baez and S. Talburt, "Governing for Responsibility and with Love," 41.
57. Ibid., 29.
58. Ibid.
59. K. Mitchell, "Educating the National Citizen in Neoliberal Times," 397 (see note 3).
60. B. Baez and S. Talburt, "Governing for Responsibility and with Love," 33.
61. E. Sharland, "Young People, Risk Taking, and Risk Making," 6.
62. B. Baez and S. Talburt, "Governing for Responsibility and with Love," 41.
63. A. Ong, *Neoliberalism as Exception*, 14.
64. Ibid.
65. All references to online and website materials in this section can be found at the Get Schooled website, http://www.getschooled.com (accessed October 1, 2009).
66. Ibid.
67. Gates Foundation, "Television Event *Get Schooled: You Have the Right Premieres* September 8th Simultaneously Across All Viacom U.S. Networks" (press release, 2009) http://www.gatesfoundation.org/press-releases/Pages/get-schooled-event-090813.aspx (accessed December 20, 2009).
68. As the initiative does not differentiate significantly between college education and postsecondary training (i.e., community college or proprietary vocational schooling), the Gates Foundation and its Get Schooled website uses the terms 'degree' and 'credentials' interchangeably.
69. J. D. Marshall, "Foucault and Neo-Liberalism."
70. E. Sharland, 255.
71. Personal email communication, October 5, 2009. I checked the website again in December 2009, but a listing of ways to get involved locally was still nonexistent.
72. A. Ong, *Neoliberalism as Exception*, 6.
73. Get Schooled, http://www.getschooled.com/about (last accessed December 20, 2009).
74. U.S. Commission on Excellence in Education, *A Nation at Risk: The Imperative for Educational Reform*, (Washington, D.C.: Author, 1983).
75. D. Berliner and B. Biddle, *The Manufactured Crisis* (Reading, MA: Addison-Wesley, 1995).
76. L. Trammell, "Measuring, Fixing, Filling and Drilling."
77. C. Torres, "Globalization, Education, and Citizenship: Solidarity Versus Markets?" *American Educational Research Journal* 39, no. 2 (2002): 367.
78. T. Hamann, "Neoliberalism, Governmentality, and Ethics," 38.
79. Ibid., 37.
80. B. Baez and S. Talburt, "Governing for Responsibility and with Love," 35.
81. Presidential debate transcript (Commission on Presidential Debates, October 13, 2004), http://www.debates.org/index.php?page=october-13-2004-debate-transcript (accessed August 16, 2010).
82. "Paige Discusses Education and the Role of Business in Improving Minority Employment Opportunities," U.S. Department of Education, September 23, 2004, http://www.ed.gov/news/speeches/2004/09/09232004.html (accessed September 10, 2009).
83. "Education," Organizing for America, http://www.barackobama.com/issues/education/index.php (accessed December 26, 2009).
84. See the Race to the Top Fund website, http://www.ed.gov/programs/racetothetop/index.html (accessed December 26, 2009).
85. For example, see K. Saltman, *Collateral Damage* (Oxford: Rowman and Littlefield, 2000), 1–33.

86. Spring, J. Education and the Rise of the Global Economy (Mahwah, NJ: Lawrence Erlbaum Associates, Inc., 1998) p.x.
87. E. Shaker, "Privatizing Schools: Democratic Choice or Market Demand," i (see note 41).
88. J. Pykett, "Making Citizens Governable," 315 (see note 14).
89. T. Popkewitz, "Pacts/Partnerships and Governing the Parent and Child," 123 (see note 11).
90. J. Pykett, "Making Citizens Governable," 313.
91. T. Popkewitz, "Pacts/Partnerships and Governing the Parent and Child," 124.
92. J. Pykett, "Making Citizens Governable," 317.

8 The Gates' Foundation and the Future of U.S. Public Education

A Call for Scholars to Counter Misinformation Campaigns*

Philip E. Kovacs and H.K. Christie

> America's high schools are obsolete . . . By obsolete, I don't just mean that our high schools are broken, flawed, and under-funded—though a case could be made for every one of those points. By obsolete, I mean that our high schools—even when they're working exactly as designed—cannot teach our kids what they need to know today . . . Training the workforce of tomorrow with the high schools of today is like trying to teach kids about today's computers on a fifty-year-old mainframe. It's the wrong tool for the times. Our high schools were designed fifty years ago to meet the needs of another age. Until we design them to meet the needs of the twenty-first century, we will keep limiting—even ruining—the lives of millions of Americans every year.
>
> —Bill Gates[1]

On February 26, 2005, governors, policy makers, and business leaders from across the nation met to discuss ways to prevent American students from falling behind their international competitors. The "National Summit on High Schools," sponsored by Achieve, marked the beginning of the conference, and Bill Gates was there to deliver the keynote address, wherein he made the above remarks. Since 1999 Achieve has received $10,921,771 from the Gates Foundation in order to "help states align secondary school math expectations with the demands of postsecondary education and work," as well as assistance for encouraging "specific states to adopt high school graduation requirements that align with college entry requirements."[2]

Indeed, the Gates Foundation has spent over $3 billion influencing American public schools, and while the donations seem laudable on some fronts, especially in an era of increased federal demands coupled with reduced federal spending, his philanthropy remains problematic. When corporate leaders shape government institutions according to their needs, countries move away from democracy and toward corporatism, a relative of, and arguably a precursor to, fascism. This chapter is no place for a complete analysis of American democracy and fascism writ large, and we believe scholars have made a compelling case for keeping corporate leaders out of our classrooms, as despite their "best" intentions, their ideology ultimately undermines the democracy our schools purportedly serve.[3] Corporations are out for corporations, whereas democratic citizens, ideally, are out for each other.

John Dewey, American philosopher and vocal critic of traditional public schools, defined democracy as a system of associated living where individuals participate in the institutions governing them.[4] In a democratic school system, parents, students, teachers, academics, and business leaders would participate in curricular decisions. Corporatism, on the other hand, requires citizen obedience to corporate demands; individual needs are ignored. In the case of U.S. public schools, CEOs have great influence on the curricula whereas parents have little to none. Individual students become products whose manufacture is subject to the whims of the market. As our society becomes more market based, we have seen stricter coordination between government and industry. This coordination often comes in the form of government-business partnerships, whereby elites from both groups decide how public institutions should be shaped and run. Ultimately, corporatism undermines the legitimacy of individual citizens and any possibility of democracy, as these elites, often unelected, make decisions for the people. This chapter problematizes the Bill and Melinda Gates Foundation's involvement with the reformation of U.S. public schools. Focusing on four organizations funded in part by the foundation, we use Chris Mooney's work on "political science abuse" to illuminate how corporate-funded think tanks and advocacy groups generate "spontaneous consent" for pro-corporate educational reform.[5] We then raise questions about the legitimacy of what these organizations say and do, with the hope that scholars will work to counter misinformation campaigns funded by corporate philanthropists such as Bill Gates.

NEOLIBERALISM AND PUBLIC EDUCATION

'Neoliberalism and public education' warrants a book of its own, and indeed there is no shortage of literature on the subject. We include a brief treatment here to help situate the activities of these four think tanks as part of an ongoing national movement to regulate and/or privatize public education. Neoliberals seek to create educational systems suited to increasing economic productivity.[6] Measuring productivity requires controlled conditions and repeated assessments, which exist today in the form of schools operating under a testing regime. Neoliberals use these tests as 'objective' proof that U.S. public schools are failing in a variety of ways. School failure, according to neoliberal logic, will result in America's loss of dominance in the global marketplace, a refrain started in the early 1980s when the neoliberal Reagan administration used *A Nation at Risk* to scare Americans into educational restructuring.[7] Indeed as we show later in this chapter, neoliberal educational reformers continue to employ fear as a tactic to drive educational change.[8]

Neoliberals believe that embracing free-market reforms will save America's schools.[9] Embarking on multiple media and political campaigns to color all schools failures (facilitated by a federal program that recently branded one out of three American schools as failing),[10] neoliberal educational reformers argue that parental choice will result in the best schools succeeding. Parents, informed through objective test scores (now available everywhere due to federal requirements), can select which schools they wish to support, and thus determine which schools survive in the market. "Public schools," explains the neoliberal Milton and Rose D. Friedman Foundation, "respond positively to competition."[11] There is no empirical evidence to support the Friedman Foundation's claim.

Despite their use of the word 'free,' neoliberals need a strong state to create and regulate markets,[12] and neoliberal reformers have been successful at using the state to meet their demands, working with local, state, and federal judicial and legislative bodies to force regulation and privatization on citizens who are, by most accounts, happy with their schools.[13] Once the market replaces the public, according to neoliberal reformers, the best schools—those with the highest test scores—will force the worst schools to shut down, and every American child will get a 'high-quality' education, which will ensure that America retains its status as a global economic superpower.

OVERVIEW OF THE FOUR ORGANIZATIONS

Examining each organization on the receiving end of Gates Foundation money is a project more suitable for a book than a chapter. Upon analyzing Gates Foundation records, we found 441 organizations received $3,369,942,557 for educational projects between 1999 and June 2007.[14] These organizations range from neoconservative think tanks such as the Thomas B. Fordham Foundation and the Manhattan Institute[15] to neoliberal think tanks such as the Education Trust and Education Sector. Gates Foundation money also went to various state departments,[16] public school districts,[17] and charter school organizations.[18] For this analysis, we chose four think tanks that used the mainstream media or testimony before Congress to forward their particular message. These organizations produce research and analysis, engage in state and national policy debate, and use the public sphere to promote neoliberal educational reconstruction. A brief examination of the individuals driving these organizations—and the language these individuals and organizations employ—will help clarify their means and ends. Toward that end, we use their words as frequently as possible in order to avoid misrepresentation.

The Education Trust: $5,076,846[19]

"Established in 1990 by the American Association for Higher Education as a special project to encourage colleges and universities to support K–12 reform efforts," the Education Trust has matured into "the #1 education advocacy organization of the decade, according to the Editorial Projects in Education (EPE) Research Center. The Ed Trust was also ranked as a top influential information source in education policy, and [their] president, Kati Haycock, was ranked as one of the most influential people in education."[20] The two most influential people in education (above Mrs. Haycock) were Bill Gates and George W. Bush, respectively.[21] From the Education Trust's website:

> **Our Mission**
>
> The Education Trust promotes high academic achievement for all students at all levels—pre-kindergarten through college. Our goal is to close the gaps in opportunity and achievement that consign far too many young people—especially those from low-income families or who are black, Latino, or American Indian—to lives on the margins of the American mainstream.
>
> **How We Advance Our Mission**
>
> Although many organizations speak up for the adults employed by schools and colleges, we speak up for students, especially those whose needs and potential are often overlooked. We evaluate every policy, every practice, and every dollar spent through a single lens: what is right for students. We carry out our mission in three primary ways:
>
> - We work alongside educators, parents, students, policymakers, and civic and business leaders in communities across the country, providing practical assistance in their efforts to transform schools and colleges into institutions that serve all students well.
> - We analyze local, state, and national data and use what we learn to help build broader understanding of achievement and opportunity gaps and the actions necessary to close them.
> - We participate actively in national and state policy debates, bringing lessons learned from on-the-ground work and from unflinching data analysis to build the case for policies that will help all students and schools reach high levels of ahcievement. URL: http://www.edtrust.org/dc/about accessed August 2, 2010.

Specifically, the Gates Foundation granted the Education Trust money to support various activities.[22] In addition to the $2.3 million "general operation" funds given to the organization between the years of 2002 and 2006, monies have been specifically allocated to the American Diploma Project and the California High School Status Report. Technical assistance support was given for the Los Angeles Unified School District to develop their high school progress report as well. Additionally, the Education Trust was awarded 2 million dollars in 2003 for research and dissemination of "effective" practices.

Education Sector: $600,000[23]

Founded in 2005 by Andrew Rotherham and Thomas Toch, "Education Sector is an independent education think tank."[24] Claiming to be "nonpartisan" and "both a dependable source of sound thinking on policy and an honest broker of evidence in key education debates," Education Sector produces both research and policy analysis and markets "outstanding work by the nation's most respected education analysts."[25] The "nonpartisan" and "independent" Education Sector's Board of Directors, Research Advisory Board, and Non-Resident Fellows include individuals such as:

- Bruno V. Mano, a trustee of the Thomas B. Fordham Foundation, and longtime advocate for charter schools.
- Ira A. Fishman, who "served as the first Chief Executive Officer of the Schools and Libraries Corporation, the nonprofit organization created to administer the E-Rate program."[26] We remind the reader that the E-Rate program was riddled with fraud and millions of tax dollars were wasted and stolen.[27]
- Eric Hanushek and Paul T. Hill, both members of the neoconservative Hoover Institute's Koret Task Force.
- Frederick M. Hess, Director of Education Policy Studies at the neoconservative American Enterprise Institute.
- Various members of the Center for Reinventing Public Education, which "engages in research and analysis aimed at developing focused, effective, and accountable schools and the systems that support them."[28]

This list of individuals makes the following, taken from Education Sector's home page, problematic at best and a flat-out lie at worst. We include this lengthy extract because it exemplifies 'doublespeak,' and we will turn to propaganda later in this chapter.

> Education policymaking in the United States suffers from a dearth of high-quality, independent analysis. Far too often, the quality of deliberation and decision-making on critical education issues is compromised by ideologically driven research and commentary. Important debates are dominated by the distorted claims and counterclaims of individuals and institutions with ideological or political agendas. Many policymakers and the public, as a result, simply don't trust much of the evidence put before them on key education questions. In a 2003 survey by the Hechinger Institute on Education and the Media, a large majority of journalists covering education dismissed most education research as "ideologically motivated." The journalists told surveyors that they "hunger for assistance from an objective, neutral source" in education debates. There is thus a tremendous need for a new, rigorously independent voice in education policymaking. Education Sector will be such a voice, an organization devoted to innovative solutions

> to the nation's most pressing educational problems, a source of sound thinking on education policy and an honest broker of evidence in key education debates in Washington and nationally. Education Sector will produce rigorous, independent research and analysis on a wide range of elementary-, secondary-, and higher-education topics. We will eschew the ideological orthodoxies that have polarized the national debate on so many education issues. We believe that public officials, journalists, business leaders, and the public at large will embrace education reform if they believe such reform is justified by solid, independent evidence. Education Sector will play a key role in producing such evidence and making it readily understandable to a broad audience of policymakers, the media, and other opinion-makers with the power to leverage meaningful change in American education.[29]

One must wonder how Education Sector can be "neutral," "rigorously independent," and "an honest broker of evidence" when its board of directors, advisory board, and fellows vocally embrace privatization and standardization. When Frederick Hess, for example, takes time off from the American Enterprise Institute to work with Education Sector, does he or can he take off his neoconservative hat to become "an honest broker of evidence" in order to "eschew the ideological orthodoxies that have polarized the national debate on so many education issues"?

THE ASPEN INSTITUTE'S COMMISSION ON NCLB: $3,263,965[30]

The Aspen Institute is one of the most recognized names in the world. It began in 1950 as a place for "CEOs, Supreme Court justices, high-tech pioneers, policymakers, and Nobel laureates to deepen their knowledge and engage in informed dialogue."[31] "Together," their website continues, "they exchange views, broaden their perspectives, and explore innovative solutions to the foremost challenges of our time."[32] Although the Gates Foundation does not directly fund the Aspen Institute, the foundation provided support for Aspen's Commission on No Child Left Behind. Co-chaired by former governors Tommy G. Thompson and Roy E. Barnes, the commission formed in order to:

> analyze the strengths and weaknesses of the No Child Left Behind Act (NCLB) and [to] make bipartisan recommendations to Congress, Administration, State and local stakeholders, parents and the general public to ensure that the law is an effective tool in spurring academic achievement and closing the achievement gap. As part of this effort, the Commission [examined] the impact of NCLB on Federal, State, and local efforts toward improving academic achievement for all students, reducing the achievement gap between disadvantaged students and their non-disadvantaged peers, improving instruction in

> core academic subjects, and recruiting and retaining a highly qualified teaching force.[33]

The commission operates under six guiding principles:

1. All children can learn and should be expected to reach high standards.
2. Accountability for public education systems in the United States must improve to enable students to excel.
3. The achievement gap between disadvantaged students and their non-disadvantaged peers must be eliminated to ensure that all children have the opportunity to succeed.
4. Education results for all students must improve in order for the United States to remain competitive in the global marketplace.
5. Parents have a right to expect their children to be taught by a highly qualified teacher. Teachers have the right to be treated like professionals, including access to sound working conditions and high-quality preparation and ongoing professional development opportunities.
6. Education reform must be coupled with additional resources, but federal, state, and local resources must be used more efficiently and effectively to ensure results in return for the increased investment.

The Gates Foundation helps the Aspen Institute achieve each of these in various ways.[34] For example, the foundation awarded the institute over a million dollars in 2005 to fund a commission of 'bipartisan' members to evaluate the effectiveness of NCLB as a gap-closing tool. The Gates Foundation also supports teacher education initiatives such as the Aspen Urban Superintendents Network, which is a series of forums for leaders in the public school system. An additional half-million dollars was used to support professional development seminars and peer-learning forums for superintendents of large, complex urban school districts. Another million dollars was awarded between 2003 and 2004 for seminars on education issues and to support the conference "From High School to College, Work and Citizenship: Learning Pathways for Youth."

EDin08 / Strong American Schools

The youngest of the four organizations covered in our analysis, EDin08 / Strong American Schools

> is a nonpartisan public awareness and action campaign offering a voice to every American who supports 'ED in 08.' [Their] goal is to ensure that the nation engages in a rigorous debate and to make education a top priority in the 2008 presidential election. [They] hope that candidates will offer genuine leadership rather than empty rhetoric and tell voters how they intend to strengthen America's schools so all students receive the education they deserve.[35]

While the organization claims to do nothing more than use its 60 million-dollar budget to start a "serious nationwide debate on education reform" amongst 2008 presidential contenders, EDin08 does in fact have an agenda and believes the candidates should focus on "three priorities that hold great promise for improving education":

- Agreeing on American education standards
- Providing effective teachers in every classroom
- Giving students more time and support for learning.[36]

As with the other organizations covered in this study, EDin08 offers a number of 'fact sheets' for individuals and organizations interested in educational reform.[37] Importantly, EDin08 has been very active in the public sphere disseminating those facts, employing celebrities to carry their messages, publishing op-eds in papers across the country, and purchasing advertisements in print, online, and on television.[38] As with the other three organizations that receive Gates Foundation funding, the 'facts' EDin08 forwards are misleading at best and flat-out lies at worst. We turn now to justification of this claim.

PROPAGANDA AND POLITICAL SCIENCE ABUSE

While not without its problems, the democratically constructed and maintained Wikipedia offers a robust and appropriate definition of the term propaganda:

> Propaganda is a type of message aimed at influencing the opinions or behavior of people. Often, instead of impartially providing information, propaganda can be deliberately misleading or using fallacies which, while sometimes convincing, are not necessarily valid. Propaganda techniques include: patriotic flag-waving; glittering generalities; intentional vagueness; oversimplification of complex issues; rationalization; introducing unrelated red-herring issues; using appealing, simple slogans; stereotyping; testimonials from authority figures or celebrities; unstated assumptions; and encouraging readers or viewers to 'jump on the bandwagon' of a particular point of view.[39]

To varying degrees, each of the organizations examined in our study engages in one or more of the aforementioned activities in their efforts to influence "the opinions or behavior of people." For example, "leave no child behind" and "closing the achievement gap" are "appealing, simple slogans" that few people can disagree with. At the same time the "achievement gap," as we will show below, is an "oversimplification of a complex issue." Bill Gates is obviously a celebrity; he travels the country encouraging people to "jump on the bandwagon" that America's public schools are failing and must be saved via a number of market-based reforms—either outsourcing education to supplemental educational service providers or closing public schools and restructuring them as private, for-profit, or charter schools.

What earns these organizations the label propagandist, however, is that while they claim to be "impartially providing information" with words such as "non-partisan," "independent," and "not for profit," they deliberately mislead voters and their representatives with narratives that are "sometimes convincing" but "not necessarily valid." This convincing takes place through a process that Chris Mooney calls "political science abuse." As explained by Mooney, political science abuse is "any attempt to inappropriately undermine, alter, or otherwise interfere with the scientific process, or scientific conclusions, for political or ideological reasons."[40] Although Mooney does not extend his analysis of political science abuse to education specifically, his framework extends to the field. We employ Mooney's terminology in an effort to detail how these organizations generate support for neoconservative and neoliberal educational reform efforts.[41]

According to Mooney, individuals and organizations engage in political science abuse in a number of ways. They might, for example *undermine science itself* by dismissing research as irrelevant or flat-out false. Frederick Hess provides an example of this with his smear of the American Educational Research Association's 2007 annual meeting, a place where scholars go to "celebrate their own awesomeness" rather than engage in substantive work.[42] Recall that Hess works for both Education Sector and the American Enterprise Institute. Educational reconstructionists may also *suppress* information while they attempt to make a convincing argument for their side. Such suppression occurred when the Department of Education attempted to hide one of its own studies critical of charter schools.[43] Similar suppression occurred when members of the Commission on NCLB traveled the country saying things such as "There is broad agreement that testing plays a critical role in education"[44] while failing to mention that hundreds of the country's most esteemed psychologists, psychometricians, and educators offer convincing evidence to the contrary. Most recently and poignantly, Sharon L. Nichols and David C. Berliner show that high-stakes testing obfuscates what actually goes on in classrooms and has in fact resulted in the miseducation of hundreds of thousands of children.[45]

One significant way these four organizations engage in political science abuse is by *rigging the process*, controlling the input of data in a policy debate by either packing a panel with scientists who are like-minded or by airing one side of the story. The most visible example of this on the national level is the scandal-ridden federally funded Reading First program.[46] The Aspen Institute's Commission on NCLB is also guilty of this abuse. As it traveled the country setting up "hearings" where witnesses discussed NCLB, the commission packed panels with neoliberal and neoconservative reformers. Although a handful of active school administrators participated, the commission did not call on a single classroom teacher to 'testify.' Instead, the commission heard testimony from individuals such as:

- Kati Haycock, director of the Education Trust
- Chris Whittle, CEO and founder of Edison Schools[47]
- Andrew Rotheram, cofounder and codirector, Education Sector
- John E. Chubb, Koret Task Force, Hoover Institution
- Michael Petrilli, vice president for National Programs and Policy at the Thomas B. Fordham Foundation
- Chester Finn, president of the Thomas B. Fordham Foundation[48]
- Michael Cohen, president of Achieve (a for-profit educational organization)
- Neal McCluskey, education policy analyst of the Cato Institute
- Susan Traiman, director of education and workforce policy, Business Roundtable[49]
- Brian Gong, executive director of the National Center for the Improvement of Assessment
- Eugene Hickok, former Bradley Fellow at the Heritage Foundation and senior policy director of Dutko Worldwide
- Aimee Guidera, director of the Data Quality Campaign
- Stuart Kahl, president and CEO of Measured Progress

It should be no surprise to readers familiar with these individuals that they called for policy changes that support neoliberal reform with a focus on data, testing, and market reform. For example, at a hearing in Hartford Connecticut, "Aimee Guidera, Director of the Data Quality Campaign, emphasized the importance of supporting state efforts to develop longitudinal data systems that track individual student performance from pre-K through 12th grade, even into postsecondary education."[50] The Data Quality Campaign, created in 2005 with a grant from the Gates Foundation, works "to provide support for and advocacy on behalf of organizations that create, collect, and use education data in an effort to improve student achievement."[51] Guidera "urged the federal government to build the capacity of all education stakeholders to use data," explaining that "educators are scared of data; data has been seen as a hammer. We want them to see it as a flashlight, as the most important tool in their arsenal."[52] Stuart Kahl, president and CEO of the for-profit Measured Progress, assured the commission that testing companies had the "capacity to handle the increased data assessment demands of NCLB" but asked that companies be given more time "to verify that each school had results for all its students."[53] Read differently: every child in every school must be tested.

During a commission hearing in Wisconsin, Eugene Hickock—formerly a Bradley Fellow at the Heritage Foundation and now the senior policy director at a multimillion-dollar lobbying firm—spoke on behalf of supplemental educational services. "SES [supplemental educational services] represents a potentially valuable educational opportunity not fully realized under No Child Left Behind."[54] He blamed the failure to fully implement SES reforms on people "who feel the money would be spent better under their direction," and he stressed that the tutoring provision "must be measured and extended over time." In Washington Chris Whittle, founder and CEO of the for-profit Edison Schools, a company that benefits directly from NCLB's sanctions, "recommended reevaluating the law's provisions that deal with corrective action and restructuring."[55] At that same meeting, long-time charter school advocate John E. Chubb suggested that responsibility for enforcing choice provisions should be "taken away from districts and put in the hands of a state education agency."[56] Chubb also argued that "eligible parents and students [should] be able to choose any regular or charter public school in any school district—provided the family handles transportation out of the district." None of the speakers at any of these hearings offered empirical evidence that any of their reforms would lead to better schools for America's children, a type of political science abuse Mooney refers to as *dressing up values in scientific clothing.*

Perhaps the most egregious way these organizations abuse science is by *hiding errors and misrepresentations.* While Mooney defines this as making false claims or distorting data, it also involves deliberately misleading individuals, using fallacies, and the oversimplification of complex issues—three hallmarks of propaganda as defined in this chapter. After analyzing the four think tanks funded by the Gates Foundation, we identified three shared claims that are misleading, contradictory, oversimplifications, or flat-out lies:

1. Other countries are outperforming America, endangering it's place in the global economy.
2. The jobs of the future require a highly skilled workforce.
3. NCLB is working.

"International comparisons show . . . "

The argument that America's students are falling behind their international peers has been forwarded since at least 1957, when conservative educational reformers blamed poor schooling for Sputnik. In 1984 *A Nation at Risk* revived the meme, and today members of both political parties return to this fallacy when discussing educational reform. One of the most common refrains forwarded by the four organizations we surveyed is that foreign students are outperforming American students, threatening America's dominance of the global economy. "International comparisons show," argues the ASPEN Commission on NCLB, "that the level of performance of American students is consistently surpassed by that of students in other countries."[57] From EDin08 we learn that "by the time they've graduated from high school, students in other countries have obtained the equivalent of one more year of education than their American counterparts."[58] More specifically, the Education Sector notes that when comparing mathematics exams, "students in Chinese Taipei, Japan, and Singapore far outperformed U.S. students on every test."[59] Most recently, Amy Wilkins of the Education Trust told the host of NPR's *On Point* that America's "most affluent kids are getting their lunches eaten by kids in other countries."[60] The men and women running EDin08 argue this country needs more rigorous testing requirements because "left unchecked, a 'race to the bottom' among states would imperil efforts to raise student achievement and put America at even greater disadvantage internationally."[61]

Each of these claims is a misrepresentation, an oversimplification, or a fallacy, and researcher Gerald Bracey spends significant amounts of time debunking all of them.[62] For example, when the commission claims students in other countries outperform American students, Bracey reminds listeners to ask which students. If we compare the top students from Singapore to students relocated to Houston after Hurricane Katrina, then obviously one group will outperform the other. Though that is not what Amy Wilkins of the Education Trust would have people believe. Recall her claim that America's "most affluent kids are getting their lunches eaten by kids in other countries."[63] This is simply not true. When Bracey disaggregated international testing data by poverty rate he found:

> for reading and science, the two categories of US schools with the smallest percentages of students living in poverty score higher than even the highest nation, Sweden in reading, [and] Singapore in science. In math, the top US category would be 3rd in the world. It is only in American schools with 75% or more of their students living in poverty where scores fall below the international average.[64]

Bracey also reminds us that there is no correlation between performance on tests and economic productivity, contrary to what each of these think tanks would have us believe. For the better part of five years, the United States has ranked first or second on the World Economic Forum's *Global Competitiveness Report*. This year the U.S. ranked sixth but not because of schools. Bracey shows that corruption, failing infrastructure, and macroeconomic instability (national debt, trade deficits, a war, and tax cuts) caused the U.S. to lose its top ranking.[65] Bracey concludes:

> American economic competitiveness with Japan and other nations is to a considerable degree a function of monetary, trade, and industrial policy, and of decisions made by the President and Congress, the Federal Reserve Board, and the federal departments of Treasury, Commerce, and Labor. Therefore, to conclude that problems in international competitiveness can be solved by educational reform, especially educational reform defined solely as school reform, is not merely utopian and millenialist, it is at best a foolish and at worse a

crass effort to direct attention away from those truly responsible for doing something about competitiveness and to lay the burden instead on the schools.[66]

"The jobs of today and tomorrow require a highly skilled workforce . . . "

Each of these four organizations argues that students must receive specific training in order to prepare them for highly skilled jobs. Writing in *Thinking K–16*, a journal published by the Education Trust, Patte Barth argues that "the Information Age set off a rush to find skilled workers in many occupations and simultaneously reduced the proportion of unskilled jobs."[67] She ominously warns, "The future holds grim prospects for young people who lack sufficient skills, for they are increasingly shut out of good, middle-income jobs. The occupations experiencing the largest growth are those that demand well-developed cognitive skills and postsecondary credentials."[68] That growth, reports EDin08 on a 'fact sheet' entitled "American Education Standards," means that "two-thirds of new jobs being created in today's economy require higher education or advanced training."[69] Those students not entering 'high-skill' jobs must receive a rigorous education heavily dosed with math and science, urges Education Sector, because "today even blue-collar jobs call for more than basic computational skills."[70] Indeed, according to EDin08, "Occupations that pay enough to raise a family—jobs like electrical work, construction, upholstering, and plumbing—now demand the same math and reading skills it takes to be successful in college."[71] The Aspen Commission paints an even bleaker picture for America's workforce, arguing that students are not prepared for either high-skilled jobs or blue-collar work. They report that "large numbers of employers and college professors say that expectations for students do not match what they need to succeed after high school."[72]

These statements are misleading at best. Recent research from the Urban Institute shows that U.S. public schools are producing more scientists and engineers than the market demands.[73] According to our own research, out of 7 million new jobs projected from 2004 to 2014, only 28.5 percent require a high school or college degree.[74] A mere 7.1 percent require graduate-level schooling (see table 8.1).

We are not arguing that students should not stay in high school, and we deny no one the right to a college education. We simply question the motives of individuals who claim that rigorous training in math, science, and reading will prepare students for a workforce that purportedly requires high levels of all three when job forecasts indicate the vast majority of jobs require rudimentary skills at most. Who benefits when there are more workers than the market requires? Who loses when children focus on one skill set, (math and science, for example) at the expense of others (say, critical media literacy or civics)?

"NCLB is working."

In a 2007 debate with Deborah Meiers, Diane Ravitch argued that "the Center on Education [CEP] Policy [which also receives Gates support][75] released a report on NCLB, concluding that it was overall having a positive effect on achievement."[76] Ravitch, although not a member of any of the organizations critiqued in our analysis, works closely with individuals such as Chester Finn, and she fiercely advocates for rigorous national standards.[77] After reading the report ourselves, we had difficulty understanding how Ravitch could make the claim, and we contacted Jack Jennings, president of the CEP for clarification. He told us Ravitch was misusing the data. "In fact," he told us, "one of our five main conclusions is that it is very difficult, if not impossible, to prove causality between state test-score trends and NCLB."[78] Ravitch was not alone in doing so.

At the Aspen Commission hearing in D.C., Deputy Secretary of Education Raymond Simon began his testimony with the claim that NCLB "has had a truly extraordinary and positive impact on our schools over the past five years."[79] When Kati Haycock, director of the Education Trust, addressed the House Committee on Education and the Workforce, she told them that "despite the shortfalls in funding and the anxiety about AYP, [NCLB] is having a dramatically positive impact on American education."[80] And while Haycock noted that "nobody thinks the law is perfect," she informed the committee that "educators in every part of this country have told [her] that this law strengthens the hands of those who are working to improve overall achievement and close the achievement gaps."[81] Haycock's conclusion: "Because of NCLB, achievement gaps are no longer simply tolerated; a culture of achievement is taking hold in our schools, and we are better poised to confront the new challenges."[82] Andrew Rotherham, codirector of Education Sector, was more reserved in his praise for NCLB, but he urged the Aspen Commission to work to make the law stronger, arguing that "the framework it offers, tying federal resources clearly to reform and results, is the most promising avenue for education policy making today and one we should improve and refine rather than jettison."[83] EDin08 has no formal position on NCLB, but they do support "rigorous American education standards" with some sort of (undefined) national enforcement in order to prevent a "race to the bottom" from states lowering their testing requirements.[84]

Is the 'achievement gap' closing? According to many researchers the answer is a resounding no. Gary Orfield, writing for the Harvard Civil Rights Project (yet another recipient of Gates Foundation funding)[85] argues "that neither a significant rise in achievement, nor closure of the racial achievement gaps is being achieved."[86] Other individuals showing that high-stakes testing has or will ultimately increase the 'achievement gap' by reducing opportunities for genuine student development and growth include esteemed researchers and scholars such as David Berliner, Sharon Nichols, Deborah Meier, Bruce Fuller, Monty Neill, Lisa Gusibond, Bob Schaeffer, Derek Neal, Diane Whitmore Schanzenbach, Linda McNeil, and

Linda Perlstein, to name a few.[87] The Aspen Commission itself acknowledges that achievement gaps remain widespread, with achievement decreasing as students move beyond middle school.[88] Most recently, Diane Ravitch changed her position on the legislation, arguing that it is fundamentally flawed and ultimately undermines public education.[89]

Retired principal and current teacher Steve Davidson asks an interesting question: is closing the achievement gap a worthy goal?[90] He argues that a shrinking achievement gap could indicate a decrease in student performance. This would occur if:

- Scores for Black students improve while White students make no improvement
- Scores for Black students improve while White students score lower
- Scores for Black students make no change while White students score lower
- Scores for both sets of students decrease with White students decreasing at a faster rate[91]

In fact, as Davidson shows, the only way the 'achievement gap' can close with benefits to both groups is for the test scores of Black students to increase at a faster rate than those of White students. Given the world we live in, this will hardly happen anytime soon.

Recall that propaganda requires the "oversimplification of complex issues" and the use of "appealing, simple slogans." Reducing the 'achievement gap' to what goes on inside of schools has proven to be an effective way for policy makers to ignore all of the other 'gaps' outside of America's classrooms. Although researcher after researcher has shown that outside influences contribute to student performance and achievement, proponents of high-stakes, standardized reforms continue to press for more 'rigor,' as if harder work alone will mitigate every external factor that influences children's lives.[92] Rather than focus exclusively on the 'achievement gap,' policy makers and educational reformers might consider policies that help reduce other 'gaps' that exist within our country. Gaps that could be narrowed in order to improve the lives and schooling of all students include but are not limited to:

- The incarceration gap, whereby six times as many African Americans are behind bars compared to their White counterparts[93]
- The homeowner gap, whereby 72.7 percent of White Americans own their homes compared to 48.2 percent of African Americans[94]
- The healthcare gap, whereby 71.4 percent of White Americans are insured compared to 53.9 percent of African Americans[95]
- The earnings gap, whereby White Americans average over $20,000 more a year than African Americans[96]
- The poverty rate gap, whereby 8.7 percent of White Americans live at or below the poverty line while 24.7 percent of African Americans do so[97]

- The unemployment gap, whereby 5.7 percent of White Americans are unemployed while 13.2 percent of African Americans are without work[98]
- The happiness gap, whereby 72 percent of White youths say they are happy with life in general compared to 56 percent of their African American counterparts[99]
- The murder gap, whereby 49 percent of murder victims in the United States are African Americans, who make up 13 percent of the population[100]

Schooling does not exist in a vacuum, and it should come as no surprise to the reader that failing schools are most often found in 'failing' communities, the majority of which are non-White. Jean Anyon (predating Gerald Bracey) argues that failing schools are "a logical consequence of the U.S. macroeconomy—and the federal [neoliberal] and regional policies and practices that support it."[101] Anyon correctly rejects neoliberal reformers who blame teachers, principals, students, and schools for the 'achievement gap.' As she explains, "an unjust economy and the policies through which it is maintained create barriers to educational success that no teacher or principal practice, no standardized test, and no 'zero tolerance' policy can surmount."[102] We agree with Anyon and Bracey: policy makers serious about narrowing the 'achievement gap' must look beyond schools and begin addressing the very real gaps that are the arguable result of replacing social responsibility and democracy with market fundamentalism.

CONCLUSION

In this chapter we have identified and problematized the claims and activities of four think tanks supported by contributions from the Bill and Melinda Gates Foundation. We have attempted to show that these contributions support scholars and research of dubious quality at best. As they engage in political science abuse, these organizations perpetuate discourses and narratives that stand in opposition to democratic school alternatives, ultimately reducing the likelihood that democratic school reform will ever take place.

Scholars who support democratic school reform must engage publicly and politically to counter the political science abuse taking place in public and political spheres. Importantly, we must do so in language that is accessible to multiple publics lest our arguments, eloquent as they may be, remain secreted away in journals or edited volumes. Gramsci clarifies what we call for here. "The mode of being of the new intellectual," he writes, "can no longer consist in eloquence, which is an exterior and momentary mover of feelings and passions, but in active participation in practical life, as constructor, organizer, 'permanent persuader,' and not just a simple orator."[103] The growing numbers of academics blogging and reaching out to mainstream media outlets is a positive step, but we have yet to become "permanent persuaders" who have the access or amplification of our counterparts housed in think tanks funded by the Gates Foundation. However, such access and amplification is not beyond the reach of scholars who

Table 8.1 BLS Jobs Projections: 2004–2014

Occupation	Job Projection	High School	College	Graduate
Retail salesperson	800,000	No	No	No
Registered nurses	700,000	Yes	Yes	No
Postsecondary teachers	500,000	Yes	Yes	Yes
Customer service representatives	475,000	No	No	No
Janitors and cleaners, except maids and housekeeping cleaners	450,000	No	No	No
Waiters and waitresses	425,000	No	No	No
Food preparation and service workers, including fast food	400,000	No	No	No
Home health aides	300,000	No	No	No
Nursing aides, orderlies, and attendants	300,000	No	No	No
General operations manager	300,000	Yes	Yes	No
Personal and home care aides	300,000	No	No	No
Elementary school teachers, except special education	275,000	Yes	Yes	No
Office clerks, general	275,000	No	No	No
Laborer and freight, stock, and material movers, hand	250,000	No	No	No
Receptionists and information clerks	250,000	No	No	No
Landscaping and ground-keeping workers	225,000	No	No	No
Truck drivers, heavy and tractor-trailer	225,000	No	No	No
Computer software engineers, applications	225,000	Yes	Yes	No
Maintenance and repair workers, general	200,000	No	No	No

envision more democratic schooling.[104] Part of the problem is academic insularity, engaging with one another while change takes place in the world housing us. Scholars are left reflecting while others act.

Although critiquing neoliberal policy is necessary for moving beyond it, we cannot limit our activities to analysis and critique alone, especially when that analysis and critique only reaches the eyes and ears of like-minded scholars. Therefore, in addition to intelligent critique, we call on the academic Left, if there is such a body, to become publicly and politically active, challenging the half-truths, misrepresentations, and flat-out lies being disseminated by organizations such as those covered in this study. This requires building relationships with reporters, bloggers, policy analysts, and members of political parties from both sides of the aisle. Importantly, as Gerald Bracey and Jean Anyon argue, education does not exist in a vacuum, and schools are subject to outside influences such as macro-economic policy decisions. Therefore, relationships must be cultivated with pro-democracy reformers in areas such as economics and urban planning, as these individuals can help us reach wider and larger audiences using language that may be unfamiliar to scholars who spend most of their time in the world of educational policy. We understand that scholars may be uncomfortable acting as constructors, organizers, and permanent persuaders, but we also recognize an evolving landscape, one dominated at present by neoliberal reformers who are not at all reserved about what they are doing or how they are doing it.

NOTES

* This chapter originally appeared in the *Journal for Critical Education Policy Studies*, http://www.jceps.com.

1. B. Gates, "National Summit on High Schools" (speech delivered February 26, 2005), http://www.gatesfoundation.org/speeches-commentary/Pages/bill-gates-2005-national-education-summit.aspx (accessed August 20, 2010).
2. See Gates Foundation, *Grants-Education: 1999–2007*, http://www.gates-foundation.org/grants/Pages/overview.aspx (accessed July 1, 2007).
3. See, for example R . Brosio, *A Radical Democratic Critique of Capitalist Education* (New York: Peter Lang, 1994); K. Emery and S. Ohanian, *Why Is Corporate America Bashing Our Public Schools?* (Portsmouth, NH: Heinemann, 2004); and D. Boyles, ed., *Schools or Markets? Commercialism, Privatization, and School-Business Partnerships* (Mahwah, NJ: Lawrence Erlbaum, 2005).
4. We base this definition on the work of Dewey and two of his biographers. For more on Dewey's understanding of democracy and education, see his *Democracy and Education: An Introduction to the Philosophy of Education* (New York: The Free Press, 1944). See also R. Westbrook, *John Dewey and American Democracy* (Ithaca, NY: Cornell University Press, 1993); and J. Martin, *The Education of John Dewey*, (New York: Columbia University Press, 2003).
5. See C. Mooney, *The Republican War on Science* (New York: Basic Books, 2005).

6. See D. Hill, "Global Neo-Liberalism, the Deformation of Education and Resistance," *Journal of Critical Educational Policy Studies* 1, no. 1 (March 2003), http://www.jceps.com/index.php?pageID=article&articleID=7 (accessed October 20, 2009).
7. For a critical history of this campaign, see D. Gabbard, "*A Nation at Risk* Reloaded: Part I & II," *Journal for Critical Educational Policy Studies* 1, no. 2 (October 2003), http://www.jceps.com/index.php?pageID=article&articleID=15 (accessed October 20, 2009).
8. For a lengthy treatment on fear and educational reform, see P. Kovacs, "The Schools Are Failing: Think Tanks, Institutes, Foundations and Educational Disaster," in *Schooling and the Politics of Disaster*, ed. K. Saltman (New York: Routledge, 2007).
9. Neoliberals, in fact, believe free-market reforms should replace a number of the democratic state's social functions, i.e., social security. See H. Giroux, *The Terror of Neoliberalism: Authoritarianism and the Eclipse of Democracy* (Boulder, CO: Paradigm, 2004).
10. M. Neill et al., *Failing Our Children: How "No Child Left Behind" Undermines Quality and Equity in Education* (Cambridge: Fair Test, 2004), http://www.fairtest.org/Failing_Our_Children_Report.html (accessed October 20, 2009).
11. See Friedman Foundation, "Frequently Asked Questions," http://www.edchoice.org/newsroom/ShowFaq.do (accessed May 10, 2010).
12. See D. Hill, "Global Neo-Liberalism, the Deformation of Education and Resistance."
13. For examples of how neoliberals work with a variety of public and private organizations to meet their ends, see P. Kovacs, "Think Tanks, Foundations and Institutes," in *Knowledge and Power in the Global Economy: The Effects of School Reform in a Neoconservative/Neoliberal Age*, 2nd ed., ed. D. Gabbard (Mahwah, NJ: Lawrence Erlbaum Associates, 2007); and P. Kovacs, "The Anti-School Movement," also in *Knowledge and Power in the Global Economy*. For Americans' feelings toward public schools, see "The 37th Annual Phi Delta Kappa/Gallup Poll of the Public's Attitudes Toward the Public Schools," *Phi Delta Kappan* 87, no. 1 (Sep. 2005). For current PDK poll, see Phi Delta Kappa's website, http://www.pdkintl.org/kappan/poll.htm (accessed May 10, 2010).
14. Gates Foundation, *Grants-Education: 1999–2007.*
15. Gates Foundation grant total: $328,575 (ibid.).
16. Gates Foundation grant total: $49,942,205 (ibid.).
17. Gates Foundation grant total: $216,250,074 (ibid.).
18. Gates Foundation grant total: $160,663,557 (ibid.).
19. Ibid.
20. Education Trust, "Education Trust Named #1 Education Advocacy Organization of the Decade," December 13, 2005, http://www.edtrust.org/dc/press-room/press-release/education-trust-named-l-education-advocacy-organization-of-the-decade (accessedAugust 2, 2010).
21. Ibid.
22. See Gates Foundation, *Grants-Education: 1999–2007*
23. Ibid.
24. Education Sector, "Our Mission and Strategy," http://www.educationsector.org/whoweare/whoweare_list.htm?doc_category_id=1970 (accessed May 10, 2010).
25. Ibid.
26. Education Sector "Board of Directors: Ira A. Fishman," http://www.educationsector.org/profiles/profiles_show.htm?doc_id=336585&attrib_id=12244 (accessed October 20, 2009).

27. For more on this, see K. Mayfield, "E-Rate Fund Hit by Rampant Fraud," *Wired*, January 13, 2003, http://www.wired.com/culture/education/news/2003/01/57172 (accessed October 20, 2009).
28. For more on this organization, see the Center on Reinventing Public Education's website, http://www.crpe.org/.
29. See Education Sector, "Our Mission and Strategy."
30. See Gates Foundation, *Grants-Education: 1999–2007.*
31. Aspen Institute, "Support the Institute," http://www.aspeninstitute.org/support (accessed March 1, 2010).
32. Ibid.
33. Aspen Institute, "Mission," http://www.aspeninstitute.org/policy-work/no-child-left-behind/reports/successful-interventions-helping-schools-achi (accessed August 2, 2010).
34. See Gates Foundation, *Grants-Education: 1999–2007.*
35. Editor's note: EDin08 closed operations in June of 2009 and no longer exists. The authors did not want to remove analysis of the initiative and elected to leave the references to the original website. EDin08, "About Us," http://www.edin08.com/AboutUs.aspx (accessed July 1, 2007).
36. Ibid.
37. EDin08, "Get the Facts," http://edin08.com/GetTheFacts.aspx (accessed July 1, 2007).
38. For an updated list of op-eds, press releases, and television commercials, see EDin08 website at http://www.edin08.com/LatestNews.aspx.
39. "Propaganda," *Wikipedia.org*, http://en.wikipedia.org/wiki/Propaganda (accessed July 1, 2007). Indeed, one of the problems with Wikipedia is that users reshape it. The definition of propaganda used for the original version of this chapter has changed substantially since 2007.
40. C. Mooney, *The Republican War on Science*, 17.
41. For a lengthier treatment of public education and political science abuse see P. Kovacs, "The Schools Are Failing."
42. See F. Hess, "A Helpful User's Guide to the 2007 AERA Conference," *Education Gadfly* 7, no. 13 (April 2007), http://www.edexcellence.net/gadfly/index.cfm?issue=285 (accessed March 1, 2010).
43. See G. Bracey, "The 15th Bracey Report on the Condition of Public Education," *Phi Delta Kappan* 87, no. 2 (October 2005): 145, http://www.america-tomorrow.com/bracey/EDDRA/ (accessed March 1, 2010).
44. See the Commission on No Child Left Behind, *Testing: Making It Work for Children and Schools; A Hearing at Saint Joseph College*, May 9, 2006, Hartford, CT, 1.
45. S. Nichols and D. Berliner, *Collateral Damage: How High-Stakes Testing Corrupts America's Schools* (Cambridge, MA: Harvard Education Press, 2007).
46. Dr. Jim Horn has done excellent work tracking the Reading First scandal. For example, see "Reading First Finding 1B: Conflicts of Interest," http://www.schoolsmatter.info/2006/09/reading-first-finding-1b-conflicts-of.html (accessed October 20, 2009).
47. For more on Edison Schools, see K. Saltman's *Edison Schools: Corporate Schooling and the Assault on Public Education* (New York: Routledge-Falmer, 2005).
48. For more on the Fordham Foundation see P. Kovacs and D. Boyles, "Institutes, Foundations, and Think Tanks: Neoconservative Influences on U.S. Public Schools," *Public Resistance* 1, no. 1 (May 1, 2005), http://www.eric.ed.gov/ERICDocs/data/ericdocs2sql/content_storage_01/0000019b/80/1b/eb/80.pdf (accessed March 1, 2010).

49. For more on the Business Roundtable, see K. Emery and S. Ohanian, *Why Is Corporate America Bashing Our Schools?* (Portsmouth, NH: Heineman, 2004).
50. Commission on No Child Left Behind, *Testing*, 5.
51. Data Quality Campaign, http://www.dataqualitycampaign.org/about (accessed March 1, 2010).
52. Commission on No Child Left Behind, *Testing*, 5.
53. Ibid.
54. Commission on No Child Left Behind, *Successful Interventions: Helping Schools Achieve Academic Success; A Hearing at Monona Terrace, Multimedia Lecture Hall,* May 9, 2006, Madison, WI, 5.
55. Commission on No Child Left Behind, *Improving NCLB: Successes, Concerns and Solutions; A Hearing at the George Washington University*, September 25, 2006, Washington, D.C., 8.
56. Ibid.
57. Commission on No Child Left Behind, *Beyond NCLB: Fulfilling the Promise to Our Nation's Children* (Queenstown, MD: Aspen Institute, 2007), 11.
58. EDin08, "More Time and Support for Learning," http://www.edin08.com/issues.aspx?id=76 (accessed July 1, 2007).
59. E. Silva, *On The Clock: Rethinking the Way Schools Use Time* (Washington, D.C.: Education Sector), 5.
60. See G. Bracey, "The Education Trust's Disinformation Campaign," *Huffington Post*, July 22, 2007, http://www.huffingtonpost.com/gerald-bracey/the-education-trusts-dis_b_57327.html (accessed October 20, 2009).
61. EDin08, "American Education Standards," http://www.edin08.com/issues.aspx?id=230 (accessed July 4, 2007).
62. For more on this, see G. Bracey, *Setting the Record Straight: Responses to Misconceptions about Public Education in the U.S.*, 2nd ed. (Portsmouth, NH: Heinemann, 2004); and G. Bracey, *Reading Educational Research: How to Avoid Getting Statistically Snookered* (Portsmouth, NH: Heinemann, 2006).
63. G. Bracey, "The Education Trust's Disinformation Campaign."
64. Ibid.
65. See G. Bracey, "Test Scores and Global Competitiveness: Does Not Compute," *Huffington Post*, January 7, 2007, http://www.huffingtonpost.com/gerald-bracey/test-scores-and-global-co_b_38035.html (accessed October 20, 2009).
66. Ibid.
67. P. Barth, "A Common Core Curriculum for the New Century: Aiming High for Other People's Children," *Thinking K–16* 7, no.1 (Winter 2003): 6. The Education Trust publishes this journal.
68. Ibid.
69. EDin08, "American Education Standards."
70. C. Jerald, *Measured Progress: A Report on the High School Reform Movement* (Washington, D.C.: Education Sector, 2006), 6.
71. EDin08, "American Education Standards."
72. The Commission on No Child Left Behind, *Beyond NCLB*, 11.
73. See V. Wadhwa, "The Science Education Myth," *Business Week*, October 26, 2007, http://www.businessweek.com/smallbiz/content/oct2007/sb20071025_827398.htm (accessed March 1, 2010).
74. See the Bureau of Labor Statistics, "Occupations with the Largest Job Growth, 2004–2014," http://www.bls.gov/emp/emptab3.htm (accessed March 1, 2010).

75. Gates Foundation award total: $962,858. See Gates Foundation, *Grants-Education: 199-2007.*
76. D. Ravitch, "The Chinese Work Ethic and Other News," http://blogs.edweek.org/edweek/BridgingDifferences/2007/06/the_chinese_work_ethic_and_oth_1.html (accessed October 20, 2009).
77. See D. Ravitch, "Every State Left Behind," *New York Times*, November 7, 2005, http://www.nytimes.com/2005/11/07/opinion/07ravitch.html (accessed March 1, 2010).
78. Personal correspondence with the author, June 7, 2007.
79. Commission on No Child Left Behind, *Improving NCLB*, 4.
80. K. Haycock, "Closing the Achievement Gap in America's Public Schools: The No Child Left Behind Act," testimony before the House Committee on Education and the Workforce, September 29, 2005, http://www2.ed.gov/nclb/overview/welcome/closing/index.html (accessed March 1, 2010).
81. Ibid.
82. Ibid.
83. A. Rotherham, "Three Fundamental Issues and Plenty to Do," http://www.educationsector.org/analysis/analysis_show.htm?doc_id=405295 (accessed October 20, 2009).
84. EDin08, "American Education Standards."
85. Grant Foundation award total: $200,000. See Gates Foundation, *Grants-Education: 1999–2007.*
86. J. Lee, *Tracking Achievement Gaps and Assessing the Impact of NCLVB on the Gaps: An In-depth Look into National and State Reading and Math Outcome Trends* (Cambridge, MA: Civil Rights Project at Harvard University, 2006), 5.
87. See S. Nichols and D. Berliner, *Collateral Damage*; D. Meier, *Will Standards Save Public Education?* (Boston: Beacon Press, 2000); M. Neill, L. Gusibond, and B. Schaeffer, *Failing Our Children: How No Child Left Behind Undermines Quality and Equity in Education* (Cambridge, MA: Fair Test, 2004); D. Neal and D. Whitmore Schanzenbach, "Left Behind by Design: Proficiency Counts and Test-Based Accountability," http://www.aei.org/docLib/20070716_NealSchanzenbachPaper.pdf (accessed March 10, 2010); L. McNeil, *Contradictions of Reform: The Educational Costs of Standardized Testing* (New York: Routledge, 2000); L. Perlstein, *Tested: One American School Struggles to Make the Grade* (New York: Henry Holt, 2007); B. Fuller, "Children Are the Losers in Polarized Debate over 'No Child Left Behind' Program," http://www.berkeley.edu/news/media/releases/2004/02/04_fuller.shtml (accessed March 1, 2010); B. Fuller et al., "Gauging Growth: How to Judge No Child Left Behind?" *Educational Researcher* 36, no. 5 (January 2007): 268–78.
88. Commission on No Child Left Behind, *Commission Staff Research Report: The State of the Achievement Gap* (Queenstown, MD: Aspen Institute, 2007).
89. D. Ravitch, *The Death and Life of the Great American School System: How Testing and Choice Are Undermining Education* (New York: Basic Books, 2010).
90. S. Davidson, "Is 'Closing the Gap' Necessarily a Worthy Goal?" *EdNews.org*, March 12, 2007, http://ednews.org/articles/is-quotclosing-the-gapquot-necessarily-a-worthy-goal.html (accessed March 10, 2010).
91. Ibid.
92. For the most recent example, see P. Sacks, *Tearing Down the Gates: Confronting the Class Divide in American Education* (Berkeley: University of California Press, 2007).

93. Prison Policy Initiative, "U.S. Incarnation Rates by Race," http://www.prisonpolicy.org/graphs/raceinc.html (accessed October 20, 2009).
94. "Homeownership Rates by Race and Ethnicity of Householder," http://www.infoplease.com/ipa/A0883976.html (accessed October 20, 2009).
95. See the Center for Disease Control, "Private Health Insurance Coverage among Persons under 65 Years of Age, by Selected Characteristics: United States, Selected Years 1984–2004," November 2006, table 133 (page 1 of 3), http://www.cdc.gov/nchs/data/hus/hus06.pdf#133 (accessed October 20, 2009).
96. U.S. Census Bureau, *Income, Poverty, and Health Insurance Coverage in the United States: 2005* (August 2006), http://www.census.gov/prod/2006pubs/p60-231.pdf (accessed October 20, 2009).
97. Ibid.
98. U.S. Census Bureau, *American Community Survey* (2005), http://factfinder.census.gov/servlet/STTable?_bm=y&-geo_id=01000US&-qr_name=ACS_2005_EST_G00_S2301&-ds_name=ACS_2005_EST_G00_ (accessed October 20, 2009).
99. Associated Press, "Young, White Americans Happier," *MSNBC.com*, August 21, 2007, http://www.msnbc.msn.com/id/20327875/ (accessed September 6, 2007).
100. See U.S. Department of Justice, Bureau of Justice Statistics, "Victim Characteristics," http://www.ojp.usdoj.gov/bjs/cvict_v.htm (accessed October 10, 2009).
101. J. Anyon, *Radical Possibilities* (London: Routledge, 2005), 2.
102. Ibid.
103. A. Gramsci, *Selections from the Prison Notebooks*, ed. and trans. Q. Hoare and G. Nowell Smith (New York: International Publishers, 1971), 10.
104. See P. Kovacs, "Neointellectuals: Willing Tools on a Veritable Crusade," *Journal for Critical Educational Policy Studies* 6, no. 1 (May, 2008), http://www.jceps.com/index.php?pageID=article&articleID=116.

9 The Giving Business

Venture Philanthropy and the NewSchools Venture Fund

Jim Horn and Ken Libby

> *Philanthropists need to take some time to really learn and understand how the policy world works. If they're interested in disruption, they need to understand that their disruptions won't ever really take root unless the whole political ecosystem embraces them. In Los Angeles, we're trying to figure out how to create political will around the idea that every high school in the city should look like a Green Dot school.*
>
> —Steve Barr, former CEO of Green Dot Public Schools[1]

INTRODUCTION

Philanthropic giving by the wealthy has a well-established history in America. In the late nineteenth century, industrialists offered up goodly portions of their millions to establish endowments that today continue to fund laudable causes such as hospitals, libraries, universities, parks, and research facilities. The self-educated Andrew Carnegie, for instance, helped establish over 5,500 public and university libraries around the world with generous gifts of cash. At the same time that he was dedicated to helping the working class to improve themselves through books, however, Carnegie also was giving large sums to establish and maintain more questionable ventures such as the Eugenics Record Office at Cold Springs Harbor on Long Island, which helped establish 'scientific racism' as the prevailing rationalization for Jim Crow segregation policies and laws during the first half of the twentieth century. Lead eugenicist Charles Davenport even became director of the Carnegie Institution in Washington, D. C., at the same time he was publishing 'scientific findings' on the dangers of race mixing. Such manipulated findings were instrumental, nonetheless, in the passage of antimiscegenation laws and the human sterilization laws in many states.[2]

Those charitable efforts during America's first Gilded Age by Andrew Carnegie, as well as those today by Bill Gates and other philanthro-capitalists, were and are aimed at achieving the public good with private funds in ways that remain consistent with the values of the givers. And while much good, then as now, has resulted from philanthropic actions, it is useful to keep in mind the distinction between giving to the public good and the wholesale purchase of public policy, which we would argue to be a chief distinction between the Era of Carnegie and the Age of Gates.

The need to maintain this distinction is particularly crucial today given the emergence of a new philanthropy paradigm built on the view of philanthropy as a social and economic venture investment aimed at shaping and steering public policy. Venture philanthropists, in fact, apply the same techniques of venture capitalists to philanthropic giving.[3] Based largely, in fact, on the success of venture capital funds during the 1990s in shaping the internet boom, today's venture philanthropy funds support social and economic expressions of entrepreneurship that remain consistent with ideological commitments to market mechanisms as the suitable engine for driving public decisions and public institutions toward increased efficiency and effectiveness, as defined by corporate values and interests.

This chapter will examine the NewSchools Venture Fund (NSVF) as a case study of modern-day venture philanthropy and social entrepreneurship aimed at educational reform. The NSVF represents the confluence of consumer capitalism, conservative antigovernment ideology, and entrepreneurial philanthropy, all aimed at disrupting public education by seeding alternatives such as corporate charter schools. NSVF operates for the simultaneous purposes of capital creation, educational policy shaping and implementation, and the steering of public institutions by for-profit and nonprofit corporations, which collect public dollars for the educational services they offer while garnering, in the case of nonprofit corporations, huge tax credits and deductions for investors to the fund. This chapter will explore, then, how NSVF represents a shift from a philanthropy based on the dispersal of capital to a kind of giving business aimed at the strategic investment of capital to seed conservative and neoliberal socioeconomic ideologies and to further business opportunities and tax savings for corporations and wealthy individuals. One may argue that the educational and social entrepreneurs who constitute the NSVF represent an effort to displace an older commitment to social giving with improvident investments in the virtue of selfishness writ large, so that public institutions whose purposes were once derived from public deliberation are now steered by vast sums of money strategically inserted to achieve the greatest return of influence by and for those philanthro-capitalists steeped in the nonsectarian theology of unregulated capitalism.

PHILOSOPHY OF THE NEWSCHOOLS VENTURE FUND

The NewSchools Venture Fund (NSVF) aims to transform public education by using private funds to leverage widespread change in one of America's most important public institutions. Convinced that market models and corporate management can provide the solution to problems of public education, NSVF attempts to derail democratic governance structures for decision making by embracing and promoting the triad of market mechanisms, consumer capitalism, and hyperindividualism. NSVF embodies the antigovernment philosophy that masks an antidemocratic ideology, and it is evidenced in both conservative and neoliberal agendas that depict public education as an inefficient, monopolized, and bureaucratic institution incapable of providing quality education for all Americans. NSVF promotes charter school alternatives that embrace their beliefs that teachers and their unions are obstacles to improvement, and that democratic, elected school boards are impediments to education reform and effective schools. NSVF's solution for improving educational quality relies on the performance measurements of standardized test scores, establishing a network of investor relationships among philanthro-capitalists, and applying techniques from venture capital initiatives to focus school-reform efforts through venture philanthropy.[4]

EARLY HISTORY

A Harvard Business School case study reveals the impetus for NSVF came from former Vice President Al Gore, who challenged technology-based entrepreneurs to come up with new ways to improve education.[5] John Doerr and Brook Byers, two Silicon Valley venture capitalists working for the 'relationship and venture capital' house of Kleiner, Perkins Caufield, and Byers (KPCB), heeded the challenge and founded NSVF in 1998.[6] Doerr's and Byers' work in venture capitalism included early funding for Amazon.com, Netscape, and Google, all training grounds that convinced the pair of the power of entrepreneurs to jarringly change, or disrupt, an entire business sector. Despite their eagerness to become involved in education reform, however, the two men had little experience in school policy, school management, school personnel, or school curriculum. They recognized, then, the need to identify education entrepreneurs, formulate a business plan, and attract capital. Using their schematic for creating change in the venture capital field as a plan for this new phenomenon that would come to be known as venture philanthropy, Doerr, Byers, and a number of other KPCB employees provided the early capital and business expertise to start NewSchools Venture Fund. Even though they lacked any clear goals related to where their ventures would lead in terms of educational results, they nonetheless set out to undermine and disrupt one of the nation's most vital public institutions in the same ways they would wage war against a mature industrial target deemed in need of entrepreneurial deconstruction.

The original funding for NSVF came from the pockets and stock holdings of KPCB employees, with a total value of less than $400,000.[7] Yet funding was only one part of getting NSVF off the ground. Doerr had limited experience in the education sector. In 1993, KPCB had invested in the

Lightspan Partnership Group, a for-profit company selling curriculum and technology-based programs for children in kindergarten through eighth grade. Doerr conducted due diligence (ongoing review) on the company, including repeated visits to schools using Lightspan materials. NSVF was going to be a much bigger fund and demanded far more experience than Doerr accumulated in this minor venture. The fund desperately needed someone with a background in education and entrepreneurship.

Dave Whorton, a fellow KPCB member also interested in education reform, recruited Kim Smith to the fund in hopes of filling the void. At the time, Smith was a second-year student at Stanford's Graduate School of Business. Like many current education entrepreneurs, Smith's involvement in education began through Teach For America (TFA), another social entrepreneurial enterprise looking for Ivy League graduates interested enough in teaching to put in a two-year commitment to work in a poor public school. Wendy Kopp, TFA's founder, had recruited Smith in 1989, hiring her as TFA's third employee long before TFA had recruited their first crop of Ivy League teacher aspirants. Smith describes her work at TFA as a transformative experience. After a stint with TFA, Smith started and ran BAYAC AmeriCorp, a volunteer organization based in San Francisco, where she lived while completing an MBA from Stanford in 1998. Teaming with Smith allowed NSVF to become a major player in the expanding field of educational entrepreneurship. Doerr, Byers, Mitchell, and Whorton recognized Smith's unique character: her commitment to school reform, background in educational entrepreneurship, strong connections to other entrepreneurs (mostly through TFA and Stanford), and a willingness to learn and apply the venture capitalist strategies practiced by KPCB.[8]

Smith began writing the NSVF business plan in 1998 with the help of Stanford professor Paul Romer, whose website cites his expertise in the "economics of ideas," which focuses on "mechanisms that can speed up the discovery and implementation of new rules, norms, and laws—ideas about how people interact." The plan incorporated Smith's knowledge of entrepreneurship, the missionary zeal of TFA, the caffeinated intellectualism of Paul Romer, and the venture capital outlook of the various KPCB employees. Ted Mitchell (current CEO of NSVF, former president of Occidental College, current president of the California State Board of Education, and previously a high-level employee of Stanford and UCLA) became involved with the venture in the late 1990s as well. Mitchell was attracted to NSVF by the entrepreneurial spirit, the new-economy approach to finding emerging markets ripe for capitalization, and the venture capital formula for driving success.[9] Mitchell held a position on the NSVF board from 1998 until his appointment to CEO in 2005. He continues to lead NSVF as the CEO, complete with a $480,000 salary (in 2007), which comes on top of his salary for his other day job as president of the California State Board of Education. With Mitchell at the helm,

Kim Smith has turned more of her attention to policy matters and continues to play an influential role for NSVF.

Much of NSVF's literature references the 'new economy' of the 1990s, and it is imperative to keep in mind the economic setting in which NSVF evolved: Silicon Valley during the tech boom in the latter parts of the twentieth century. In particular, the founders of NSVF promoted the belief that the public schools were not producing graduates capable of competing in the 'new economy.' Cofounder John Doerr is on record as telling a gathering at the Harvard Business School in 2000 that "40 percent of eight-year-olds can't read" and that "if you can't read, you can't run a Web browser."[10] This 'new economy' demanded faster learning—both in the classroom and in the new jobs created by the tech boom. NSVF's twin obsession with technology-based learning and technology as a measurement tool reflects the fund's origins in the tech-obsessed world of 1990s Silicon Valley. Doerr's early and significant successes in molding California education policy include efforts in the late 1990s to pass laws in favor of charter schools and to repeal laws that were not. In Doerr's words, "four million dollars and some lobbying efforts . . . resulted in one thousand schools and three billion dollars invested over ten years. That's big, scalable social change, and that's just one story. It's the kind of work that should go on throughout the country."[11] That kind of leveraging of relatively small sums (in venture capital terms) to produce large social changes remains the model that NSVF prefers to emulate.

NSVF thrives on targeting urban schools, playing the role of 'knight in shining armor' willing to swoop in purportedly to save oppressed populations from bad schools. Meanwhile, the problems faced in America's ghettos and struggling schools are exacerbated by efforts that effect the disempowerment of minority groups, the elimination of most social safety nets, corrosive and persistent poverty, and the silent terror of neoliberalism.[12]

NSVF's biggest supporters include Microsoft cofounder Bill Gates, SunAmerica and KB Homes founder Eli Broad, the Walton family, the Fisher family of Gap, Inc., and a host of other global capitalists with hundreds of millions in tax-deductible dollars to spend on conservative educational 'choice' options. These philanthro-capitalists wield strong media influence, and their network of connections with powerful players in the urban education world include D. C. chancellor Michelle Rhee; New Orleans superintendent Paul Vallas; New York chancellor Joel Klein; and Secretary of Education Arne Duncan. As a nonprofit venture philanthropy firm, NSVF offers one important avenue to move funds in ways that yield the biggest bang for the buck, while exploiting a tax structure that gives back thirty-three cents on every dollar to these wealthiest of givers.[13]

Kim Smith elaborated the essential philosophy of the organization during a 2003 appearance at Stanford's Entrepreneurial Thought Leader Speaker Series.[14] Arguing for public education's need for competition from an outside source to improve public schools through "co-opitition," Smith indicated that NSVF was less interested in funding for-profit school ventures than in establishing a parallel charter school system that would influence the public system to change in terms of organization, financing, and management. The public image of for-profit schools has remained a public relations minefield, but social entrepreneurs could, rather, open up markets in education through nonprofit charter ventures, which in turn often hire for-profit educational management organizations (EMOs) to operate those schools. In the future, Smith would like to see a public education system wherein all schools resemble charter schools: "Every public school will have a performance contract where those people running it will have the freedom they need to manage it well, hire and fire based on performance, to design their schools in a way that is successful for their faculty and their kids, and if they're successful they get to continue. If they're not successful, they should be closed."[15] In effect, NSVF's reform agenda consolidates power in fewer hands without public oversight or accountability, depends upon market mechanisms to introduce and sustain improvement, and embraces standardized performance measures as the royal road to curricular and instructional accountability and evaluation.

FIRST FUND

NSVF requires organizations seeking funds to file a business plan, rather than a grant proposal. Such plans must show how the venture, if funded, would "produce measurable outcomes, be scalable (eventually self-sustaining), fit with NSVF's investment strategy, and benefit from the fund's investment."[16] NSVF's first fund, lasting from 1998 to 2002, invested in only three management organizations. NSVF was comfortable investing in both for-profit and nonprofit corporations, including for-profit charter management organizations (CMOs) and school management organizations (SMOs). However, the fund saw entrepreneurship opportunities outside of school management as well. The rest of their investments targeted developing 'human capital' (Teach For America, Teachscape, and New Leaders for New Schools), increasing publicity and advocacy research for school choice (Greatschools.com and policy studies through the Center for Policy Studies and the National Center on Education and the Economy), and instructional materials (Carnegie Learning and Success for All). Of the three management organizations that received grants during the first round of funding, only one was considered a success, Aspire Public Schools. High Tech High and LearnNow both failed to meet NSVF's goal of creating management organizations capable of going to scale. This willingness to invest in a variety of types of organizations was consistent with the investment strategies of venture capitalism.

In 1999, NSVF cohosted a conference with the Stanford Graduate School of Business and Education aimed at creating "a network among education entrepreneurs and addressing the resource needs,"[17] the first of what would become an annual event for social entrepreneurs and venture philanthropists looking to build the business-model infrastructure necessary to offer charter alternatives to traditional public schools. The 1999 summit was attended by TFA founder Wendy Kopp, KIPP cofounder and TFA alumnus Michael Feinberg, GreatSchools president Bill Jackson, University Public Schools founder and CEO Don Shalvey, and LearnNow cofounder and CEO Gene Wade.[18] The annual event offered a venue for exchanging ideas, discussing the challenges faced by education entrepreneurs, and (tacitly or explicitly) establishing the national policy agenda favoring the corporate charter-school movement. Since 1999 the invitation-only event has grown in attendance and prominence that coincides with NSVF's expansion. NSVF's annual summit now regularly attracts education entrepreneurs, high-level public policy makers, foundation representatives, and influential think tank denizens, both neoconservative and neoliberal.

NSVF's first direct funding to charter schools also began in 1999, with a $500,000 grant to the University Public Schools (UPS), along with the promise of future funding based on meeting performance targets. UPS founder Don Shalvey, an experienced teacher and superintendent of the San Carlos School District, had created California's first charter school in 1994 and believed the presence of the school improved the entire district. Shalvey articulated his views on improving education when he appeared on television with Smith in 2005 as a guest of Charlie Rose, suggesting "public education is indeed a monopoly that has not yet been broken to the degree where we can have competition and choice and higher standards to serve kids well."[19] Shalvey felt the public school system would be pressured to change if charters were able to attract 10 percent of a district's students, a theory shared by Smith and the NSVF. UPS is now known as Aspire Public Schools (APS) and has dramatically expanded. APS's website shows the nonprofit now receives significant funding through NSVF, as well as from the foundations of Gates, Broad, and the Walton family. The Gates Foundation alone has donated over $10 million to Aspire through three different grants (in 2000, 2003, and 2009), and the charter chain was a beneficiary of part of a $60 million grant awarded to five charter schools in 2009. APS has been one of NSVF's most successful ventures and is mentioned as a high-quality model by many pro-charter reformers. In 2009, the Gates Foundation announced that Shalvey would join their education team and work with the foundation's director of education.

NSVF also experienced a few failures during the early years. LearnNow, a for-profit company started by Gene Wade and Jim Shelton, originally started as a nonprofit school management organization. However, Wade and Shelton had difficulty raising funds and switched to the for-profit model in an attempt to attract capital. NSVF was one of the early backers of the young organization. Just six months after investing $500,000, LearnNow ran into financial trouble and faced the possibility of shutting down. NSVF was forced to provide additional assistance in the form of funding and organizational guidance. The failure of LearnNow would have brought negative public relations to the charter-school movement, a risk NSVF was unwilling to take.[20] The financial turmoil of LearnNow came to a close when Edison Schools purchased the company in July of 2001 for 1.4 million shares of Edison's class-A common stock, which was trading at $22.37 per share. NSVF managed to make over a million dollars in profit from the sale of Edison stock during 2001. However, the fund sold their stock in Edison at various points of the year, a year in which Edison's stock plummeted after their deal to run Philadelphia schools fell through. Although NSVF managed to turn a profit on their LearnNow investment, they ultimately failed to produce a model of scalable sustainability.

Jim Shelton's floundering with LearnNow did nothing to damage his own personal stock, however. He was put in charge to lead the NSVF East Coast division and then worked for the Gates Foundation until 2009, when he was appointed to lead the Office of Innovation and Improvement under Secretary of Education Arne Duncan. In his new role, Shelton will have a $650 million Innovation Fund to drive the corporate brand of education reform, this time using federal dollars to do so.

High Tech High (HTH), another management organization receiving investment funds from NSVF, provided the fund with a different set of challenges. HTH represented NSVF's early attempt at a franchise model of nonprofit charter schools. However, by 2003 the franchise model, described by Smith during a presentation for the Stanford Business School's Entrepreneurial Thought Leader Speaker Series, was viewed as an unfeasible model because it lacked consistency of product.[21] Smith compared the franchise model in education to groups like the Boys and Girls Club and the YMCA, all of which have varying degrees of quality across sites. NSVF felt the inconsistency would eventually hurt the charter brand, as well as NSVF's reputation. NSVF, which embraced the venture capitalist model of only investing in what can expand in the market, did not feel HTH could be taken to scale. HTH currently operates eight schools and has not received NSVF funding since 2001. NSVF no longer supports the for-profit model or franchise charter model largely due to their experience with LearnNow and High Tech High.

In 1999, the fund also invested in Carnegie Learning, a private company started by Carnegie Mellon professor John Anderson. The for-profit company produced a variety of math curricula integrating their computer-based programs, textbook, online tutors, and teacher professional development. The algebra program, aimed at ninth-grade students across the nation, involves students using the computer-based tutor for three days a week and meeting with a teacher and class during the other two days. This appeal of technology-based learning is twofold for NSVF: 1) a replicable strategy for improving scores on standardized tests would be tremendously valuable under a law like No Child Left Behind; and 2) a test-based learning curricula like Carnegie's variety of computer-based lessons could be copied and pasted into other NSVF's charter schools—which would, in turn, increase the value of Carnegie Learning. Additionally, the program's limited instructional commitment by teachers could lower the costs of running a school by limiting the need for instructional personnel. Carnegie's program could also attract other Silicon Valley venture capitalists, who share a widely held belief that technology-assisted teacher proofing may help minimize the negative effects from public school teacher incompetence. But NSVF is only one of Carnegie's many enthusiastic supporters: the Chicago Public Schools used $770,000 of a $21 million Gates Foundation grant to adopt Carnegie's algebra program in 2006.[22]

In September 1999 the fund provided Success for All, a nonprofit program, with a five-year, $1 million loan with a 3 percent interest rate. The Success for All program targeted at-risk children through rigorous reading instruction, research-based curricula, and staff professional development. Investments in curricula, particularly programs aimed at increasing math and reading scores on high-stakes tests, could possibly help future ventures while adding diversity to the NSVF portfolio. However, the Department of Education's implementation of No Child Left Behind and Reading First directed funding toward its own preferred list of providers. Success for All was implemented in only two of the 4,800 schools eligible for Reading First funding, despite being listed as an 'approved' program in many states.[23] NSVF no longer funds Success for All.

Teach for America (TFA), New Leaders for New Schools (NLFNS), and Teachscape were the other three educational entrepreneur organizations supported by NSVF during their first round of funding. TFA, NLFNS, and Teachscape promised to provide the new kind of leaders and teachers needed for the charter-school movement. These fast-track programs assume an effective teacher need only a grasp of the material they teach and the willingness to implement scripted and boxed curriculum. The importance of pedagogical coursework for teachers is greatly discounted, offering as it does the theoretical, political, and historical contexts that could bring under scrutiny the ironclad reformist assumptions that otherwise go unquestioned by neophytes without the benefit of any foundational knowledge of American education.

Teachscape provides educational professional development services by using recorded case studies to train prospective teachers. According to tax filings, NSVF provided the for-profit venture with a $500,000 interest-free loan in 2000. The early funding helped Teachscape expand services toward offering an alternative to the more traditional avenue of practice teaching. However, the program is a case of tech industry veterans assuming that great teachers simply need to see other great teachers in action (in this case, through recorded case studies). Mark Atkinson, CEO and founder of Teachscape, worked as a television producer for NBC and CBS prior to his work in educating future educators. The passive learning method of Teachscape's tech-based education may help to create a pipeline of marginally prepared teacher candidates willing and often eager to depend upon scripted curricula.

NSVF provided Teach for America with significant grants in 2001, 2002, 2003, and 2004. Most important, NSVF provided Wendy Kopp and her organization with opportunities for expansion. Both NSVF and TFA have focused their reform agenda by targeting California; New York; Washington, D.C.; New Orleans; and Chicago. These urban centers that house some of America's most impoverished neighborhoods are sites where philanthro-capitalists can target the weakest links in public education, while simultaneously pushing top-down free-market privatization agendas focused on providing narrowed curriculums of rote learning and total compliance for the poor. Young TFA corps members provide culturally irrelevant, sycophantic, and temporary labor for school districts looking to minimize personnel costs for charter schools.

Some TFA alumni, then, are recruited into the entrepreneurial-philanthropic complex to further corporate America's charter school agenda. KIPP, one of the nation's largest charter school chains with over eighty locations, has former TFA corps members as principals in 60 percent of its schools.[24] Although it is beyond the scope of this chapter to offer further details, TFA has adopted corporate techniques into the way they train future teachers and in their expectations for a temporal teaching profession. This mentality appeals to NSVF investors, a group guided by venture capitalists, funded by philanthro-capitalists, and managed by people thoroughly uninterested in questioning the pedagogical consequences of their ventures or for correcting the socioeconomic conditions in America's economically depressed and underserved communities.

New Leaders for New Schools (NLFNS) received over $750,000 during NSVF's first round of funding. NLFNS provides training for future leaders of urban public schools. The organization operates under the same corporate assumptions as the philanthro-capitalists driving education reform and the social entrepreneurs willing to implement their goals: change school through new leadership steeped in the corporate ethos and psychological techniques, eliminate due process and tenure restrictions in personnel matters, and apply market-based strategies to running schools under the control of a CEO/principal. CEO and cofounder Jon Schnur, a long-time supporter of the Democratic reform efforts and former insider in the Clinton administration, served as an advisor to the Obama campaign and briefly as an advisor to Arne Duncan's Department of Education before returning to NLFNS in May of 2009.

SECOND FUND

NSVF's Second Fund began in 2002 and lasted through 2006. The group's earlier work had established a clear course of action: invest more resources toward developing 'human capital' and nonprofit charter schools. With the Second Fund, Teach for America and New Leaders for New Schools continued to garner support that expanded yearly. The Charter Accelerator Fund and Performance Accelerator Fund were established as part of the Second Fund, driving expansion of charter schools and data-based assessment tools. While the Charter Accelerator Fund had wide appeal and attracted large amounts of venture philanthropy from philanthro-capitalists, the Performance Accelerator Fund, which was focused on the development and expansion of computer-based assessment tools, pulled in less than $3 million and fell short of NSVF's hopes.

Totaling around $70 million, NSVF's Second Fund was fueled largely by the Bill and Melinda Gates Foundation. Tax filing show the Gates Foundation made a $22 million contribution in 2003 and provided another $33 million in 2006. Collectively, the Gates-Walton-Broad trio contributed most of the $70 million. More important, the collective agendas of Gates-Walton-Broad continued to coalesce around the deprofessionalization and deskilling of teaching, the application of corporate strategies to public school governance and management, and the continued exploitation of technology for testing and evaluation. In most cases, the aforementioned foundations invested in the same charter schools as NSVF, effectively using NSVF's management consulting as a way to further leverage changes that fit within the overarching corporate theology. The U.S. Department of Education under George W. Bush chipped in to the cause for the taxpayers, when the department issued a $1.99 million grant to NSVF in 2003 for their charter school reform efforts. Such use of public funds to establish corporate control of public institutions went unmentioned in either the regular or academic presses.

The Second Fund saw an explosion in funding of charter schools. The for-profit LearnNow and High Tech High disappeared from the NSVF's agenda in favor of nonprofit corporations. Far from the original concept of charter schools as incubators of innovation directed by educators and parents, NSVF began pushing a limited number of 'proven choices' based on standardized curriculum, instruction, and assessments. In 2003, Aspire Public Schools received continuation funding, while new monies were awarded to the Green Dot Public Schools in Los Angeles and the Leadership Public Charter Schools in the Bay Area. Schools closed or otherwise restructured under NCLB sanctions became targets for charter conversions, even as the opening of new charter schools effectively created a market for 'choice' parents, thus strengthening the corporate charter-school movement as a whole.

The biggest impediment to charter expansion now and earlier in the decade was the limited availability of affordable facilities, a burden that could be partially eased with financing from venture philanthropy until public policy could be adapted and molded to better serve the corporate charter-school agenda. The Second Fund recognized, then, the limited availability of cost-efficient buildings available for charter schools, and the fund aggressively invested in real estate. On the policy front, the National

Alliance for Public Charter Schools recently published a guide to revising charter schools laws that encourages the creation of additional public loans for charter schools that have access to outside funding, a stipulation that almost always excludes the local version of community-based cooperative charter schools in favor of those with corporate backing.

In 2003, Kim Smith led an NSVF effort to start Pacific Charter School Development (PCSD), an organization aimed strictly at financing and developing spaces and facilities for future charter schools. PCSD would come to serve many of the other charter organizations receiving funding and guidance from NSVF, including Green Dot, Alliance, Aspire Public Schools, KIPP, Partnership to Uplift Communities, and the Inner City Education Foundation. PCSD has received nearly 7 million dollars in venture philanthropy from the Gates Foundation, $12.47 million from the Broad Foundation, and $75 million in equity funding from the Walton Family Foundation. James Wilcox, a former NSVF employee and current CEO of Aspire Public Schools, serves on the Board of Directors for PCSD, along with NSVF partner Julie Mikuta and the Broad Foundation's COO, Kevin Hall. By the end of 2010, PCSD will have funded the facilities development of forty-one schools seating over 15,000 students.[25] The inbred monetary relations of NSVF and PCSD exemplify the incestuous flood of tax-deductible dollars washing back and forth across the permeable borders of these various nonprofit foundations, venture philanthropy firms, and social entrepreneurial corporations.

NSVF also invested in a facilities development organization based in New York known as Civic Builders, a nonprofit corporation started in 2002 to provide real estate opportunities to a variety of service agencies, including charter schools. In 2003 New York mayor Michael Bloomberg announced $250 million available for charter school infrastructure development and included Civic Builders as a partner in the expansion project. NSVF's tax filings for 2003 declares the fund received over $80,000 from the New York Department of Education for "education consulting" services between September 2002 and September 2003. This partnership provides an example of how philanthro-capitalists leverage control of public policy issues to concentrate power through a labyrinthine maze of financial exchanges that effectively use public dollars to reduce tax liabilities while increasing business opportunities. NSVF offers a two-way conduit for the transfer of cash that always ends up benefiting a small group of philanthro-capitalists with tremendous financial capital and staffs of financiers and attorneys skilled in charging government institutions for services that favor NSVF's antipublic agenda to seed future ventures aimed at shrinking the public space and increasing corporate profits, all the while using more public dollars to fund democracy's demise.

A similar organization appeared in Washington, D.C., in 2006. Tax filings for EdBuild, a nonprofit providing support for 'data-based learning,' shows the organization was incorporated by four individuals: CEO of the

Federal City Council John W. Hill; NSVF partner Jordan Meranus; former general manager of Comcast Donna Rattley Washington; and former D.C. administrator LeGrande Baldwin. EdBuild almost received a $57.6 million no-bid contract from the D.C. school board to implement new curricula, provide professional development, and rehab four buildings that could later be leased to charter schools. Even though funding was cut from the D.C. schools budget at the last minute, Kim Smith and NSVF received compliments for their work on the effort from the American Enterprise Institute, a conservative think tank that advocates limited government and free-market economics.[26]

NSVF used the bulk of Second Fund resources to open new charter schools in a number of cities. The fund continued to focus on California, particularly the Los Angeles and Oakland Unified School Districts, by supporting Education for Change, Aspire Public Schools, Leadership Public Schools, Alliance, Green Dot, Inner City Education Foundation, and Partnership to Uplift Communities. Achievement First, Lighthouse Academies, and Uncommon Schools all received contracts for charter management in New York. NSVF has worked with pro-charter D.C. chancellor Michelle Rhee while providing support to Friendship Public Charter School, D.C. Prep, Lighthouse Academies, and KIPP D.C. Noble Network of Charter Schools, Perspectives Charter Schools, Academy for Urban School Leadership, and Lighthouse Academies all operate in the Chicago area and expanded greatly under Chicago Public Schools CEO, Arne Duncan.

The Second Fund saw the successful development of a variety of charter school management organizations in a number of large cities, almost all with mayoral control of education. NSVF helped establish charter schools in Chicago; New York; Washington, D.C.; and in a number of California municipalities. Additionally, Ted Mitchell, president of the California Board of Education, assumed the role of CEO for NSVF in September 2005, even as Kim Smith retained a powerful shaping influence in the organization. During this time, the fund increasingly operated as a lever for reform efforts directed through consulting services, commissioned research and advocacy studies to advance its agendas, close networks of entrepreneurs and government officials, and a strategic guidance system for staggering sums of financial resources.

OTHER FUNDING

The bulk of NSVF's funding now goes to supporting nonprofit charter management organizations, developing the human capital necessary to run them, and establishing facilities for future charter schools. Importantly, though, NSVF has also sponsored advocacy-group studies to advance its agenda through the Institute for the Study of Knowledge, the Progressive Policy Institute, Center for Policy Studies, Center for Education Reform,

Institute for the Study of Management in Education, and the National Center on Education and the Economy.

Tax records show NSVF provided a $75,000 grant to the National Center on Education and the Economy (NCEE) in 2000 to create a school leadership institute, the National Institute for School Leadership (NISL). This program was an $11 million investment by NSVF, the Broad Foundation, the Carnegie Corporation, the Stupiski Foundation, and the NCEE. NISL aims to bring the leadership knowledge from the military, corporate America, the legal field, and the medical profession to public education.[27] NCEE is best known for the 2006 publication, *Tough Choices, Tough Times*, which was partly funded by the Gates Foundation.

The Progressive Policy Institute (PPI) also received grants from NSVF. In 2003, tax records show NSVF made a $23,400 grant to PPI for a conference and publication aimed at strengthening the charter-school movement. The event and publication, cofunded by the Annie E. Casey Foundation, Standard and Poors, and Connections Academy, brought together many of the most powerful players in education reform. Among the attendees were Jim Shelton of the Gates Foundation, NSVF's Kim Smith, Aspire's Don Shalvey, and NYC councilmember Eva Moskowitz. PPI continues to support much of NSVF's agenda, aimed as it is toward mayoral control, expansion of charter schools, market-based reform efforts, high-stakes standardized tests, and performance pay for teachers based on test scores. Andrew Rotherham, one of PPI's main education experts and high-ranking Democratic education policy advisor for the Clinton administration, has worked with the Obama administration through informal and formal channels. Until recently, Rotherham worked for EdSector, a New Democratic think tank funded with at least $600,000 in Gates Foundation grants. The connection to PPI and new players within Democrats for Education Reform (DFER) means NSVF will likely continue to enjoy a highly visible presence within the Washington establishment.

THIRD FUND

Now operating in its Third Fund, NSVF continues to fund charter school expansion and operates with the energetic support of the Secretary of Education and other high-powered federal and state education officials. The fund asserts that it supports 124 schools with nearly 38,000 students and plans to expand to 200 schools with some 75,000 students during the next few years.[28] In a statement accompanying a Gates Foundation investment in 2006, funders maintain that NSVF hopes to serve "hundreds of thousands of students" by 2015.[29]

The Third Fund, beginning in 2006 and continuing to the present, unfolds during a turbulent time in education reform. The economic climate will tighten funding for the nonprofit sector, but the full effects of the financial crisis remain unclear for charter school corporate operators and management firms. Although Gates suffered an $18 billion loss during the recent financial turbulence, the Gates Foundation plans on increasing donation levels in the near future.[30] The Walton family appears poised to continue playing an influential role in education reform, given Wal-Mart's continued strength in the current economic climate. Obama administration support for unlimited charter-school expansion, teacher performance pay, and 'postpartisan' partnerships between the public and private sectors indicate favorable conditions for an expanded role for the NSVF agendas.

The Innovation Fund in the American Recovery and Reinvestment Act of 2009 devotes $650 million specifically for education entrepreneurs. Secretary of Education Arne Duncan tapped former Gates Foundation employee and LearnNow cofounder Jim Shelton to lead the Office of Innovation and Improvement. According to their website, the Office of Innovation and Improvement created under President George W. Bush bills itself as the "nimble, entrepreneurial arm of the Department of Education." The Obama administration's Department of Education appears, in fact, to be picking up where venture philanthropy leaves off, its own agenda for innovation largely indistinguishable from that of NSVF and the multiple millions in tax-deductible 'investments' it manages.

The $4.35 billion Race to the Top Fund (RTTF) is the largest fund ever distributed solely at the discretion of the Secretary of Education and his advisors. Duncan recruited NSVF COO and partner Joanne Weiss to lead the fund, another clear indication of NSVF's favorable positioning with the new administration. Duncan intends to use this fund to fundamentally alter public education: "Joanne will help us push a strong reform agenda that is entrepreneurial in spirit, providing carrots and sticks, to change the way we do business, and fundamentally turn around underperforming schools in ways that last for decades," Duncan told an audience at NSVF's 2009 annual summit via videoconference. He continued: "We may never have an opportunity like this again to dramatically improve our country's educational system with huge investments in a few strategic areas to make changes that are deep and foundational."[31] Weiss and Duncan will be able to use the RTTF to reward states for adopting the agenda now embraced by venture philanthropists and the Obama DOE, aimed specifically at removing state restrictions on charter school expansion, adopting national testing and data systems, altering teacher preparation programs by curtailing pedagogical content, and establishing teacher-performance pay systems based principally on standardized test scores.

During the past dozen years, NSVF has shown itself to be an effective agent for using venture capitalist methods to disrupt the public education system and to back the efforts of funded entrepreneurs with more money than knowledge to apply business and technology solutions to educational and social problems. In so doing, NSVF has shown itself as a valuable conduit for the movement of intellectual capital, human capital, and investment capital aimed at sustaining a social and economic dogma that remains immune to empirical or philosophical challenge. At the same time, the devotees of the corporatist state whom NSVF serves remain undeterred by either argument or evidence from a mission that would appear destined to make democracy safe for the corporate world. For the corporate and political Elect, "they base their decisions on established beliefs, such as the primacy of an unregulated market or globalization, which are accepted as unquestioned absolutes."[32] And even as there is little to no evidence to recommend the preconceived solutions to the public education system that must be dismantled in order to make way for the entrepreneurial replacements, the disruptors and the leveragers press on with renewed vigor in their war against any public institution or public space that is not steered and controlled by the unquestioned and unmonitored virtues of corporate interests.

The general public has very little understanding of the current complexities of public education in the United States, represented as it is by a complex web of government offices, business organizations, think tanks, nonprofit corporations and foundations, venture philanthropy outfits, and educators. Meanwhile, the failure of mainstream journalism to post questions of the new disruptive reformers mirrors the larger widespread failure of media coverage of America's foreign policy escapades. The promises of quick school turnarounds and increasing test scores provide media fodder that is alluring for a public that views the corporate charter movement in a favorable light, particularly in the historically oppressed communities of America's urban apartheid communities. Nonprofit corporate chains like KIPP and the KIPP knock-offs that are supported by NSVF thrive by focusing their educational efforts at increasing test scores in reading and math for those who remain willing and able to withstand the demands of these total-compliance charter organizations. By appealing to the 'no excuses' mantra that has found its way even into President Obama's speech to commemorate the 100th anniversary of the NAACP, these academic chain-gang charters that are funded by NSVF and billed as replacements for urban public schools have located, finally, the ultimate excuse needed to abandon those brown, Black, and poor children whose educational failure is deemed a personal or cultural shortcoming.

CODA

Citizen involvement at the local, state, and national levels can counteract the shift toward centralized corporate control of public schools. That involvement will only be engaged, however, by an informed public and by informed professionals who understand what is at stake when the public loses the controlling interest in one of the largest enterprises that we citizens own. The need for informed media coverage of education policy matters is desperately needed, and the engagement by researchers in uncovering the current sociological, psychological, and political realities in schools is of paramount importance. Concerned educators at all levels must help the public become informed about current threats to the public schools and to the historical civic purpose of education that Thomas Jefferson demanded, while at the same time offering policy alternatives that will generate the commitment to humane, effective, and efficient public schools aimed to preserve and expand our democracy and to assure our children's competence in assuming their adult roles. At the core of those alternatives must be the acknowledged necessity for public control over one of the most important of America's public institutions.

NOTES

1. P. Tough, "How Many Billionaires Does It Take to Run a School System?" *New York Times Magazine*, March 9, 2008, http://www.nytimes.com/2008/03/09/magazine/09roundtable-t.html (accessed June 1, 2009).
2. E. Black, *War against the Weak: Eugenics and America's Plan to Create a Master Race* (New York: Basic Books, 2003).
3. S. Katz, "What Does It Mean to Say that Philanthropy Is "Effective? The Philanthropists' New Clothes," *Proceedings of the American Philosophical Society* 149, no. 2 (2005): 123–31.
4. P. Frumkin, "Inside Venture Philanthropy," *Society* 40, no. 4 (2003): 7–15.
5. N. Tempest, "Case Study 3.2: NewSchools Venture Fund," in *Entrepreneurship in the Social Sector* (Thousand Oaks, CA: Sage Publications, 2007), 114.
6. J. Scott, "The Politics of Venture Philanthropy in Charter School Policy and Advocacy," *Educational Policy* 23, no. 1 (2009): 123.
7. NewSchools Venture Fund, *NewSchools Venture Fund Summit, 1999*, http://newschools.org/files/Summit1999Brief.pdf (accessed June 22, 2009).
8. N. Tempest, "Case Study 3.2," 120.
9. Ibid., 117.
10. S. Wolf, "VC Luminary John Doerr: Education Reform Critical to Success of New Economy," *Harvard Business School Bulletin*, June 2000, http://newschools.org/about/news/articles/John-Doerr-article (accessed June 22, 2009).
11. Ibid.
12. H. Giroux, *Against the Terror of Neoliberalism* (Boulder, CO: Paradigm Publishers, 2008).
13. S. Perry, "Obama's Plan to Reduce Charitable Deductions for the Wealthy Draws Criticism," *The Chronicle of Philanthropy* (News Updates), February 26, 2009, http://philanthropy.com/news/updates/7244/obama-plans-to-reduce-charitable-deduction-for-wealthy-donors (accessed September 2, 2009).
14. "Kim Smith, NewSchools Venture Fund," eCorner: Stanford University's Entrepreneurship Corner, 2003, http://ecorner.stanford.edu/authorMaterialInfo.html?author=54 (accessed June 22, 2009).
15. K. Smith and D. Shalvey, "A Discussion about Improving Public Education with Kim Smith and Don Shalvey," *The Charlie Rose Show* (New York: Rose Communications / Bloomberg Television News and Thirteen/WNET New

York, 2005), http://www.charlierose.com/view/interview/886 (accessed June 2, 2009).

16. J. Scott, "The Politics of Venture Philanthropy in Charter School Policy and Advocacy."
17. NewSchools Venture Fund, *NewSchools Venture Fund Summit, 1999.*
18. Ibid.
19. K. Smith and D. Shalvey, "A Discussion about Improving Public Education."
20. G. Dees and B. Andersen, *NewSchools Venture Fund (B)* (Palo Alto, CA: Stanford University Graduate School of Business, 2001).
21. K. Smith, "Scalability and Sustainability in the Non-Profit Sector," eCorner: Stanford University's Entrepreneurship Corner, 2003, http://ecorner.stanford.edu/authorMaterialInfo.html?mid=625 (accessed June 22, 2009).
22. Gates Foundation, "Chicago Schools Purchases Carnegie Learning Math Curricula with Bill & Melinda Gates Foundation Funds, 2006" (press release), http://www.carnegielearning.com/company_press_detail.cfm?pressreleaseid=86 (accessed June 22, 2009).
23. M. Grunwald, "Billions for an Inside Game on Reading," *Washington Post*, October 1, 2006, http://www.washingtonpost.com/wp-dyn/content/article/2006/09/29/AR2006092901333.html (accessed March 1, 2009).
24. Teach for America, *Teach for America and KIPP: Where Great Teachers Become Great School Leaders*, 2008, http://www.teachforamerica.org/assets/ documents/2008-09.SLI.KIPP.Draft4.pdf.
25. Pacific Charter School Development, "Clients," 2008, http://www.pacific-charter.org/clients (accessed June 22, 2009).
26. B. Hassel and F. Hess, "Entrepreneurs in Education Meeting: Growing the Human Capital Pipeline," EdFunders.org, October 13, 2006, http://www.edfunders.org/downloads/AEI_entrepreneurs_10-13-06.pdf (accessed June 22, 2009).
27. National Institute for School Leadership, "Professional Development for School Leaders: What We Do," http://www.nisl.net/about/.
28. NewSchools Venture Fund, "Charter Management Organizations: NewSchools Venture Fund," 2007, http://newschools.org/portfolio/impact/charter-management-organizations (accessed June 22, 2009).
29. Gates Foundation, "Major New Investment Supports NewSchools Venture Fund's Effort to Provide 200 High-quality Charter Schools for 100,000 Low-Income Students," (press release, 2006), http://www.gatesfoundation.org/press-releases/Pages/newschools-charter-school-management-061009.aspx (accessed June 22, 2009).
30. L. Kroll et al., "The World's Billionaires," *Forbes*, March 11, 2009, http://www.forbes.com/2009/03/11/worlds-richest-people-billionaires-2009-billionaires_land.html (accessed June 22, 2009).
31. United States Department of Education, "Secretary Duncan Sets Tone for 'Race to the Top' by Naming Innovative New Leader" (press release, 2009), http://www.ed.gov/news/pressreleases/2009/05/05192009c.html (accessed June 22, 2009).
32. C. Hedges, *Empire of Illusion: The End of Literacy and the Triumph of Spectacle* (New York: Nation Books, 2009), 98.

10 Dear Bill

'Grokking' Education*

Patti Lather

August 2009

Dear Bill:

I understand from a 2006 *Newsweek* article that you hope to "grok" "this mysterious thing" called education.[1] I have read your 2008 and 2009 annual reports and note your desire to use data toward innovation in pursuit of increased impact.[2] I see your commitment to creating an environment where your staff can do its best work, including listening more closely to your partners in the field on the basis of a recent survey of 'grantee perception' of how relations are and are not working.

Good for you (and your foundation, more specifically) for remaining committed to the reform of U.S. secondary education in spite of disappointments and setbacks.[3] Especially good for you for recognizing that new forms of program evaluation are necessary in moving forward. "Change comes so slowly and is so hard to measure," you say in regards to your goals for changing America's schools.[4] "It is hard to test with scientific certainty," you go on to say, in recognizing the need for "better tools" to measure progress.

In deepening and extending the foundation's impact, clearly we need new ways of looking at old issues. Although easy to overlook, the too often left-to-the-instrumentalists arena of program evaluation knows well that how assessment happens in school reform is a key part of understanding 'what works' and what does not. This entails addressing how narrow ideas of research and program evaluation design may be contributing to your disappointments in terms of how one 'measures' becoming.

Advances in program evaluation are an important part of Gates Foundation initiatives. Several authors in a recent edited collection trace lessons learned from the $10 million spent on school reform by the Annenberg Challenge that yielded few results but did call for better methods of program evaluation.[5] Your foundation has picked up such lessons but in rather fugitive ways, as captured by a friend of mine who works for a Gates Foundation-funded, Houston-based project on effective teachers. In a request for help in making sense of her experience in the project, she reports "I'm thinking that there's something different here in what we're doing." She is referring particularly to a way of using mixed methods whereby both quantitative and qualitative data are well respected for what they bring to the table. This bodes well for advances in program evaluation.

I'm especially glad that the impact of classroom teachers is coming back into focus, but I worry about your alignments with what is emerging as President Obama's agenda. I know he's got a lot on his plate, but I had hoped he would at least have put people in place who would move away from standardized testing instead of expanding it to 'performance pay' for teachers. However 'highly effective teachers' are made, defined, and rewarded, let it not be through measurement alone but through means that include parents, kids, teachers, and administrators in what gets listened to. Your report of a visit to Hidalgo Early College High School demonstrates the power of your listening to students and teachers, and my interest is in how this might be translated into a more sustained focus on how such "listening" methods can be systematically built into your "maniacal focus on drawing in the best talent and measuring results."[6]

"The new science" you call upon worries me.[7] Leaving alone the question of whether the same kind of science works in health care and agriculture as in education, "the strength of our evidence"[8] would be expanded by recognizing that some things are not perceivable in orthodox ideas of science. This is philosophy and morality. But there are philosophies and moralities embedded in scientific practices, whether we acknowledge these or not. Many qualitative researchers across many disciplines have been busily writing about how the rhetoric of 'the best scientific evidence available' elides the contested nature of science. Assumptions of 'objective knowledge' free from political, social, and moral considerations limit the kind of social interventions that are thinkable, doable, and quite underway in many contexts. Take two examples, when researchers at Duke University ask people to "tell their stories" of emergency room use in order to restructure its family medicine unit[9] and when David Kennedy does fieldwork to find out how to reclaim teenage drug sellers from the streets:[10] these are interventions grounded in fieldwork, not measurement. Practice-oriented research that focuses on differences, challenging power and constraint, and encouraging new possibilities can be of much use in resisting norms and bringing about substantial change. The limits of standard practices of inquiry are precisely the key. Research that helps change thinking might get us further to where we want to be than research that focuses overmuch on that which is tidily and easily measurable. Such research can revitalize critique as an important step forward.

In reforming schools, I would also urge you toward an ecology of different models, each insufficient unto itself, that perform and cultivate a democratic counterculture "from a variety of different angles across a variety of different registers" that weave together "for more sustained engagements."[11] Build large and growing coalitions; fashion a radical democratic structure; set up receptive practices to hear multiple voices; enact communities of difference; enable pragmatic research of various sorts on particular issues. I am urging that a diversity of approaches be instituted, each a factor in a complex web that builds capacities for micropossibilities instead of all this big bang, scaling-up stuff. What would an accumulation of changes look like that could disrupt current norms? What are the possibilities of deliberate reform that gives enduring body to democratic possibilities, mobile ecologies, building on those already engaged? Perhaps this is where the "hive" of "mind share" that you are invested in for internet culture is brought to education reform.[12]

There are many areas working on such issues: ecology, urban development, applied anthropology, participatory program evaluation, deliberative development in international contexts. Taking the last area as but one example, political scientist Peter Evans has surveyed such efforts and found strong theoretical and empirical arguments for new policy frameworks that address the disappointing results of earlier development efforts.[13] His urging is toward participatory models of "thick democracy" instead of the imposition of "one-best-way" models. What he means by this is small-scale experiments whereby people can form and transform their perspectives in more information-intensive forms of deliberation to address the " 'hollowed out democracy' "[14] to which superficial electoral democracy has accustomed us. Eliciting and aggregating local input and experimentation, public discussion, and exchange, the goal is to build democratic capacity, particularly the fundamental ability to choose. This is a capability approach that "raises the bar" in terms of transparency and accountability toward wasting fewer resources and supporting "precious occasions of genuine change."[15]

After witnessing the town halls around health care, the risk of 'messiness' has to be faced for what it is: democracy in action. One could hope that your foundation could foster a more information-rich environment for such occasions and the sort of infrastructure that would seed a micropolitics to work against seeking confrontation in a way that yields more static than debate. Perhaps learning to deal with this sort of messiness is part of the capacity building for 'deep' democracy to which your work might contribute.

The "steep learning curve" you have encountered in agricultural interventions in Africa will be good practice for you in "the hardest science of all": education reform.[16] You make clear that you want to be open to changing your approach, to learning and moving ahead. Michel Foucault, the philosopher and historian of ideas, is debatably the most-cited figure of those who have written about these matters. In an interview from almost thirty years ago, he nails everything I have been trying to say and provides 'food for thought' in a way perhaps best offered by philosophers (and science fiction novelists).

> Years, decades, of work and political imagination will be necessary, work at the grass roots, with the people directly affected, restoring their right to speak. Only then will we succeed, perhaps, in changing

> a situation that, with the terms in which it is currently laid out, only leads to impasses and blockages . . . It's a matter of working through things little by little, of introducing modifications that are able if not to find solutions, at least to change the given terms of the problem . . . to bring about so that, in the very workings of society, the terms of the problems are changed and the impasses are cleared.[17]

To 'grok' is to merge knower and known, to absorb and blend into an entangled understanding beyond language. This kind of knowing comes from being immersed in a context, from listening, and from working all that goes beyond what numbers can capture in moving toward a deeper understanding. As you increasingly focus on what makes an effective teacher, the sustained development of frameworks for program evaluation that bring into practice a kind of knowing through engagement might end up being one of your biggest success stories in fostering educational change.

Sincerely,

Patti Lather

NOTES

* This chapter originally appeared in P. Lather, *Engaging Science Policy: From the Side of the Messy* (New York: Peter Lang, 2010).

1. S. Levy (2006) in *Newsweek* quotes Gates using Robert Heinlein's term from *Stranger in a Strange Land* (1961) wherein 'grok' came from a Martian language and meant an internalized way of knowing. According to Wikipedia, the term is common in hacker culture.
2. Gates Foundation, http://www.gatesfoundation.org/.
3. Since 2000, $4 billion have been spent.
4. B. Gates, *Gates Foundation 2009 Annual Report*, 11.
5. R. Bacchetti and T. Ehrlich, eds., *Reconnecting Education and Foundations: Turning Good Intentions into Educational Capital* (San Francisco, CA: John Wiley and Sons, 2007).
6. B. Gates, *Gates Foundation 2008 Annual Report*, 3.
7. B. Gates, *2009 Annual Report*, 12.
8. Ibid., 16.
9. As reported in "The Healthcare Equation" blog by R. Bazell, NBC News chief science correspondent, January 26, 2009, http://www.gatesfoundation.org
10. As reported by S. Smalley, "Always on My Mind," *Newsweek*, February 9, 2009, 53.
11. R. Coles, "The Wild Patience of Radical Democracy: Beyond Žižek's Lack," in *Radical Democracy: Between Abundance and Lack* (Manchester: Manchester University Press, 2005), 80.
12. "After Bill: Briefing Microsoft after Gates," *The Economist*, June 28, 2008, 76–78.
13. P. Evans, "Development as Institutional Change: The Pitfalls of Monocropping and the Potentials of Deliberation," *Studies in Comparative International Development* 38, no. 4 (2004): 30–52.

14. Ibid., 37.
15. Ibid., 46.
16. David Berliner came up with this phrase. See D. Berliner, "Educational Research: The Hardest Science of All," *Educational Researcher* 31 (2002): 18–20.
17. M. Foucault, "Interview with Michel Foucault," in *Power: Essential Works of Foucault 1954–1984*, vol. 3 (New York: The New Press, 2000), 288.

11 An Open Letter to Bill Gates, Jr. (with a Message to My Colleagues)

David Gabbard

Dear Mr. Gates,

As you well know, efforts toward bringing substantive changes to the institutional patterns and practices of public schooling can very quickly be frustrated by any number of seemingly intractable challenges. For example, when citizens here in North Carolina visit the website of the state's Department of Public Instruction, they could walk away with the impression that our schools function as model teaching and learning environments, grounded in high-principled and thoroughly researched standards that guide the work of administrators, teachers, and students.[1] If those same citizens, however, after reading about and understanding those standards, ventured into the schools and classrooms in this state, they would be hard pressed to find any real presence of those high-minded standards in the professional cultures of those schools. Only rarely would they meet teachers whose curricular and instructional practices upheld those standards in any meaningful way. Yet sadly, the mere pronouncement of newer and higher standards satisfies the concerns of most citizens and their governmental representatives for the quality of public schools. Any serious efforts toward implementing and enforcing those standards, meanwhile, goes neglected. Under these circumstances, school reform reforms nothing but the paper on the package. What's inside the box never changes, and no one notices because no one looks. New standards come with new slogans, but the lack of any serious measures to enforce them reduces those standards to the status of political gimmicks.[2]

Those of us in teacher education are required to align our curricula with those standards, but as early as their first field experiences in public schools, our students hear teachers tell them to forget what they learn in their university classes. And so begins their resocialization into the historically dominant patterns and practices of public schools. (I say 'resocialization' because, after all, the vast majority of our teacher education candidates have already received thirteen years of socialization into those patterns and practice during their time as students in the public schools.) To make matters potentially far worse, we now hear national- and state-level officials calling for efforts to begin holding teacher educators accountable for student achievement, not for the achievement of our students in teacher education but for the achievement of the students in our graduates' classrooms. Perhaps we would be more inclined to embrace this model of accountability if the professional culture of schools actually supported teachers in teaching in accordance with the professional standards to which the state requires us to align our curricula. The truth, however, as previously noted, is that the professional cultures of those schools fall far short of this.

In other words, Mr. Gates, teacher educators have good reason to empathize with the frustrations of people such as yourself, Eli Broad, Don Fisher, and others regarding public schools' resistance to reform. Personally, I understand how that reform-resistance motivates the perhaps well-intended efforts of wealthy philanthropists such as you are to use your financial wealth and social status to advance strategic initiatives designed to circumvent that resistance (e.g., charter schools).[3] Sadly, I and many of my colleagues in academia have often failed to recognize that circumvention as a possible motivation behind those initiatives, have chosen instead to uncritically vilify their promoters by casting their motives as primarily, if not solely, profit driven. Concomitantly, we frequently cast those efforts to circumvent the reform-resistance of public schools as just more corporate attacks on American democracy. In doing so, however, we also commit the error of uncritically, and sometimes even blindly, defending public schools and the highly imperfect democratic forms governing them.[4] Without denying the validity of our concerns, democratic intellectuals, myself included, must learn to better monitor the spirit in which we express them.

CRITICAL CONSCIOUSNESS AND THE PROBLEM OF TRANSFORMATION

Honesty forces me to concede, Mr. Gates, that our indictments of educational reforms supported by corporate and/or political elites sometimes undermine our own professed goals and values. This holds especially true for those of us claiming to embrace the principles of critical pedagogy developed by Brazilian educator Paulo Freire. In his *Pedagogy of the Oppressed*, Freire writes that "while humanization and dehumanization are real alternatives, only the first is *the people's* vocation [my emphasis]"[5] or calling. In aligning ourselves with Freire, we implicitly stake claim to our own humanity and commit ourselves to restoring that humanity to those who have had it denied to them. We also commit ourselves to an individual and collective declaration of solidarity with those whose humanity is threatened by the forces of dehumanization in whatever form they may take. These commitments, however, mean nothing unless we hold ourselves accountable to their underlying principles. Specifically, what does it mean for us to stake claim to our humanity? To what are we staking a claim? What is our humanity?

In Freire's view, becoming or being human entails the activation and exercise of two distinctly human capacities that function together to constitute what he calls *praxis*. It is through this praxis that we become human. Praxis, or humanization, begins with an act or moment of what he terms *conscientização* (conscientization), or critical consciousness. Exercising this first capacity enables us to recognize our social reality as the product of human ideation and action on the part of concrete historical actors, not as something natural or as having divine origins that render it immutable. This leads directly to our recognition of the second capacity. Since our social reality is the product of human ideation and action, since it is not fixed and immutable, we can exercise our capacity for creative action to transform and shape the world. We need not accept the world nor our position in the world as a given. We can change it!

As outlined in *Pedagogy of the Oppressed*, Freire's notion of critical pedagogy takes awakening people to these capacities as its central aim. This awakening, however, occurs not through didactic lessons on how to achieve critical consciousness and engage in creative action to transform the world, but through *dialogue*. Dialogue facilitates the activation of those capacitates by engaging people in naming the world and the dehumanizing *limit situations* that confront and oppress them. By contrast, the traditional model of pedagogy, which Freire refers to as the *banking model*, represents a dehumanizing form of education. It suppresses the emergence of people's critical consciousness through its reliance on monologue. Teachers present prefabricated representations of the world, and student success hinges on being willing and able to memorize and regurgitate those representations. The oppressive nature of this situation is made worse by the fact that because schools are agencies of the state and because the primary function of the state is to serve and protect the interests of society's dominant institutions, the forms of knowledge and the representations of the world deposited in the heads of schoolchildren most typically serve and protect those same interests.

In establishing this background, Mr. Gates, I hope to have provided some context for helping you understand the appeal that Freire's ideas hold for those of us most deeply committed to America's deepest democratic traditions and values and who aspire to see those values more authentically nurtured in our public schools. I've also sought to help establish some common ground between us. We share your frustrations over the reform-resistance of public schools, though we clearly don't share the resources that allow you to sponsor educational reform measures that circumvent such resistance.

In establishing this common ground, I hope to clear a space for dialogue between you and those of us who hold a vision of school reform tied less to your concerns for America's economic future and more to a concern for the future of American democracy. Those of us operating within the Freirean and other critical traditions within educational theory seldom have a voice at any table where educational reform or policy decisions are discussed. This is a shame because we offer many important insights into some of the most pressing issues confronting teachers and students in today's classrooms. Although it might be tempting to suggest to you that we are marginalized from such discussions due to our political leanings, I think too many of us have contributed to our own marginalization for too long.

For Freireans, this tendency may be rooted in Freire's writings themselves. We forget that Freire's context, working to help poor peasants in Brazil during the 1960s to gain not only literacy skills but also political voice, differs significantly from our own. Through his writings, we may have learned to concern ourselves solely with the humanization of 'the people'—the oppressed. In doing so, however, we violate one of the most basic Freirean principles, thus ignoring the humanity of those we identify as oppressors. In Freire's own words:

> Dehumanization, which marks not only those whose humanity has been stolen, but also (though in a different way) those who have stolen it, since it is a *distortion* of the vocation of becoming more fully human . . . Because it is a distortion of being more fully human, sooner or later being less human leads the oppressed to struggle against those who made them so. In order for this struggle to have meaning, the oppressed must not, in seeking to regain their humanity (which is a way to create it), become in turn oppressors of the oppressors, but rather the restorers of the humanity of both.[6]

Even in cases where antidemocratic ideologies and/or the quest for profit do motivate the educational reform agendas supported by wealthy corporate heads/philanthropists, we Freireans should not lose sight of their humanity. Doing so only diminishes our own. If we believe their humanity has been distorted, then we must also believe it can be restored. We must never assume it does not exist.

Most significantly, we have learned to ignore our own humanization, perhaps because we mistakenly take our own humanity as a given, as something we have already achieved, and therefore we allow it to remain unexamined. Again, for most of us who would identify ourselves as Freireans or as members of some other branch of the critical democratic tradition of educational thought, our context bears very little similarity to that of Paulo Freire when he was conducting the work that lead him to write *Pedagogy of the Oppressed*. For the most part, we do not work with peasants to help them achieve political consciousness and empowerment through critical literacy programs. We are, by and large, middle- to upper-middle-class university professors. When we look at the condition of our own humanity, our training and our vocation contributes a great deal toward the steady maintenance of our critical consciousness, but our capacity for creative action to transform the reality revealed to us by our critical consciousness goes undeveloped and unexercised.

For many of us, myself included, these circumstances have taken their toll. Critical consciousness can be a heavy burden to carry, especially when applied to the study of how the tensions between capitalism and democracy have played themselves out in U.S. society throughout history. And that burden only grows heavier across time, as we gain more consciousness of capitalism's historic efforts to subvert and even deny the existence of a common good. The weight of this knowledge alone is difficult to bear, but it grows heavier with our frustrations over our inability to take, or even determine, the actions necessary to impede those efforts. For most of us, teaching and writing constitute the limits of our creative action. And frankly, many of us have grown weary—intellectually, emotionally, and spiritually fatigued by how little change those forms of action have produced over the years. Several of my closest colleagues and I have shared stories of how that fatigue has recently pushed us into a state of professional paralysis. No matter how hard we try, we can't find the energy or the motivation to carry on. Even the most familiar work that used to give our lives meaning no longer satisfies us. Sensing this work is no longer ours to do, we look to lay it down and find something else to fill the void we feel within us. The centrality that *Pedagogy of the Oppressed* once held for us has given way to a need for a 'pedagogy of the depressed,' as we try to understand what has happened to us and what we can do to dig ourselves out of this hole.

Parker Palmer's "The Politics of the Brokenhearted" offers us some important clues both for understanding our condition and for finding our way out of its darkness. From Palmer's perspective, critical consciousness is heartbreaking. To appreciate this point, we must know that he uses the notion of heart to signify the core of our sense of self, not our emotional center. Our society teaches us one thing about what it means to be Americans, but that story does not hold up under any serious scrutiny. It leads us to believe that our political institutions define our character and that these institutions were built upon and operate under democratic principles and values. Plato would have characterized this story as a 'noble lie,' taught to the young in order that they learn to tie their own identity to the state that governs them in order to render them more governable as adults. Therefore, we can see how Palmer's notion of heartbreak applies to our situation. Critical consciousness breaks our hearts in the sense that it fractures our sense of self. We, along with the government we grew to identify ourselves through, are not what we were told.

Palmer also informs us that "there are at least two ways to picture a broken heart." First, we can view it in a conventional manner as "a heart broken by unbearable tension into a thousand shards—shards that sometimes become shrapnel aimed at the source of our pain. Every day, untold numbers of people try to 'pick up the pieces,' some of them taking grim satisfaction in the way the heart's explosion has injured their enemies. Here the broken heart is an unresolved wound that we too often inflict on others."[7]

BROKEN-HEARTEDNESS AND HUMANIZING OURSELVES

For many of us (and again, myself included) the academy offers both a safe haven to steal away with our hearts broken by critical consciousness and a bunker from which to fire our shrapnel at our enemies. Our words become our weapons as we set upon a tragically Quixotic quest to vanquish our enemies through our books, chapters, and articles. In the end, however, our broken hearts go unhealed; and our humanity, in the full Freirean sense, goes unfulfilled because no matter what or how much we write, the world remains unchanged. In my own case, I entered teacher education over twenty years ago with aspirations of changing what and how children learned for the better and in greater keeping with democratic values and principles. And yet when I look at schools today, not only have I made no difference, but the conditions and content of schooling are worse than when I began my career.

But Palmer offers us another way to view a broken heart. "Imagine that small, clenched fist of a heart 'broken open' into the largeness of life, into greater capacity to hold one's own and the world's pain and joy. This, too, happens every day. Who among us has not seen evidence, in our own or other people's lives, that compassion and grace can be the fruits of great suffering? Here heartbreak becomes a source of healing, enlarging our empathy and extending our ability to reach out."[8]

What would shifting from 'hearts broken apart' to 'hearts broken open' mean for those of us who long to see America and its schools move closer to realizing the promise of our professed democratic values and principles? It would mean learning to better hold the tensions between American capitalism and American democracy. We cannot deny that America has always been and remains a capitalist nation. As such, many of our citizens own and control vast sums of wealth, while others control or own very little if anything. Although we might work to minimize or eliminate the latter, the former show no signs of going away anytime soon. In keeping our hearts closed to them, we deny them the opportunity to hear our concerns and our ideas. We also greatly diminish our own ability to participate in shaping whatever changes come to pass, and this will only prolong our feelings of frustration and marginalization.

Am I advocating a shift from a grassroots model of social transformation to a treetops model? No. As so effectively dramatized in his new novel, *Only the Super Rich Can Save Us*, Ralph Nader has also come to understand that we need both the grass roots and the treetops working together. We forget that America's wealthiest citizens are still citizens, and many of them share our concerns for the health of the planet, the state of American democracy, and the growing income disparities that reproduce countless other social ills. As Palmer argues:

> The capacity to hold tensions creatively is the key to much that matters—from a life lived in love to a democracy worthy of the name to even the most modest movement toward peace between nations. So those of us who care about such things must work to root out the seeds of violence in our culture, including its incessant drive toward control. And since culture is a human creation, whose deformations begin not 'out there' but in our own inner lives, we can transform the culture only insofar as we are inwardly transformed.
>
> As long as we are mortal creatures who love other mortals, heartbreak will be a staple of our lives. And all heartbreak, personal and political, will confront us with the same choice. Will we hold our hearts open and keep trying to love, even as love makes us more vulnerable to the losses that break our hearts? Or will we shut down and lash out, refusing to risk love again and seeking refuge in withdrawal or hostility?[9]

INVITATIONS TO LISTEN, REQUESTS TO BE HEARD

When setting out to research this chapter, I sought out sources that I hoped would give me greater insights into you other than your status as cofounder and former CEO of Microsoft and richest person on the planet. One of those sources was your father's book, *Showing Up for Life: Thoughts on the Gifts of a Lifetime.* It says a great deal about the man that he includes among those gifts the lessons he learned from your mother and from raising you and your two sisters. I also found it touching that in your short foreword to that book you wrote: "Dad, the next time somebody asks you if you're the real Bill Gates, I hope you say, 'Yes.' I hope you tell them that you're all the things the other one strives to be." That certainly is asking a lot of yourself; he has lived an amazing life and given a great deal back to his country and the world. I don't know how many people realize that the Bill and Melinda Gates Foundation, which he continues to codirect at the age of eighty-three, originated from his William H. Gates Foundation.

What I found most interesting in his book was his chapter on education.[10] As educated and knowledgeable as he is on most things, and as progressive as his politics are on most other issues, it startled me to discover how lacking his knowledge is on the issue of education. Given his relationship with President Carter, whose election benefited greatly from the support he received from the teachers unions after promising and actually creating the U.S. Department of Education and elevating its head to a cabinet-level position, I found it surprising that Bill Sr. would cite the Reagan administration's 1983 report *A Nation at Risk* as being so influential on his thinking.

As many of us in critical educational studies have pointed out through our research, that report functioned as part of very elaborate propaganda campaign aimed blaming the alleged poor performance of our schools for the deteriorating economic conditions and sliding standard of living created by the structural adjustments being imposed by policies oriented toward the deindustrialization of the U.S. economy. According to the logic of the report, the U.S. economy achieved global supremacy in the post–World War II era due to the excellence of our public schools. Due to the liberal reforms of the 1960s and '70s, however, our schools lost their commitment to high standards such that by the early 1980s, the poor quality of our high school graduates weakened the quality of our workforce. In turn, because U.S. corporations had such a hard time hiring qualified workers, those corporations lost their competitive edge in world markets; and this loss of competitive edge brought about the weakened economy that cost so many U.S. workers their jobs and started the standard of living plummeting for those fortunate enough to retain their jobs.

Sadly, the deterioration in the quality of journalism that now plagues our body politic had already been set in motion, and not a single journalist questioned any of the claims made by the authors of *A Nation at Risk*. When I pose the questions to them, my undergraduate teacher education majors have no difficulty, without even the benefit of any research, in deconstructing that logic and revealing its lack of credibility. In the first place, they know that the decimation of the economic infrastructure of our traditional competitors during World War II was what allowed for the rise of the U.S. economy to global supremacy in the 1950s. It was hardly attributable to the high quality of our workforce. During the 1950s, only about 35 percent of American workers had graduated from high school. The also know that by the early 1970s, those former competitors had rebuilt their economic infrastructures. So therefore, the drop in U.S. corporations' competitive advantage had far less to do with the quality of our workforce and much more to do with the fact that for the first time since before the start of World War II, they faced real competition in the global marketplace. To offset that competition, they began searching out cheaper sources of industrial labor overseas, which meant sending American jobs overseas. Outsourcing had begun. Amazingly, given the logic of *A Nation at Risk*, the bulk of those jobs were being shipped to nations whose school systems could not be fairly equated with ours. Although *A Nation at Risk* sought to convince the public and policy makers that the superior test scores of students in Europe and South Korea placed the U.S. economy at risk, our jobs were not flowing to Europe. They were flowing to countries with much inferior educational systems (e.g., Mexico). Furthermore, the report did not reveal that students in South Korea are handpicked by the government there to take the tests. They consider it a national honor. Imagine how favorably our students might look in international comparisons if we selected which students would be honored with the opportunity to take the tests.

Moreover, your father's discussion of schools, much like your own comments, conveys the message that our teachers and schools have failed America. Like you and your father, I believe that our schools can and must do better. However, I would submit the opposite thesis. Our schools have not failed America; America has failed the value of education. In the first place, from their origins, America's public schools were never intended to educate anyone, but rather to discipline future workers into the proper behaviors and attitudes deemed necessary to adapt to the boring and monotonous work of the factory floor. If they could be coerced to perform dull, repetitive work at school in exchange for grades, then they would be well prepared to accept such work in the factory in exchange for a wage. This legacy still continues. As I tell my students at the start of each semester, as they sit in their desks scanning the syllabus I've just handed them, "I know that none of you is here because you *want* to be, but because you *have* to be in order to complete your program in teacher education. I also know that as you, or at least many of you, scan over the syllabus, your mind is conducting a sort of economic calculation. You are trying to discern how much energy you will have to expend in order to get what you want from this class. And what you want from this class is not learning or education, but credit hours. This is the game as you have learned how to play it. You learned to do what you need to do to earn and collect enough credit hours so that you can exchange them for a diploma and get out of school as quickly as you can." While this may sound severe, most of them are honest enough to admit that I am correct in my assessment of the situation before me. The ones who contest me, the ones who have come with an authentic interest in learning something, prove to be my best students. They are in the minority. Sadly, both they and the students in the majority, those not particularly interested in their own education, wish to become teachers. Though they may or may not be interested in their own education, they all want the government to license them to become entrusted to care for the education of others.

These young people do not deserve our scorn, Mr. Gates. If anything, we deserve theirs. For they are the products of the world we have passed on to them. Like everything else, school is just a commodity to them. It's something to be consumed and collected so as to increase their own use-value in the labor market. Its sole value, for too many people, lies in its status as an economic value. Is this how we want out children to experience and interpret the meaning of education?

Not only has America failed the value of education, it has also failed the Enlightenment project more generally. Not only have we devalued education, defined as the quest to understand ourselves, the world around us, and our place within that world, we have also devalued truth and the pursuit of truth. I am not discussing truth here as a fixed or final entity. Our children should understand science as a process through which we perpetually move beyond established truths to develop deeper, richer, and more accurate understandings of things in generating even newer truths that will later be challenged by ensuing generations. But truth represents a noble pursuit, and we have betrayed its nobility in a host of different ways. In politics as in marketing, truth has become whatever you can dupe people into believing.

As pointed out by Richard Hofstadter[11] and, more recently, by Susan Jacoby,[12] America has a long history of anti-intellectualism. But the fervor of anti-intellectualism today has grown so intense that anything said by anyone is taken to be just as valid and legitimate as something said by someone who might actually know what they are talking about. To challenge this popular relativism opens one to charges of elitism. Former vice president and Nobel Prize winner Al Gore tackled these issues in his book *The Assault on Reason*.[13] Others including Morris Berman and, more recently, Charles Pierce have broached the same topic. As Pierce points out in his book *Idiot America: How Stupidity Became a Virtue in the Land of the Free*,[14] and as Bill Maher featured in his film *Religulous*, there is actually a Creation Museum in Hebron, Kentucky where dinosaurs are depicted with saddles and being ridden by people. Why? Because some of us take the creation story in the Bible so literally that they truly believe the earth is only 6,000 years old and that dinosaurs coexisted at some point with humans.

I could continue at great length on other evidences of America's abandonment of the Enlightenment project, but I trust you've heard enough to get my point. Our students, teachers, and schools will always reflect the ideas and values of the larger society surrounding them. We should not, then, expect any substantive reform of our public schools until the larger society learns to value education as more than just an economic value.

CONCLUSION

In conclusion, we cannot allow the historic status quo of compulsory schooling to persist, but neither can we continue along the current path of reform. That path, with its emphasis on raising students' scores on high-stakes standardized tests in the name of achievement, reforms nothing. Its simplistic logic of bottom-line accountability to pressure teachers into producing such narrowly defined results strengthens the most deadly elements of the status quo by feeding the prevailing culture of vulgar pragmatism in most school systems. Ironically, the quest to raise achievement scores reduces the value of education, unless we are willing to restrict our own understanding of that value to the most base economic terms. If we treat education as a commodity, then our children and grand children will continue to do so. However meaningless the process may seem to them as they pass through it, the most compliant of them will endure its stifling boredom in return for the promise of increased economic security. The rest will fall out or be pushed out, and the majority of them will take their places in the unemployment lines and the penal system.

We could, of course, choose a different path. One place we could look, Mr. Gates, for ideas to help us envision that new direction would be the school that you attended in Seattle, Washington. The Lakeside School asserts that its mission "is to develop in intellectually capable young people the creative minds, healthy bodies, and ethical spirits needed to contribute wisdom, compassion, and leadership to a global society. We provide a rigorous and dynamic academic program through which effective educators lead students to take responsibility for learning." It goes on to state that it "fosters the development of citizens capable of and committed to interacting compassionately, ethically, and successfully with diverse peoples and cultures to create a more humane, sustainable global society. This focus transforms our learning and our work together."[15]

Reading this mission statement leads me to think that such a vision would not only provide inspiration and direction for reforming our public schools but also for transforming our national culture writ large. The enormity and complexity of this endeavor would demand operating on multiple fronts, beyond either of our lifetimes. We have to understand, however, that our schools will always reflect the dominant values, beliefs, and ideals of the larger society. We cannot succeed in moving the former until we have sufficiently initiated the process of transforming the latter. I hope that you, Melinda, and your father can recognize the imperative for the scale and scope of the project I am suggesting here. You can trust that I will be working to continue our conversation from my end. I hope that you will be interested in joining the conversation from your end.

NOTES

1. `North Carolina Professional Teaching Standards Commission, *North Carolina Professional Teaching Standards* (Raleigh, N.C.: Department of Public Instruction, 2008), http://www.ncptsc.org/Final%20Standards%20Document.pdf (accessed October 29, 2009).
2. D. Gabbard and M. L'Esperance, "Revisiting Reform in North Carolina: Responding to 'First in America'—An Open Letter to Former Governor James B. Hunt Jr.," *Educational Forum* 66 (4): 340–46.
3. As a board member of a local charter school here in eastern North Carolina, I have assembled a team of fellow teacher-educators from the College of Education at East Carolina University to support the CEO/principal in building visionary leadership among teachers, students, parents, and community members to create a school culture that is both more culturally responsive to the community it serves and a more professionally and educationally rewarding for the teachers and students who work there. Although that culture remains a work in progress, that work would never have begun without the vision, wisdom, and dedication of those who initiated it, coupled with the freedom to pursue that vision provided by the historic ambivalence of county and district officials toward the population served by our school (99 percent African American, 85 percent receiving free or reduced lunch).
4. Recently in a local community here in eastern North Carolina, for example, a mother ran for and won election to the local school board solely because

she was upset that the district's school uniform policy prohibited her daughter from wearing pink polo shirts to school. Pink was not among the district approval colors. Once elected, the girl's mother succeeded in adding pink to that list, along with a certain style of khaki pants that she favored. We do not know much this woman knew or cared to learn about other matters concerning federal, state, or local school policy. Seldom do local electorates scrutinize candidates for local school board elections.

5. P. Freire, *Pedagogy of the Oppressed*, 30th anniversary ed. (1970; reprint, New York: Continuum, 2001), 43.
6. Ibid., 44.
7. P. Palmer, "Politics of the Brokenhearted: On Holding the Tensions of Democracy," in *Essays on Deepening the American Dream*, ed. Fetzer Institute (Kalamazoo, MI: Fetzer Institute, 2009), 232, http://www.couragerenewal.org/images/stories/pdfs/politicsbrokenhearted.pdf (accessed October 29, 2009).
8. Ibid.
9. Ibid.
10. B. Gates Sr., *Showing Up for Life: Thoughts on the Gifts of a Lifetime* (New York: Broadway Books, 2009), 112–17.
11. R. Hofstadter, *Anti-Intellectualism in American Life* (New York, Knopf, 1963).
12. S. Jacoby, *The Age of American Unreason* (New York: Pantheon, 2008).
13. A. Gore, *The Assault on Reason* (New York: Penguin, 2007).
14. C. Pierce, *Idiot America: How Stupidity Became a Virtue in the Land of the Free* (New York: Doubleday, 2009).
15. Lakeside School, "Mission Statement," http://www.lakesideschool.org/podium/default.aspx?t=122165 (accessed October 29, 2009).

12 Why Current Education Reform Efforts Will Fail

Marion Brady

> Now what I want is Facts. Teach the boys and girls nothing but Facts. Facts alone are wanted in life. Plant nothing else, and root out everything else. You can only form the minds of reasoning animals upon Fact; nothing else will ever be of any service to them . . . In this life, we want nothing but Facts, sir, nothing but Facts!
>
> —Schoolmaster Thomas Gradgrind in Charles Dickens' 1854 novel, *Hard Times.*

Anyone who's ever tried to lose weight, squeeze out more miles per gallon, or attract customers to a business knows something about the law of diminishing returns. The first few pounds usually come off fairly easily. A little more air in the tires will make an immediate difference in mileage. A half-page ad in the newspaper may bring in fifty new customers.

After that, it gets tougher. The closer a system gets to its peak performance, the harder it is to make a difference. After a while, the payoffs aren't worth the additional money, time, or trouble. When that happens, a whole new approach may be necessary—exercise to go along with the diet, buying a different car, moving the business to a better location.

American education began to run up against the law of diminishing returns at a serious level around 1950, about the time I took my first teaching job. In the years since, I've watched and sometimes participated in efforts to respond to the institution's flat performance. I've seen 'open-space' schools built and abandoned; flexible and block scheduling tried; 'new' math, language arts, social studies, and science instructional programs written then shelved; observed experiments with mixed age groups, teacher teams, homogeneous and heterogeneous grouping and tracking; and followed the fates of schools 'without walls,' inquiry and discovery learning, rubrics, mainstreaming, outcome-based education, looping, year-round schools, community service, and learning centers (just to begin a list). Most of those efforts had potential, and here and there some continue, but none did more than skim the surface of the institution.

A parallel stream of opinion and advice from the general public and mainstream media accompanied those educator-initiated fads and reforms. Years of writing newspaper columns for Knight-Ridder/Tribune Information Services—columns to which my email address was attached—brought reams of opinion and advice. Readers told me that 'things were better in the good old days,' that what schools needed were really tough discipline policies, that social promotion should be outlawed and teachers unions shut down. I was made to understand that socialist influences needed to be rooted out, the remaining traces of John Dewey and the Progressives obliterated, schools of education disbanded, irresponsible parents fined or jailed, and the Ten Commandments prominently displayed in every classroom. Readers said school uniforms should be mandatory, zero tolerance policies rigidly enforced, and 'frills' eliminated. I was told that reading is the key to academic success and phonics instruction is the key to reading, that either too much or not enough money was being spent on schools, and that tomorrow's technology was about to come riding to the rescue (again, just to begin a list).

In 1983, during President Reagan's administration, a National Commission on Excellence in Education entered this confused picture with a report called *A Nation at Risk.*

The report's tone was ominous. "The educational foundations of our society," it said, "are presently being eroded by a rising tide of mediocrity that threatens our very future as a Nation and a people." It continued with, "If an unfriendly foreign power had attempted to impose on America the mediocre educational performance that exists today, we might well have viewed it as an act of war."[1]

Educators thought the report's assessment of the quality of American education was based on a misinterpretation of data, and a subsequent federal study from Sandia Laboratories confirmed their view.[2] However, by the time the Sandia report was released, the 'public schools are broken' tape had been played so often and so loudly that it was firmly fixed in the public consciousness and had become an indisputable fact in the minds of American leaders of business and industry. Long accustomed to cold-war tensions and apprehensive about the growing economic performance of Japan and other nations, those leaders decided American education was too important to be left in the hands of educators. Working through state governors and then Congress and demonstrating the Golden Rule—that whoever has the gold makes the rules—business leaders threw educators off the education reform boat and took over education policy.

The thrust of the reform program they put in place can perhaps best be summed up by the inspired slogan 'standards and accountability.' It implied that prior to their efforts, there had been neither standards nor accountability; that therefore educators weren't to be trusted; that there was work to be done, and business leaders, not educators or the general public, should shape America's educational future. National education meetings were convened to which professional educators weren't invited.

What was needed, the new leaders said, was 'rigor.' Schools should be like those they remembered attending. What had happened, they believed, was that America's teachers, once first-rate, were no longer getting the job done. Over time they'd gradually slacked off, probably suffering from 'the soft bigotry of low expectations.' Those who replaced educators as policy makers demanded and got a souped-up core curriculum—more required higher math and more science, less social studies, art, music, and other non-core subjects. Standards for all school subjects needed to be put in place, business leaders insisted, and standardized tests had to be administered at regular intervals, with reading and math emphasized above all other subjects. Educators were still to do the grunt work, but they weren't allowed in the pilothouse of the education ship.

Steering a right course, the new leaders believed, was fairly simple. Educating well, they said, wasn't very complicated, mostly a matter of distributing information—transferring it from those who know to those who didn't know. If information wasn't being distributed, it must either be because (a) teachers didn't know what information to distribute, or (b) they weren't trying hard enough.

In either case, the new leaders assumed the two problems had easy solutions. If teachers didn't know what to teach, then detailed 'standards' would tell them. And if they weren't trying hard enough, then market forces—competition, merit pay, choice, vouchers, charters, publicity, fear of job loss, labeling and grading of schools, and so on—would pressure them to shape up. Competition, of course, required precise scorekeeping, hence the need for constant testing.

The officers on the bridge of the education ship—wealthy leaders of business and industry, state governors, big-city mayors, and a few state legislators and members of Congress—have now been in control for a full K–12 educational cycle. How are things going? According to Louis V. Gerstner, former CEO of American Express, RJR Nabisco, IBM, and the Carlyle Group and winner of many awards for his efforts to reform American education, not very well. In a December 1, 2008, Wall Street Journal op-ed, he said, "We must start with the recognition that, despite decade after decade of reform efforts, our public K–12 schools have not improved."[3]

But he has an explanation for the failure. He thinks the standards and accountability procedures Congress pressured the fifty states to put in place are lousy—too local, too political, too varied—to allow direct comparisons of performance. What's needed, he believes, are national standards and national and international tests.[4] In 2008 the Gates Foundation-funded EDin08 would pour millions of dollars into a national media campaign calling for a common set of standards for U.S. schools. By the time this book leaves the printer, those standards will have been hammered out by individuals with little to no background in schools or cognitive psychology but plenty of boardroom experience.

If the new captains of American education are right and the educators down on the deck doing the actual work either don't know what to do or aren't motivated to do it, then the last two decades of 'standards and accountability' screw-tightening make good sense. But if they're wrong, the screw-tightening has been counterproductive, akin to 'the beatings will continue until morale improves' leadership strategy.

As I said ten years ago: "The closer a system gets to its peak performance, the harder it is to make a difference. After a while, the payoffs aren't worth the additional money, time, or trouble. When that happens, a whole new approach may be necessary."[5]

But the new leaders aren't ready for that. They're sure 'the system' is basically sound, that it just needs the discipline of standards and the pressure of market forces to make it 'world class.'

Their confidence comes from a series of firmly held myths. Here are seven of them.

MYTH: AMERICA'S SCHOOLS USED TO BE BETTER

It's likely that since the dawn of civilization, members of the older generation have rolled their eyes at how little they think the younger generation knows. The young manage to supply the elders with enough evidence to perpetuate the traditional belief, and the elders take note.

In 1988, two Washington think tankers, Diane Ravitch and Chester E. Finn Jr., gave the tradition a booster shot. They wrote a book titled *What Do Our 17-Year-Olds Know? A Report on the First National Assessment of History and Literature.*[6] As one could guess, they wrote the book because they believed the answer was 'not very much!' and they wanted others to reach the same conclusion. Mixed in with the text, sometimes on every page, are bordered gray blocks that each contain a multiple-choice question asked of a sample of eleventh graders, followed by their averaged scores.

When *What Do Our 17-Year-Olds Know?* was published, newspapers across the country carried examples of the questions (e.g., 'Who wrote *The Return of the Native*?') and listed student scores. Emphasized, of course, were those questions newspaper editors thought their readers could answer that were muffed by lots of high school juniors. Public hand-wringing rose to a level that made political interest and exploitation inevitable.

Prodded by all the media attention, the hand-wringing was predictable, but the consternation was an overreaction. Not in recent centuries have two generations shared a broad spectrum of knowledge. Social change sees to that. However, to think this is a bad thing is to fail to understand the adaptability that social change makes necessary. If there's ever a generation that knows only what the generation immediately preceding it knows, then it can kiss its chances of survival goodbye.

Valid generalizations about the actual differences in quality of schools from one generation to the next aren't possible, so I'll make none. I do, however, have an opinion based on my seventy-seven years in education, at various times as student, public school teacher, college professor, contributor to academic journals, author of textbooks and professional books, consultant to publishers, education columnist for Knight-Ridder/Tribune Information Services, and visitor to schools across America and around the world. Without hesitation I'll say that in most schools, the kind of work students are expected to do hasn't changed significantly since the public-school movement began around 1850. What's changed in recent years isn't the nature of the work but the amount. It would surely be revealing to weigh each generation's textbooks in the required core subjects. Kids—at least those willing to participate—are doing what they've always done, just doing more of it.

A couple of years ago, gathering material for a newspaper column, I went to my nearest middle school and borrowed popular eighth-grade textbooks for math, science, language arts, and social studies. Assuming that the glossaries of the books contained the main ideas the authors and the textbook selection committees thought were important, I counted them. There were 1,465 important ideas. That comes out to a brand new idea about every twenty minutes, and no going back for review. I need only raise my eyes and look around the room to see example after example of authors who thought it took a whole book to explain just one idea.

Given all the variables, it's not possible to compare the quality of two schools in the same town on the same day, much less all schools across America over decades or a century. It's reasonable to suppose, however, that 'the good old days' in education never were. For extensive research on this point, see Richard Rothstein, *The Way We Were? The Myths and Realities of America's Student Achievement.*[7]

MYTH: GOOD TEACHERS ARE THE PRIMARY DETERMINANT OF EDUCATIONAL QUALITY

That teachers differ greatly in effectiveness goes without saying. My mother was a long-time teacher of the fifth grade in an elementary school that, insofar as possible, kept classes together as they moved up through grade levels. Every year, as the school year drew to a close, the sixth-grade teachers in her school did everything but attempt to bribe the principal to give them the class my mother had taught. When the new reformers push merit pay or pay-for-performance schemes, it's people like my mother they want to reward and to hold up as models for others to emulate.

But quantifying the qualities that made her an outstanding teacher would have been impossible. When educators try to explain that accountability isn't nearly as simple as its advocates think, the new leaders respond with 'No excuses!'

San Francisco doctor Mark Filidei, summing up research,[8] says millions of kids younger than age six are exposed to lead in paint, plumbing, and pesticides. Lead levels in the body, he says, contribute to learning disabilities, hyperactivity, aggressive behavior, temper tantrums, fearfulness, and attention-deficit disorders. Children with high levels are much more likely to drop out of school and even to exhibit criminal tendencies.[9] Mercury is worse than lead, and airborne particles of it reached an all-time peak about the time today's fifteen-year-olds were born. Should teachers be held accountable for learning problems caused by heavy-metal contamination?

A study of second graders by Gordon Shaw, a physics professor at the University of California–Irvine, found that music training affects brain functioning and increases the likelihood of success in school.[10] In his experiments, as little as four months of piano lessons improved certain math skills such as working with fractions and proportions. Exposure to music apparently meets a brain-development need. Should teachers be held accountable for failure to provide musical instruction to all students?

Typing a few words into Google brings a bundle of research about relationships between physical conditioning—muscle strength, body fat, flexibility, cardiovascular endurance, and so on—and the kinds of brain functioning necessary for learning.[11] Although schools that cut out recess and 'phys ed' to devote more time to test preparation should have some explaining to do, getting kids in shape has never been considered the schools' main job. Should teachers be held accountable for the poor physical conditioning of America's young?

It hardly needs to be said that there's a relationship between toddlers' TV exposure and learning problems. The more time spent staring at the tube, the greater the likelihood of problems.[12] Should teachers be held accountable for excessive TV viewing?

Between 1940 and 1990, the U.S. population shot up from 132 million to 249 million. In that same fifty years, the number of public schools went from 200,000 down to 62,000. Do the math: 132,000 fewer schools serving 117 million more people! Should teachers be held responsible for building schools the size of which require them to be run like medium-security prisons?

Three of every four high school students work more than fifteen hours a week, many far longer. Studies say the workplaces themselves often contribute to depression, poor self-esteem, tension, fatigue, insomnia, illness, a greater likelihood of drug and alcohol use, higher rates of delinquency, loss of parental control, and other conditions affecting academic performance.[13] Should teachers be accountable for the conditions of their students' workplaces and their schedules?

It's pretty hard, educators say, to teach a parade. Americans move a lot and take their school-age kids with them. The better-off are usually following the job market; the worse-off are often trying to stay ahead of the rent collector. Whatever the reason, about 35 percent of moved-around kids are more likely to fail a grade, and about 77 percent are more likely to have behavior problems.[14] Should teachers be held accountable for how America's economy functions?

Should every teacher be held accountable? Of course. But so should everyone else directly or indirectly responsible for decisions the end products of which are: lead, mercury, no music, poor physical conditioning, too much television, gigantic impersonal schools, teenage work and family demands, population mobility, neglected sight and hearing problems, hunger, language difficulties, social class differences, childhood experiences, personality disorders, innate ability or lack of it, cultural deprivation, class size, insane amounts of paperwork, creativity-stifling bureaucracy, sneaky manipulation of school performance statistics, policy makers with political agendas, and state legislatures that pile ever-greater responsibilities on public schools generation after generation.

Hold teachers accountable? Sure. But they're parts of a vast system over which they have almost no control. To put the accountability monkey on their backs is scapegoating, pure and simple.

MYTH: COMPETITION, PAY FOR PERFORMANCE, THE REWARDS OF WINNING, AND OTHER MARKET FORCES ALWAYS BRING OUT THE BEST IN PEOPLE

From the farmhouse where I once lived, it was pretty much a straight shot up Ohio Route 14 to Lincoln Electric on the east side of Cleveland. Fifty years ago, it was about an hour's drive. Lincoln Electric manufactured electrical equipment, mostly electric welders. A neighbor, friend, and father of one of my students worked there. He rarely missed an opportunity to remind me that he made about three times more money assembling electric welders than I made teaching his daughter. I knew the way to Lincoln Electric not because I was interested in changing jobs but because the agricultural teacher Bruce and I were talking to someone there about a project we thought could improve the high school where we were teaching.

By just about any measure, Lincoln was progressive. In 1914 they created an Employee Advisory Board made up of elected representatives from every department. In the next few years, long before most other companies, everybody got free life insurance, paid vacations, stock ownership plans, bonuses for useful suggestions, automatic cost-of-living raises, and continuous employment guarantees. During the worst years of the Great Depression, average pay for employees more than doubled.

What particularly interested us about Lincoln, however, was the company's Incentive Bonus program. Simply put, the better job you did, the more you got paid.

Merit pay! We loved the idea! We began an effort, blessed by the school board, to bring merit pay to our school.

It was a real challenge. Every problem we solved seemed to create two or three new problems. Month after month we talked about 'the devil in the details.' Finally, notwithstanding our initial enthusiasm, notwithstanding a year of effort, notwithstanding how commonsensical the whole idea seemed, notwithstanding how 'American' the idea of merit pay, we concluded that the gulf between manufacturing things and teaching kids was unbridgeable. The devil wasn't in the details; the devil was in the fundamentals.

Here are some of the reasons we gave up. They're still relevant:

1. Every kid is different. In industry, quality controls discard unsatisfactory 'raw material.' Teachers have to work with whatever the local

parent population produces—smart and slow, motivated and lazy, clever and clueless, sick and healthy, friendly and hostile.

2. Every class is different. Two classes of the same size studying the same subject in the same room at the same time of day and year will have different 'collective personalities' and have to be taught differently.
3. Every subject is different. A performance evaluation for a band director won't work for a teacher helping kids learn how to give impromptu speeches in an English class or to analyze propaganda in a social studies class or to study milk production on a local dairy farm in an agriculture class.
4. Every teacher is different. Some come on like Marine drill sergeants, others like Mary Poppins. Both approaches, and everything in between, can succeed for teachers who build on their strengths and minimize their weaknesses. How a particular style works will be different for every student, and the results may not be known for years.
5. Every work environment is different. Some administrators treat teachers as professionals, encouraging independence, growth, and creativity. Others are authoritarian and controlling or even see teachers as enemies. Not surprisingly, teachers function differently in different environments.
6. Every resource base differs. There's no standardization of the kinds and amounts of instructional tools and materials available; of monies for supplies and enrichment activities; or for the ability and willingness of parents or volunteers to share their knowledge, experience, and support.

That's six major variables affecting teacher performance, only one of which is controlled in any way by the teacher.

I can think of no way to bulldoze all those variables into a level playing field for all teachers. And in the more than fifty years since Bruce and I tried and failed, I've never seen anyone else do it. Most politicians and much of the public think bringing market forces to bear via merit pay is a great idea, and a couple of states have put teachers in positions where they have no choice but to adopt some form of it, but that doesn't make it fair or functional.

But even if some genius figures out how to do what we couldn't do, it won't solve the problem. Merit pay is based on an assumption about basic human nature, that *competition is the ultimate motivator*, and the behavior of most teachers I've known says that just isn't true.

In *Zen and the Art of Motorcycle Maintenance,* Robert Pirsig persuasively argues that *creating quality* is a deeper human drive than acquisitiveness.[15] Sure, teachers want enough to live decently. But the teachers whom most parents and grandparents should want teaching their kids and grandkids are those for whom quality work is more important than making more money than the teacher in the next room. If the opportunity to do quality work is missing, then raising salaries enough to keep teachers in the profession will trigger a nationwide tax revolt.

MYTH: TEACHING IS A RELATIVELY SIMPLE PROCESS.

Schoolmaster Gradgrind has a lot of disciples among those now shaping education policy. One of the new leaders' favorite terms is 'rigor,' and the relationship of 'facts' to 'rigor' is extremely close. It's a knowledge of facts that allows the test taker to fill in the blanks on worksheets and pencil in the proper ovals on the standardized test items. It's a knowledge of facts that earns parental praise when little Johnny or Jane is asked, 'What did you learn in school today?' It's facts that get highlighted or underlined in textbooks, noted in notebooks, or typed into laptops as a teacher's lecture proceeds.

In traditional schooling, facts have a life of their own. They're almost tangible—capable of being 'stuffed' into heads, 'crammed' in preparation for an exam, or made to 'come alive' by a history teacher. They're 'hard,' can be 'stored,' 'filed,' and 'mixed up.' Kids who don't have enough of them are 'empty headed,' while others can have so many they have 'facts running out their ears.'

The simplistic notion that teaching is primarily a matter of moving facts out of books and teachers' heads or off the internet and into learners' heads is an extremely destructive idea. Of all the assumptions the new makers of education policy brought with them, this is almost certainly the most destructive. It implies that teaching is so easy that if it weren't for difficulties related to discipline and classroom management, just about anyone who knows something could teach, that teaching is primarily a matter of telling, and learning is primarily a matter of remembering.

If that's what educating means, class size makes no difference. With a good sound system, it's as easy to distribute information to 300 or 3,000 as it is to 30. If that's what educating means, programs like Teach for America that put new college graduates into classrooms for a couple of years as a kind of public service before they move on to 'real' work is a good idea. If that's what educating means, it's hard even to make a case for having schools and teachers at all.

As Socrates repeatedly demonstrated, however, teaching is incredibly complex. It isn't rocket science; it's much harder—a complicated, intellectually challenging matter of analyzing the flawed models of reality in learners' minds, then trying to help them align those models more closely with the real thing. 'Telling' rarely does anything of consequence. What needs to happen if learning is to take place happens in the learner's mind. And if it happens, it's almost always a consequence of a question that doesn't have a factual answer, often some version of 'but how does what you're saying square with, say, such a rapid increase in the temperature of the material?' or 'isn't what you're saying inconsistent with what you said yesterday?'

Teaching is tough, and telling doesn't cut it. I have in my files a video shot at a Massachusetts Institute of Technology graduation ceremony. Several students, still in their caps and gowns, are handed a short section of a tree limb and asked how the piece of wood was made. What was the usual response of the graduates? Some version of "it's made mostly from stuff the tree sucked up out of the ground." Well, of course, it wasn't. It came from an invisible gas in the air. Sunlight, by way of photosynthesis, turned carbon dioxide into the solid material of the tree.

The point of the video wasn't to expose the ignorance of graduates from a top-flight university, but to bring attention to the inadequacy of the belief that educating is just a matter of dumping information into kids' empty heads. Almost certainly, every single one of those MIT graduates had studied photosynthesis in elementary school, middle school, high school, and college. To get into MIT, it's a safe bet they aced the photosynthesis questions on standardized tests.

Why, then, did they give interviewers a totally wrong theory about the origin of the wood? Because the explanation they'd dreamed up early in life based on 'common sense' never got matched up with and reorganized by books and teachers. Teaching as 'telling' and learning as 'remembering' skip critical steps—surfacing and challenging deeply embedded but flawed models of reality, then following through to monitor the evolution of those models. The process is personal, individual, different for every learner in every class.

The new leaders of education policy ask, "Is the kid getting the information?" To that question, standardized tests provide accurate, satisfying answers, answers often drilled and drilled into kids' heads until they produce near-automatic responses. But that doesn't mean anything has been learned. Socrates wanted to know if the learner was *making sense* of the information, and no standardized, machine-scored test can come even close to finding out what any experienced teacher who's spent weeks or months in direct dialog with learners knows.

MYTH: AMERICAN EDUCATION AS A SOCIAL INSTITUTION IS BASICALLY SOUND; IT JUST NEEDS A GOOD DOSE OF RIGOR

Imagine a bus with twenty-two steering wheels and twenty-two drivers, each with a different destination in mind. The result? Paralysis or chaos. The bus would either go nowhere or go nowhere in particular. Hugh Arnold, a professor at the University of Nebraska, dug back through official government publications and found twenty-two different aims for America's involvement in the Vietnam War.[16] Yes, *official* government publications. And yes, twenty-two different aims. North Vietnam, on the other hand, had a single aim: Get the foreigners out.

Everyone knows how that story turned out.

If you're trying to do something, it helps to know precisely what that something is. In matters educational, my quick survey of educational literature turned up about three dozen steering wheels on the education bus. Is a general education supposed to introduce the core disciplines? Prepare the young for democratic citizenship? Teach 'the basics'? Raise standardized tests scores? Encourage tolerance? Create informed consumers? Develop character? Transmit societal values? Encourage creativity? Prepare students for useful work? Promote love of country? Improve problem-solving skills? Explore key concepts? Address 'eternal' questions? Teach thinking skills? Instill a love of learning? (Just to begin a list.)

Don't say "all the above," because every one of those aims, efficiently pursued, calls for distinctive instructional materials, distinctive teaching methods, distinctive tests. It's no more possible to teach effectively to multiple aims than it is to simultaneously arrive at multiple destinations. Forget political rhetoric about educational progress. 'Progress' must be measured by the amount of movement toward an agreed-upon overarching institutional aim, and American education has no such aim. 'The system' runs on inertia.

When I was young and working in construction, if a question was raised about the quality of work being done, the standard facetious response from someone on the crew was, "It'll look okay from the street." There are exceptions, but much of American education looks okay from the street. In place and functioning are buildings, sophisticated technology, trained administrators, dedicated teachers, a range of optional studies, elaborate testing systems. Buses run, bells ring, classes meet, assignments are given, and grade cards get sent home on schedule. People are doing what they're expected to do.

And that's the problem—people doing what they're expected to do. What America expects is what it has: a system for doing what it does, and what it does is 'cover the material' in a handful of school subjects.

But keeping operational a system for covering school subjects is no more an aim than maintaining a standing army is an aim. Both are *tools*. You don't pick up a tool then wander around looking for something to fix. You have something that needs to be fixed, and you find or fashion the tool you need to fix it.

In education, the aim—doing the job that justifies the social institution—isn't teaching school subjects. Neither is the aim to get kids ready to do well in a chosen college major or in a particular profession or field of work. The job that needs doing is helping learners live life more thoughtfully and productively. To that end, passing a standardized math exam misses the point by a mile. Making *sense* of math also misses the point, not by as much, but misses it nevertheless. The aim of schooling as it relates to math is *making sense of math that makes sense of daily life. Right here, right now!*

To be viable, a system for educating must have a purpose, a goal, an aim. And that aim needs to be thoroughly understood and accepted not just by policy makers, not just by the writers of items on standardized tests, not just by school superintendents and principals, not just by editorial writers and parents, but by every kid walking down every school hallway. Lacking that, what we can expect is what we have: a system for educating held together not by a deep-seated, natural desire to make more sense of experience and the human condition, but by habit, inertia, mindless bureaucracy, mandatory attendance laws, threats, promises, and efforts to collect more state and federal dollars.

MYTH: THE FAMILIAR, TRADITIONAL 'CORE CURRICULUM' IN NEAR-UNIVERSAL USE IN PUBLIC, PRIVATE, PAROCHIAL, MAGNET, AND CHARTER SCHOOLS IS UP TO THE CHALLENGES THE FUTURE WILL BRING

In 1892, when Harvard president Charles Eliot's Committee of Ten (men) standardized the present 'core curriculum,' the biggest new idea in American industry was mass production. Concentrated wealth financed giant factories, standardization of parts made it possible for those factories to make everything from nails to railroad rails rapidly and far less expensively, and wave after wave of immigrants were available to do the physical labor.

That labor, of course, was usually rather mindless. It could take years to learn how to make a pair of shoes by hand, but it took only minutes to learn how to operate a punch press that could turn out shoe soles or heels by the thousands. Mass production required a few thinkers and a lot of doers.

Not surprisingly, the approach to educating blessed by Eliot's committee reflected the thinking of the time. But times have changed. America's thousands of silent factories testify to the end of that simpler era. Today's enterprises must contend with mind-boggling technological complexity; unpredictable global markets; mobile populations; fluid capital; political potholes; multiple regulatory agencies; rapidly changing physical environments; and frictions stemming from differing national, regional, and social-class values and beliefs. Only those enterprises capable of continuous adaptation can now survive and prosper. And, as the failure rate of businesses and industries routinely demonstrates, adaptation isn't easy. Wisdom in the form of foresight, insight, ingenuity, creativity, and flexibility are essential, with educational implications not just for managers but for all citizens and therefore for all students.

The foundation of that wisdom must be built in America's schools, and it isn't happening. The curriculum is where the rubber meets the road, and the familiar math, science, language arts, and social studies curriculum isn't doing the job. Its problems and inadequacies are myriad and specific. In addition to its lack of an overarching aim, it fails to take adequate account of the fact that knowledge is expanding at a geometric rate with no criteria in place saying which new knowledge to teach and what old knowledge it's acceptable to omit.

The brain needs order and organization,[17] but the traditional curriculum dumps random information on learners in volumes and at velocities far beyond even the best student's ability to cope, assuring that what's 'learned' will never make it beyond short-term memory, much less be available for use years into the future.

Learners aren't moved smoothly through ever-increasing levels of conceptual difficulty. The words get harder and the sentences longer, but the ideas themselves don't 'pyramid' to ever-greater levels of complexity.

Difficult moral and ethical dilemmas that bear importance to everyday life aren't even discussed, much less pursued to reasonable, workable conclusions.

Thought processes other than the easily tested process of recall—processes essential to routine functioning and problem-solving such as inferring, hypothesizing, generalizing, relating, valuing, and so on—get little or no attention.

The interpretation and manipulation of textual and numerical symbols used to model reality have become more important than making sense of the reality the symbols represent.

The separate-subject curriculum not only denies the seamless, systemically integrated, mutually supportive nature of knowledge, it has so thoroughly compartmentalized the profession by disciplines educators can hardly communicate effectively about the task they share.

The reality a general education attempts to model is dynamic and constantly changing, but no mechanisms force the curriculum to take note of those changes, much less adapt to them.

The young are assigned passive, seat-bound roles at odds with their basic nature. The real world in all its richness lies all around them, and they sit confined in a room, 'covering the material' in a pale, shallow, secondhand, two-dimensional shadow of that world on the pages of textbooks.

That barely begins a list of problems with the 1893 curriculum. Any one of them, and many others, are serious enough to warrant a summit conference of the best minds, and the traditional curriculum suffers from all of them.

In the 1960s, educators were beginning to make real progress in designing a replacement for the traditional curriculum. General Systems Theory as it had emerged from World War II made it possible to see that all fields of study were parts of a systemically integrated, mutually supportive structure of knowledge; and research into brain functioning showed how the human brain selects, organizes, integrates, manipulates, and creates knowledge.[18]

When, in the 1980s, leaders of business and industry, working though governors and other politicians, pushed professional educators aside and took over,[19] a quarter century of progress in curriculum design became irrelevant. The new leaders, convinced the system that had brought education to a precarious state was nevertheless basically sound, moved the clock back to the 1950s.

And that's where it now stands. Locked in place by means of 'standards and accountability' it is a relic of a bygone era, a curriculum adopted in 1893, the original purpose of which was to make the task of college admissions officers easier by standardizing the transcripts of the tiny percentage of students likely to graduate from high school and go on to college.

Double-locking that curricular relic in place are the calls for 'rigor'; for increasing the number of required higher math and science courses; for moving such courses down one or two grade levels; for abandoning music, art, recess, and other 'frills'; for ignoring the incredible benefits of human variability and forcing every kid to jump through the same ancient hoops. As it is currently laid out, this seems like it remains part of the lost "myth."

CHARTING A NEW COURSE

If the new leaders get their way and the state standards and tests keyed to the 1893 curriculum are replaced by national standards and tests keyed to that same curriculum, then the institution will be permanently paralyzed, incapable of providing the young with the intellectual tools essential to their survival in an increasingly complex, dynamic, dangerous world. I want to close by proposing an alternative vision, one aimed at transforming the future rather than repeating the past.[20]

1. Take the phrase 'neighborhood school' seriously and design around it. Choose local adult-student steering committees to locate, rent, or lease centrally located community centers, churches, houses, or other facilities.
2. Set maximum school size at thirty to forty students for morning classes and another thirty to forty for afternoon or evening classes.
3. Hire a three- or four-person teacher team, based on interviews and the team's written program proposal.
4. Right up front, spend whatever is necessary to test and fix sight and hearing problems. It's a waste of money to try to educate kids who're functioning at less than peak potential because they don't hear or see well.
5. Find out who each kid really is. It mystifies me how, with straight faces, we can simultaneously sing the praises of 'American individual-

ism' while we force all kids through the same narrow program. For a fraction of the cost of present standardized subject-matter tests, every kid's distinctive strengths and weaknesses can be explored using inexpensive, proven inventories of interests, abilities, personalities, and learning styles.

6. Eliminate grade levels. Start with where kids are, help them go as far as they're able, and give them a diploma describing what they've done and can do.
7. Eliminate textbooks. They're relics of a bygone era, cost a lot of money, are out of date the day they're printed, and they're the main support of simplistic ideas about what it means to teach and learn.
8. Stop chopping knowledge up into 'subjects.' Knowledge is seamless, and the brain processes it most efficiently when it's integrated.
9. Push responsibility for teaching specific skills and knowledge on to users of those skills and knowledge: employers. Specialized, occupation-related instruction such as that now being offered in magnet schools will never be able to keep up with either the variety or the rate of change. Employers will resist, so sweeten the pot with subsidies as necessary. (A bonus: Apprenticeship and intern arrangements will go a long way toward smoothing the transition into responsible adulthood.)
10. Eliminate school buses, food services, athletic departments, athletic fields, cops on campus, nonteaching administrators, attendance officers, extracurricular activities. (And add into the tax savings much of the $50,000 and more it costs each year to keep poorly educated kids locked up in prisons.)
11. Strip away all the nonacademic roles and responsibilities state legislators piled on schools during the twentieth century. Create independent municipal support systems for neighborhood-level, multiage programs for art, dance, drama, sports and anything else 'extracurricular' for which a local need or interest is apparent.
12. Drastically shrink central administrations. Have them coordinate the forming of teacher teams, and relieve those teams of paper shuffling, resource acquisition, and other noninstructional tasks.

School doesn't need to take all day, every day. Suggestions 5 through 9 will make it possible to accomplish more in three hours than is now being accomplished in six. The special interest, personal learning project which every student should always have underway can be done on her and his own time.

Not incidentally, I'm concerned with matters in addition to functional schools: the creation of a sense of neighborhood and community, the expansion of community service activities, and vastly increased contact between generations. Cutting out all the nonacademic responsibilities will open up time for all kinds of fascinating new growth-producing activity.

NOTES

1. National Commission on Excellence in Education, *A Nation at Risk: The Imperative for Educational Reform* (U.S. Department of Education, April 1983),http://www.google.com/url?sa=t&source=web&cd=1&ved=0CBIQFjAA&url=http%3A%2F%2Fdatacenter.spps.org%2Fsites%2F2259653e-ffb3-45ba-8fd6-04a024ecf7a4%2Fuploads%2FSOTW_A_Nation_at_Risk_1983.pdf&ei=4s9ZTLLGFMiGsAbkitj8Cw&usg=AFQjCNHidls9SwaMYx03ix6ftlVnLcPe7g (accessed August 4, 2010).
2. For more on this, see T. Ansary, "Education at Risk: Fallout from a Flawed Report," *Edutopia,* http://www.edutopia.org/landmark-education-report-nation-risk (accessed May 20, 2010).
3. L. Gerstner, "Lessons from 40 Years of Educational 'Reform,'" *Wall Street Journal,* December 1, 2008, http://online.wsj.com/article/SB122809533452168067.html (accessed August 29, 2010).
4. Ibid.
5. See M. Brady, "Education Reform: The Long Hard Road," *Orlando Sentinel*, March 6, 2000, http://articles.orlandosentinel.com/2000-0306/news/0003060132_1_education-reform-things-differently-diminishing-returns (accessed May 20, 2010).
6. D. Ravitch and C. Finn Jr., *What Do Our 17-Year Olds Know? A Report on the First National Assessment of History and Literature* (New York: Harper and Row, 1987).
7. R. Rothstein, *The Way We Were? The Myths and Realities of America's Student Achievement* (New York: Century Foundation Press,1998).
8. M. Filidei, "Toxic Metals and Mental Health," *International Guide to the World of Alternative Mental Health,* Safe Harbor, http://www.alternative-mentalhealth.com/articles/toxicmetals.htm (accessed August 4, 2010).
9. Ibid.
10. F.H. Rauscher et al., "Music Training Causes Long-Term Enhancement of Preschool Children's Spatial-Temporal Reasoning," *Neurological Research* 19 (1997): 2–8.
11. See, for example, C. B. Taylor, J. F. Sallis, and R. Needle, "The Relation of Physical Activity and Exercise to Mental Health," *Public Health Reports* 100, no. 2 (March–April 1985): 195–202, http://www.ncbi.nlm.nih.gov/pmc/articles/PMC1424736/ (accessed August 4, 2010).
12. D. Christakis et al., "Early Television Exposure and Subsequent Attentional Problems in Children," *Pediatrics* 113, no. 4 (April 2004): 708–13.
13. R. Rothstein, "Lessons—Linking Poor Performance with Working after School" (Washington, D.C.: Economic Policy Institute, 2001), http://www.epi.org/publications/entry/webfeat_lessons20011031 (accessed August 4, 2010).
14. Z. Xu, J. Hannaway, and S. D'Souza, "Student Transience in North Carolina: The Effect of School Mobility on Student Outcomes Using Longitudinal Data" (Washington, D.C.: Urban Institute, 2009), http://www.urban.org/url.cfm?ID=1001256. Accessed August 4, 2010.
15. R. Pirsig, *Zen and the Art of Motorcycle Maintenance* (New York: William Morrow, 1974).
16. See H. Arnold, 'Official Justifications for America's Role in Indochina, 1949–1967,' Asian Affairs 3, no. 1 (September–October, 1975): 31–48.
17. D. Ausubel, *The Psychology of Meaningful Verbal Learning* (Oxford: Grune and Stratton, 1963).

18. For more on General Systems Theory, see L. Skyttner, *General Systems Theory: Perspectives,Problems, Practice*, 2nd ed. (Hackensack, NJ: World Scientific Publishing Company, 2006).
19. M. Vinovskis, *The Road to Charlottesville: The 1989 Education Summit* (Washington, D.C.: National Education Goals Panel, 1999).
20. A version of these twelve points originally appeared in M. Brady, "Cheaper by the Dozen: 12 Ways to Save Money at High Schools," *Orlando Sentinel*, May 7, 2005, http://articles.orlandosentinel.com/2005-05-07/news/0505070146_1_save-money-knowledge-ways-to-save (accessed May 20, 2010).

Contributors

Deron Boyles is professor of philosophy of education in the Department of Educational Policy Studies at Georgia State University. His research interests include school-corporate nexes, epistemology, pragmatism and the philosophy of John Dewey, and critical pedagogy. His work has been published in such journals as *Educational Studies*, *Philosophical Studies in Education*, *Philosophy of Education*, *Social Epistemology*, *History of Education Quarterly*, and *Educational Theory*. With Benjamin Baez, he is also coauthor of *The Politics of Inquiry: Education Research and the "Culture of Science,"* which was named a CHOICE Outstanding Academic Title for 2009. He is also the recipient of the 2010 James and Helen Merritt Award for Distinguished Service to Philosophy of Education. Boyles received his PhD from Vanderbilt University, is a Fellow in the Philosophy of Education Society and John Dewey Society, and serves as president of the American Educational Studies Association and the Advisory Board for Chrysalis Experiential Academy.

Marion Brady began his career in education in 1952, teaching in a semirural high school in northeastern Ohio. Since then he has taught at every level from sixth grade through the university, been a county-level school administrator, publisher consultant, teacher educator, textbook author, contributor to professional journals, author of professional books, writer of instructional materials, visitor to schools across America and abroad, and long-time education columnist for Knight-Ridder/Tribune.

H.K. Christie is a doctoral student at the University of Minnesota in the program of Curriculum and Instruction majoring in Culture and Teaching with a minor in Political Psychology. Christie has a Master of Arts in public policy and leadership from the University of St. Thomas and a dual Bachelor of Arts degree in philosophy and theology from St. Catherine University. Her work focuses on political literacy and the pedagogical practices that support participatory democratic student learning outcomes. Her research has been featured in the *Journal of Critical Educational Policy Studies* and *The Gift of Education: Public Education and*

Venture Philanthropy by Kenneth J. Saltman, for which she conducted the data collection and analysis of the Gates and Broad Foundations' tax forms. She has been a speaker at the American Educational Studies Association (AESA), her most recent talk titled "Dare We Transform AESA: A Call to Activism" at the 2009 national conference.

David Gabbard is professor of educational foundations in the Department of Curriculum at East Carolina University. His publications include *Knowledge and Power in the Global Economy: The Effects of School Reform in a Neoliberal/Neoconservative Age* (Routledge, 2008) and *Education Under the Security State*, with E. Wayne Ross (Teachers College Press, 2008).

Leslee Grey is lecturer of educational foundations at Queens College, the City University of New York. In addition to critiquing neoliberal and market-based education reforms, her research interests include the educational implications of genderqueering, the unconscious processes of learning, and the liberatory (im)possibilities of youth cultures.

Jim Horn is the keeper of Schools Matter, a blog devoted to the preservation and renewal of public education in America. He is also associate professor of educational leadership and foundations at Cambridge College. He has over three decades of experience as a K–12 educator and professor of social foundations and qualitative researcher. His theoretical research agenda focuses on understanding complexity in educational systems, and his applied research ranges from exploring teacher renewal to understanding the effects of high-stakes testing and privatization in urban school settings. He is strongly committed to renewing the democratic purposes of public education, and he advocates for the social justice mission of schools here and abroad.

Aimee Howley is senior associate dean and professor of educational research and evaluation at Ohio University. She received her Bachelor of Arts degree in philosophy from Barnard College, her Master of Arts degree in special education from the West Virginia College of Graduate Studies, and her Doctorate of education in educational administration from West Virginia University. Prior to coming to Ohio University, Dr. Howley worked as a special education teacher and administrator in the Jackson County Schools in West Virginia. She also worked in various higher education institutions in West Virginia as a professor, director of teacher education, and college-level administrator. For the past several years, Dr. Howley has worked on research that explores the intersection between social context and educational practice, and she has used both quantitative and qualitative methods to investigate a wide range of questions relating to rural education, instructional improvement, recruitment and retention of school administrators, school size, education of the gifted, and parent involvement. In addition, she has written numerous critical analyses of educational policies and practices focusing on topics such as the intellectual aims of schooling, the sense in which rurality constitutes a social context, and the relationship between educational theory and practice. Dr. Howley is the coauthor of five books and the author or coauthor of more than fifty referred articles.

Craig B. Howley, adjunct associate professor in the Ohio University College of Education, is the coauthor of fifteen books and book chapters and fifty peer-reviewed research articles. He currently directs the research initiative of an NSF center devoted to rural mathematics education (ACCLAIM). In previous lives, he directed an ERIC Clearinghouse and worked as a research and development specialist at a Regional Educational Laboratory; he began teaching in a special education school in a state mental hospital, the site of which is now occupied by a Wal-Mart. He holds a Bachelor's degree in English and comparative literature from Columbia College, a Master's degree in gifted education from WVCOGS, and a Doctorate degree in educational administration from West Virginia University. Howley is particularly interested in connections between schooling and everyday life in rural places and cultures. He wonders, still, if there is an overlap between schooling and education per se. He entertains the possibility even now. Recent activities include cowriting with Aimee Howley two book chapters, including the one in this volume, and one dealing with social class and rural identity (forthcoming from Penn State). The previous year, as well, finally saw publication of an article about rural education research bearing the strange title "Doing Science Right." The Howleys own and operate a small farm in Albany, Ohio, raising a gratifying profusion of animals and crops for food, without commercial fertilizers and pesticides. They have three children (two in education) and four grandchildren.

David Hursh is an associate professor at the Warner Graduate School of Education, University of Rochester. His interests include education policy, school reform, political theory, and environmental sustainability and social studies curriculum. His most recent book is *High-Stakes Testing and the Decline of Teaching and Learning: The Real Crisis in Education* (Rowman and Littlefield), which situates the rise of high-stakes testing within the debates over pedagogy, economics, and governance, and specifically examines the Chicago Public School reforms during the Arne Duncan regime (coauthored with Pauline Lipman). Overall, he has over seventy journal publications and book chapters. He has been politically active resisting the rise of high-stakes testing in New York and mayoral control in Rochester, New York. Fourteen years ago he cofounded Rochester's Coalition for Common Sense in Education, a group actively fighting for progressive pedagogy, democratic governance, and equitable funding. He can frequently be heard on public radio and at local venues.

Michael Klonsky, PhD teaches in the College of Education at DePaul University and currently serves as the national director of the Small Schools Workshop and the Center for Innovative Schools. Dr. Klonsky is a teacher educator who has spoken and written extensively on school-reform issues with a focus on urban school restructuring. His latest book (with Susan Klonsky), *Small Schools: Public School Reform Meets the Ownership Society* (2008), is a critique of top-down school reform and the push toward privatization of public schools. He is also the author of *Small Schools: The Numbers Tell a Story* (University of Illinois Small Schools Workshop) and coeditor of *A Simple Justice: The Challenge for Teachers in Small Schools* (2000). His blog SmallTalk can be found on the web at http://michaelklonsky.blogspot.com/.

Philip E. Kovacs is assistant professor of education at UAHuntsville. While his theoretical work focuses on the role(s) of foundations, think tanks, and institutes in implementing educational policy changes, he is now working with local schools on initiatives that seek to increase the amount of schooling spent teaching toward intelligent behavior. To that end, he is interested in transdisciplinary action research that employs alternative pedagogies geared toward student, teacher, school, and community transformation. Dr. Kovacs was instrumental in helping a group of concerned scholars, teachers, and educational advocates organize and protest the No Child Left Behind Act from 2004 to 2006. The petition they launched continues to receive signatures in support of dismantling the legislation.

Patti Lather is professor of education at the School of Educational Policy and Leadership at Ohio State University, where she teaches courses in qualitative research, gender in education, and feminist methodology. Her books include *Getting Smart: Feminist Research and Pedagogy with/in the Postmodern* (Routledge, 1991), *Troubling the Angels: Women Living with HIV/AIDS* (coauthored with Chris Smithies; Westview, 1997), *Getting Lost: Feminist Efforts Toward a Double(d) Science* (State University of New York Press, 2007), and *Engaging Science Policy: From the Side of the Messy* (Peter Lang, 2010). Lather's research interests include (post)critical policy studies, feminist methodology, and poststructural theory. She is an AERA Fellow and recipient of the AERA Division B Lifetime Achievement Award.

Ken Libby recently completed his Master's degree in the art of teaching from Lewis and Clark's Graduate School of Education and hopes to either find a teaching job or pursue further studies in the field of education. He currently works with parent groups organized around education issues in Portland, Oregon.

Kenneth J. Saltman is a professor in the Educational Policy Studies and Research Department at DePaul University in Chicago. He is the author most recently of *The Gift of Education: Public Education and Venture Philanthropy* (2010) and *Capitalizing on Disaster: Taking and Breaking Public Schools* (2007). He edited most recently (with David Gabbard) *Education as Enforcement: the Militarization and Corporatization of Schools*, Second Edition (Routledge, 2010); and *Schooling and the Politics of Disaster* (2007).

Jessica Shiller is an assistant professor of education at Lehman College, City University of New York where she has taught courses in historical foundations, social studies methods, and urban education. Her research interests include urban school reform policy and practices, social justice education, and the role of race and class in schooling.

Index

For Product Safety Concerns and Information please contact our EU representative GPSR@taylorandfrancis.com
Taylor & Francis Verlag GmbH, Kaufingerstraße 24, 80331 München, Germany

www.ingramcontent.com/pod-product-compliance
Ingram Content Group UK Ltd.
Pitfield, Milton Keynes, MK11 3LW, UK
UKHW022000180926
475701UK00003B/125

* 9 7 8 0 4 1 5 5 3 6 6 3 9 *